HAWKINS'  TORIES

HAWKINS' TORIES

A REGIMENTAL AND SOCIAL HISTORY OF THE
7th TENNESSEE VOLUNTEER CAVALRY USA
IN THE CIVIL WAR

PEGGY SCOTT HOLLEY

BRAYBREE
Publishing

Published by BrayBree Publishing Company LLC
FIRST EDITION

Cover: Issac R. Hawkins (military records), Silhouettes (istockphoto.com),
American flag (istockphoto.com)
Frontispiece: Issac R. Hawkins (military records)

ISBN: 978-1-940127-04-0

Printed in the United States of America

BrayBree Publishing Company LLC
P.O. Box 1204
Dickson, Tennessee 37056-1204

Visit our website at braybreepublishing.com

Dedicated to my father, William Benjamin Scott,
who knew many of these soldiers and passed their stories on to me.

CONTENTS

ILLUSTRATIONS

PREFACE

Although the country as a whole soon forgot the southern Unionists, their memory was often kept alive among descendants. I have always known about my family members who fought "for the North." My father knew many of the 7th Tennessee Cavalry soldiers who lived into the early 1900s in Carroll and Henderson Counties and recounted their stories to me. Other families in the area passed down the traditions as well, especially those that centered on the horrors of prison life. For that reason, the first paper I wrote was "The Seventh Tennessee Volunteer Cavalry: West Tennessee Unionists in Andersonville Prison" published in *The West Tennessee Historical Society Papers*, Volume XLII, Spring 1988.

Still knowing little about the early years of the regiment, a search began for more information. The few times the 7th Tennessee received attention in secondary sources generally concerned 1) Ingersoll's evaluation of their performance at Lexington; 2) their surrender to Forrest at Trenton; or 3) their gullibility in believing Colonel W.L. Duckworth's ruse at Union City. The latter references almost always include Quaker cannons, fake artillery calls, and rescue troops "only six miles away."

It is my hope that this manuscript will help the reader appreciate that the 7th Tennessee Cavalry USA has been the victim of some rather shallow research and general neglect. In an effort to produce a more balanced account, some attempt has been made to show the men contributed significantly more than is usually credited to them. No attempt, however, has been made to turn the men into saintly heroes. Whether the 7th ever receives recognition or appreciation, however, matters little in the final analysis. Theirs, after all, was not a "Lost Cause."

I am indebted to the National Archives and to the many descendants of the soldiers who shared their family stories, photographs and copies of military records. Special thanks to my husband Ed Holley, who helped me in numerous ways, and to Kevin D. McCann, who encouraged me to publish this volume and worked to make it presentable.

PEGGY SCOTT HOLLEY
MAY 2013

HAWKINS'
TORIES

———— • ————

CHAPTER ONE

RECRUITMENT AND ORGANIZATION

Loyalists from Whom the Union Recruited the 7th Tennessee Cavalry

Voting Against Secession

A t the beginning of the debate over secession from the Union, most Tennesseans expressed support for the federal government. An election in February 1861 to mandate the calling of a convention on secession failed to pass. Tennessee's pro-Confederate Governor, Isham G. Harris, dissatisfied with the outcome of the first vote, called a second election in June of 1861. This time voters could choose either "Separation" or "No Separation" from the Union. The developing sentiment in favor of secession exerted pressure on the supporters of the federal government to either change their vote or stay away from the polls for the second vote.[1]

---

1. Thomas L. Connelly, *Civil War Tennessee* (Knoxville, TN: University of Tennessee Press, 1979), 1–6.

Of the three divisions of Tennessee, West Tennessee had the highest percentage of the population in favor of secession.[2] On the eastern side of West Tennessee near the Tennessee River, however, several counties contained citizens with a strong attachment to the federal government. These loyalists became unpopular with their neighbors. Some supporters of separation attempted to prevent the public presentation of the loyal view. For example, they stopped Emerson Etheridge, a popular Weakley County politician of known Union sentiments, from speaking in Henry County between the two elections and, at another assembly, killed one Union supporter and wounded four more.[3]

Individuals disagreeing with the majority could be in danger as well. Nathaniel Brewer, a yeoman farmer of Carroll County, declared it of "general report" that "every Union man who offered to vote would be shot" and he "believed it." In Brewer's district, rebel soldiers from Union City guarded the polls.[4] Williamson Younger, a plantation owner with land in both Carroll and Gibson counties who eventually supported the Confederacy, voted against secession in the first election but decided to remain at home for the second.[5] Mr. Horton, who lived near Paris, Tennessee recalled that he told the rebel inquirers he could not "spare time" to attend the election. He knew he would be prevented from voting for the Union a second time.[6] Citizens loyal to the Federal Government lost their assurance of voting secretly when some newspapers, including the popular *Memphis Daily Appeal*, encouraged secessionists to leave their ballots unfolded so people voting against separation could be identified.[7]

In spite of the risk involved, a small majority of voters in Weakley, Carroll, Henderson, Decatur, and Hardin counties, plus loyal pockets

2. West Tennessee also had the highest percentage of slaves among the three sections of the state.

3. U.S. War Department, *The War of the Rebellion: A Compilation of the Official Records of the Union and Confederate Armies, 128 vols* (Washington, D.C.: Government Printing Office, 1880–1901) Series 1, Vol. 1, Part 2. Gideon Pillow to L. P. Walker, April 24, 1861. Hereafter: *OR*, 1, LII, (2), 69.

4. "Nathaniel Brewer," *Southern Claims Commission Disallowed Claims, 1871–1880.* National Archives Microfiche Publication M140 RG 233, Fiche #881. There were ten Brewer men in the 2nd/7th Tennessee.

5. Williamson Younger, "The Diary of Williamson Younger," *West Tennessee Historical Society Papers* 13 (Memphis: West Tennessee Historical Society, 1959): 60.

6. Charles C. Nott, *Sketches of the War: A Series of Letters to the North Moore Street School of New York* (New York: Charles T. Evans, 1863; reprint, Paris, Tennessee: The Guild Bindery Press), 67.

7. *Memphis Daily Appeal*, May 12, 1861. *Nashville Union and American*, May 11, 1861.

in nearby counties, continued to vote "No Separation" on the second vote even though the majority of Tennesseans opted for "Separation."[8] It took strong convictions to remain supportive of the federal government in a division of the state where secessionists outnumbered and outvoted them. The Union recruited the 1st (later 6th) and 2nd (later 7th) West Tennessee Volunteer Cavalries, plus members of several other Tennessee and northern regiments, from among these determined loyalists.[9]

Reasons for Loyalty to the Union

Finding documents stating reasons these particular Unionists determined to take a stand against prevailing opinion proved difficult. A few references, however, seem to indicate that they valued their nation more than their section. A late memoir by Samuel Brown recalled that circumstances forced him, and other young men meeting at minister John Neely's home in Carroll County, to choose between North and South. They chose North because they "were all a bunch of loyal men and could not fight against the Union."[10] William L. Sanders, a civilian throughout the war, wrote in an 1866 letter to his brother that he had "always been a Union Man and remained "eternally, invincibly and unalterably opposed to secession, separation from or division of the best government in the world." He even added that John Calhoun of South Carolina should have been hanged for high treason for threatening secession back in 1832.[11] Hosea Preslar, a Henderson County Methodist preacher, thought division

8. *Goodspeed's General History of Tennessee*, reprint from *Goodspeed's History of Tennessee*, 1887 (Nashville: Charles and Randy Elder Booksellers, 1973), 534. These counties were part of a larger area of Union sentiment that included Wayne County in Middle Tennessee and some of Northern Alabama.

9. *Compiled Service Records of Volunteer Union Soldiers of Tennessee*, National Archives Microfilm Publication M395 RG094 rolls 63-69 (hereafter *Compiled Service Records 7th Tennessee*). These muster rolls show recruitment primarily in Weakley, Carroll, Henderson, Decatur, McNairy, Gibson, Henry, and Hardin Counties in West Tennessee, plus a few volunteers from Middle Tennessee and Western Kentucky.

10. Samuel Brown, "The Family History," *McKenzie Banner*, May 25, 1972, 9. These young men joined northern regiments before the formation of the West Tennessee Union regiments. Neely, minister at the Christians' Chapel Christian Church, became a captain in the First West Tennessee Infantry.

11. William L. Sanders, letter to Benjamin Sanders, July 1, 1866. Unpublished, available at Gordon Browning Library, McKenzie, Tennessee.

of the country unnecessary as long as religious freedom existed.[12] Private Andrew Jackson Bonds wrote his wife that he looked forward to living again "under the old constitution and in the union." In another letter he hoped she would think he had "bravely fought" to maintain "our freedom and rights," a typically southern phrase, but in support of the Union.[13]

Dr. Ashton W. Hawkins, later Captain of Company F of the 2nd West Tennessee Cavalry and a cousin to the colonel of the regiment, expressed himself in more detail than most. In a prewar letter to his father-in-law Hawkins said the "Cotton States" (lower South) bore responsibility for disunion and would "drag the border slave states into the whirlpool of secession." He thought at first that Tennessee should attempt to remain neutral like Kentucky. After the war began, Hawkins said he joined because he believed "it was right."[14]

If the loyalists primarily resisted disunion, the question arises if a secondary motive might have been disapproval of slavery. This, however, seems highly unlikely. Their most prominent leaders tended to be of the slaveholding class. Isaac R. Hawkins, who raised the 2nd West Tennessee Cavalry, owned three slaves.[15] Fielding Hurst of McNairy County, who raised the 1st West Tennessee Cavalry, owned twenty-three people and reportedly took two or more with him on campaign.[16] William H. Cherry, with whom General Grant stayed in Savannah before the battle of Shiloh, made speeches against secession[17] while owning thirty-two people. Emerson Etheridge, a slaveholder in Weakley County who continued to represent the 9th district Unionists in the US Congress during the war, presented a petition to exempt Tennessee from the emancipation

12. Hosea Preslar, *Thoughts on Divine Providence or a Sketch of God's Care Over and Dealings with his People together with a concise view of the causes of the late war in the US*. Printed by the author, 1867, 233.

13. Andrew Jackson Bonds to Elizabeth Bonds, 1863, Camp Jackson, April 9, 1863.

14. Ashton Hawkins, letter to Colonel Lilly, May 24, 1861, in *Ansearchin' News* (Winter 1995): 148.

15. 1860 Census, Carroll County Slave Schedule.

16. James R. Chalmers, report, *OR*, 1, XXXII, 1, 57. Confederate General Chalmers even claimed to have captured Hurst's black and white mistresses at the battle at Bolivar. *OR*, 1, XXXII, 622.

17. W. H. Cherry, obituary, *Savannah Courier*, September 18, 1885.

of slaves.[18] Reverend Samuel Clark, the largest slave owner in Carroll County, professed pro-Union sentiment until he feared Lincoln would free the slaves.[19]

Some officers of the 2nd/7th Tennessee had servants with them while serving in the military. Assistant Surgeon Edward Arbuckle retained a servant named Emily Dark. Lieutenant Franklin Travis took a slave named Emmons.[20] Both Lieutenant Samuel W. Hawkins and John T. Robeson each had a servant along. The enlisted men, however, fended for themselves. A study of slaveholding in Carroll County indicates that only 5% of the Union soldiers' families owned slaves.[21] A survey of the other Unionist counties supports a similar conclusion. For the vast majority of the loyal men, taking servants to war was not an option.[22]

Although most West Tennessee Unionists failed to actively oppose slavery, evidence of some limited opposition, or at least sympathy, for slaves existed. William L. Sanders of Carroll County felt that no man should own a slave who would oppose being held a slave.[23] Reverend Hosea Preslar of Henderson County felt slavery to be unjust and a hindrance to religious progress.[24] Both men had relatives in the 2nd/7th Tennessee. Some members of the regiment encouraged slaves to run away to Union lines which might be construed as sympathy for the slaves. It could also, however, be merely a means of punishing wealthy, non-combatant Confederate supporters.[25] The small number of slaves in the Unionist

18. John Cimprich, *Slavery's End in Tennessee 1861-1865* (Tuscaloosa: University of Alabama Press, 1985), 101.

19. Molly Owens, memoir of one Unionist family's experiences. Available at Gordon Browning Library, McKenzie, Tennessee.

20. "Edward Arbuckle" and "Franklin Travis" in *Compiled Service Records 7th Tennessee*, Roll 395-69, #1788. Dark may be a description rather than last name. Emmons became a Union soldier.

21. Peggy Scott Holley, "Unionists in Eastern West Tennessee 1861-1865," http://www.rootsweb.com/~Tennesseecarrol/UnionistsWTennessee.pdf.

22. This was true of most CSA soldiers as well. Only about one in three families in South owned slaves.

23. William L. Sanders, letter to Benjamin Sanders, July 1, 1866. Gordon Browning Library, McKenzie, Tennessee.

24. Hosea Preslar, *Thoughts on Divine Providence.*

25. Williamson Younger, "The Diary of Williamson Younger," *West Tennessee Historical Society Papers* 13 (1959): 30. Lt. Newton Cox of the 2nd/7th Tennessee convinced two of Younger's slaves to run away to Humboldt. Younger said the Tennesseans were doing this.

communities may have caused the average yeoman farmer to be little concerned with the issue on any level.

Social Interaction within the Recruitment Area

Since a large proportion of the Unionists resided in defined areas with those of like-mind, it seems highly unlikely that they made uninfluenced, individual decisions about which side to support. The question therefore arises as to whether there might have been cohesion among the loyalists long before the war. An examination of Henderson and Carroll County, home to the majority of the 2nd/7th, indicates this to be the case. The future loyalists tended to live in enclaves, usually with those of the same economic class. They married each other and attended church together. Several groups within the larger group immigrated together in the 1820s and 30s. As a result of the cohesion amongst the groups that would later volunteer for Union regiments, the companies almost seem like clans. Numerous cousins, uncles, fathers, sons, brothers and brothers-in-law enlisted together. When nearly 400 of these men died during the war, some communities lost a high percentage of their males of military age.

Although most Unionists lived somewhat apart from the majority of those who became Confederates,[26] little evidence exists for open hostility between the groups before the war began. As to their relationship with the slave owners, it seems much the same. When questioned in the early 1900s[27] if slaveholders and non-slaveholders in their neighborhoods had friendly feelings or antagonism toward each other before the war, some surviving members of the 2nd/7th replied that good feelings existed. James Taylor of Company I mentioned, however, that slave owners seemed "rather distant."[28] Since few slave owners resided in the sections of the counties that remained loyal, distance lowered the probability of friction.[29] Social interaction appears to have been on a superficial level. Antagonism increased rapidly on both sides, however, when fighting

26. Determined by plotting Union and Confederate families on 1860 census and consulting marriage and church records.

27. Gustavus W. Dyer and John Trotwood Moore, compilers, *The Tennessee Civil War Veterans Questionnaires* (Easley, SC: Southern Historical Press, Inc., 1985) Reprint.

28. "James Taylor," *The Tennessee Civil War Veterans Questionnaires*, 125.

29. 1860 Census Carroll and Henderson Counties plus Slave Schedules.

began. Those of military age who supported the federal government had difficult decisions to make.

Unionist Choices Early in the War

Leaving for the North was the first option. When Tennessee became part of the Confederacy, the eastern West Tennessee Unionists found themselves behind enemy lines. No matter how burning their patriotism to save the country, little opportunity to be of service presented itself early in the war. During this period some families sent their military age sons north. This removed the young men from the peer pressure of surrounding Confederates and from the later Confederate draft. During the 1850s there had been migrations from West Tennessee into southern Illinois. The father of Felix and James Moore sent his sons to Vienna in Washington County, Illinois because their aunt resided there. Although the father opposed secession he told the boys "to keep out of either army," advice they ignored when they joined the Union Army as it invaded West Tennessee.[30]

When General Ulysses S. Grant entered Tennessee at Forts Henry and Donelson in February of 1862, West Tennessee loyalists received their first opportunity to join the Union Army on home soil. Eager young men from the area volunteered for placement in northern regiments. Grant estimated that over 500 loyal Tennesseans joined his army around this time. The enlistments led him to the conclusion that "union sentiment seems to be strong in the south part of the state."[31]

The 500 loyal Tennesseans included the previously mentioned Samuel Brown and his friends. They crossed Carroll and Benton Counties, traveling at night and hiding in the daytime in the homes of known Union sympathizers. Floating in a raft down (north) the Tennessee River they eventually made their way to Grant's army at Fort Donelson. Recruiters assigned them to Illinois, Indiana and Iowa[32] units. Some fought in the

---

30. Felix Wisdom Moore, "Moores-Pattons," Unpublished manuscript. Available at Gordon Browning Library, McKenzie, Tennessee.

31. William B. Feis, *Grant's Secret Service: The Intelligence War from Belmont to Appomattox* (Lincoln, NE: University of Nebraska Press, 2002), 90–91. A few of the 500 might have been from Middle Tennessee. Grant to McLean, March 15, 1862, *OR*, 1, X, (2), 39.

32. The group with Samuel Brown joined the 5th Iowa and 52nd Indiana.

Battle of Shiloh in April 1862 before they received uniforms.[33] Brown and his friends, remained in the northern units throughout the war, as did many others. Military markers in cemeteries all over the Unionist counties bear silent testimony to their service. A few men, however, transferred to Tennessee regiments when they organized.

President Lincoln wanted loyal citizens within the seceding states placed in regiments with state designations as soon as possible. Southern regiments fighting for the Union under their own state's name would show the conflict to be more than North versus South. The President indicated that he would value loyal troops raised in Tennessee more highly than a like number from almost anywhere else because they would be at the very place in need of protection. He wanted Andrew Johnson to do what he could to raise Tennessee troops and to "do it quickly."[34]

West Tennessee units formed as soon as recruitment centers could be organized in the period following Grant's victories at Fort Henry, Fort Donelson and Shiloh. The enforcement of Confederate conscription in Tennessee beginning in April of 1862 forced Union men to flee, join federal units or be drafted into the rebel army. Eventually the Federals raised at least one battalion for the Union Army in every southern state except for South Carolina.[35]

In this era prominent men customarily applied for commissions from the government to recruit and lead new regiments. In West Tennessee Isaac Roberts Hawkins qualified. A forty-four year old Huntingdon lawyer, Mexican War veteran, delegate from Tennessee to the Peace Conference of 1861, and a judge of the Tennessee Circuit Court, Hawkins received the authority from General Grant to raise a unit.[36] At first listed with both infantry and cavalry ("Hawkins' Horse"),[37] the regiment became the 2nd West Tennessee Volunteer Cavalry and eventually the 7th Tennessee Volunteer Cavalry.

33. Samuel Brown memoir, *McKenzie Banner*, May 25, 1972, 9.

34. Abraham Lincoln to Andrew Johnson, July 3, 1862, *Collected Works of Lincoln* 5 (New Brunswick,NJ: Rutgers University Press, 1953), 303.

35. Richard Nelson Current, *Lincoln's Loyalists* (New York: Oxford University Press, 1992), 5.

36. Jacob Fry to Stephen A. Hurlbut, telegraph, August 1862. "Isaac R. Hawkins," Roll 395-65, #79, *Compiled Service Records 7th Tennessee.*

37. U.S. Grant, November 10, 1862, *OR*, 1, XVII, (2), 341–342.

Organizing the Second West Tennessee Volunteer Cavalry USA

Expectations for a Union Cavalry Regiment

A regiment, at least in theory, consisted of twelve companies of 100 men each or about 1200 men with a colonel in command and a lieutenant colonel second in command. A company included a captain, 1st and 2nd lieutenants, 1st sergeant, quartermaster-sergeant, commissary sergeant, 5 sergeants, 8 corporals, 2 teamsters, 2 farriers, 1 waggoner, 1 saddler, 2 musicians and about 70 privates. A regiment divided into three battalions of four companies each with a major in charge. The regimental field and staff organization consisted of the colonel, lieutenant colonel, sergeant major, quartermaster-sergeant, commissary sergeant, saddler sergeant, chief farrier (blacksmith) and two hospital stewards.[38]

The 2nd West Tennessee, however, never came near meeting the standard expectations. Recruitment in primarily Confederate West Tennessee proved difficult. Instead of the expected twelve, only eight companies, A–H, formed in 1862. Several of these companies never reached the full quota of men. The number of recruits in 1862 totaled 679, over 500 men short of a full regiment. Companies I, K, and M formed in 1863, adding about 200 new men. The total for a very short time reached about 880 men in eleven companies. In the fall of 1863, however, the mustering-out of the one-year companies subtracted 287 men. By the end of 1863, the regiment contained about 590 men organized into nine companies, or only about one-half the number in a normal regiment. Although about 1300 men served in the unit from 1862–1865, the 2nd/7th Tennessee never contained 1,200 men at any one time.[39]

The regiment also lacked a full complement of officers. Hawkins' active rank remained lieutenant colonel, rather than full colonel, all through the war. Field and Staff made do with assistant surgeons plus one hospital steward rather than one surgeon and one assistant surgeon. Sergeants and corporals, however, numbered about as expected in the larger companies. One teamster, nine farriers, three saddlers, two wagon

---

38. H.C.B. Rogers, *The Confederates and Federals at War* (Conshohocken, PA: Combined Publishing, 2000), 52–53.

39. *Compiled Service Records 7th Tennessee*, M395 RG094 rolls 63-69.

masters, several acting orderlies and three buglers served the regiment during its existence.[40]

Recruitment and Muster

By June of 1862 Colonel Hawkins had begun recruitment of his regiment. He received help from Humboldt, Tennessee Post Commander Major Brackett and Provost Marshall Captain Young of the 5th Iowa.[41] Lieutenant William F. Allender, who enlisted on August 7, 1861, in Metropolis, Illinois, joined Hawkins as an assistant. Huntingdon in Carroll County, Lexington in Henderson County, Jackson in Madison County and Trenton in Gibson County served as the primary recruitment stations for the 1862 volunteers.

A newspaper published in August 1862 by the 12th Wisconsin Battery at Humboldt gave a vivid description of loyalist volunteers arriving at the post. It would have included the men from companies E and B of the 2nd West Tennessee congregating there during the late summer.

> We have observed a number of ragged fellows about the village lately and wondered what their business might be. Think [*sic*] it treachery, but were very agreeably disappointed to find that they were loyal Tennesseans, forming a company for service under the "stars and stripes." These poor fellows have been compelled to lie out in the bush to preserve their lives from their traitorous neighbors, for days and weeks, but have finally gathered to offer their services for their country. We welcome you, loyal men, and are proud of your patriotism. It is not the counterfeit that stays at home, trying to preserve neutrality, but the genuine that says "he that strikes my country, strikes me"—would to God there were more such.[42]

40. *Ibid.*

41. *Iowa Adjutant General's Office: Together with Historical Sketches of Volunteer Organizations, 1861-66* 4 (Des Moines, IA: E. H. English Publisher, 1908–1911), 848.

42. Newspaper published by 12th Wisconsin Battery from July through September 1862 at Humboldt, Tennessee, Vol. 1, No. 4, August 23 and September 4, 1862. Newspaper is on microfilm in genealogy room of the Humboldt Library.

Northern officers who mustered the 1st West Tennessee Cavalry, a regiment raised in generally the same area, gave another description of the dress of the southern recruits. They reported them as "having on every conceivable type of uniform" with their colonel in a "tall silk hat, a long coat with brass buttons, baggy jeans pantaloons, and an old sword." An officer asked General Granville Dodge[43] if he expected to "muster in such a crowd as that."[44] These northern comments about the appearance of the new loyalist volunteers seem somewhat condescending. However inappropriately dressed, placement in regular companies had already begun.

Composition of the 1862 Companies

Company E: The First Company Organized (June 1862)

Huntingdon provided the enlistment center for Company E, the first company of the 2nd to volunteer. This company required a three years commitment. John Bond of Carroll County, who enlisted in Huntingdon on June 21, 1862, led the way. By the end of June, 60 men had volunteered. Over half of the 100 men who would serve in this company enlisted in the eight days from June 21-28, 1862. They came mainly from southeastern Carroll County, northeastern Henderson County and southwestern Benton County. This first group of recruits mustered in at Humboldt, Tennessee in August 62 with the assistance of the 5th Iowa and 12th Wisconsin.

The first officers of Company E were:

Captain Pleasant K. Parsons (age 40)
Lieutenant James Wyley Morgan (age 29)
Sergeant Joel B. Madaris (age 34)
Sergeant William G. Palmer (age 30)
Sergeant Jasper Richardson (age 22)
Sergeant James Franklin Smothers (age 24)

---

43. General Grenville M. Dodge of the 4th Iowa Infantry commanded the Central Division, Army of Tennessee. He headquartered at Trenton in the summer of 1862. After the war, he oversaw the building of the transcontinental railroad from Omaha to Utah. Dodge sometimes asked specifically for the 6th and 7th Tennessee Cavalries and made use of their services.

44. Jacob R. Perkins, *Trails, Rails and War, The Life of General G. M. Dodge* (Indianapolis, IN: Bobbs-Merrill Company, 1929), 109–110.

Sergeant Granville Trout (age 25)
Sergeant John A. Norden (age 23)

Three-Year Enlistments of Original Companies A, B, C, and H for August and September 1862

August was by far the month in which the 2nd West Tennessee received its largest number of volunteers. Six companies organized, including three with three years enlistment (original A, B, and C) and three one year companies (D, F, and G). About 413 men enlisted in this month, nearly one-third of the enlistment for the regiment. Perhaps the Union's successes at Shiloh, Corinth and Memphis gave the loyalists hope for a speedy Union victory.

Company A enlisted its first recruit, Barney Dunn (age 54) of Henderson County in July of 1862. Four of his sons would later join other companies of the 7th. Lexington and Jackson provided the primary enlistment stations for this company. By mid August twenty-nine men had joined. August 18th added thirty-eight more making a total of seventy-two by the end of the month. Twelve more enlisted by the end of 1862 giving a total of eighty-five. About three fourths of these recruits furnished their own horse and equipment. During the first two years the majority of these men hailed from Henderson County. Of those whose records listed an occupation, all claimed to be farmers except for one shoemaker and one dentist.

The first officers of Company A were:
Captain Thomas Atlas Smith (age 45)
Lieutenant Alexander T. Hart (age 36)
Lieutenant Frank M. Reed (age 20)
Sergeant Annanias Boatwright (age 25)
Sergeant William P. Bolton (age 27)
Sergeant Martin V. Burnes (age 29)
Sergeant Willis H. Cunningham (age 48)
Sergeant John M. Rhodes (age 33)

Company B enlisted primarily in Carroll County and the majority of the men lived there. A few, however, hailed from western Benton County. By the end of August 1862 the company contained seventy-five men. Nine more volunteered from September to December of 1862 making a total of eighty-two.

The original officers of Company B were:

Captain James M. Martin (age 36)
Lieutenant Newton Cox (age 27)
Sergeant Stephen F. Dill (age 28)
Sergeant William R. Norvell (age 45)
Sergeant Elbert N. Royall (age 24)
Sergeant Thomas E. Pasteur (age 24)
Sergeant Robert M. Pruett (age 32)
Sergeant James M. Spellings (age 36)

Company C had two enlistments in Huntingdon in July of 1862 but most of the fifty-one men who registered in August did so at Lexington, Tennessee. Many of these men lived in the Bear Creek area of northeast Henderson and northwest Decatur Counties and followed the lead of Asa Hayes who became captain. The enlistment at Lexington seems to have been reaffirmed later at Jackson, Tennessee. By the end of 1862 this company had ninety-seven members.

The original officers of Company C were:

Captain Asa N. Hays (age 46)
Lieutenant William F. Allender (age 24)
Lieutenant Mark M. Renfro (age 53)
Sergeant Lawson Boren (age 29)
Sergeant George Cole (age 23)
Sergeant William H. Dennison (age 38)
Sergeant George Frizell (age 19)
Sergeant Samuel L. Hays (age 33)
Sergeant Britoen Smith (age 35)

Company H signed up about twenty-six men at Lexington on September 24, 1862. The first day volunteers turned out to be over half of the forty-six volunteers who joined this smallest company in the 2nd West Tennessee. Most men mustered in at Trenton on September 28, 1862. The company never really organized. Their captain, Wesley Derryberry, served only a short time before being demoted to private. Derryberry and at least nineteen more of these soldiers eventually transferred into

Company I. Some also later served in companies E, B, and C. Twenty-two men, however, kept the Company H designation all through their enlistment.

The company lacked a captain, a lieutenant and originally even sergeants, having only three corporals, a farrier and a bugler. How this small company operated within the regiment remains unknown. It may have eventually acted in conjunction with another company, probably Company I.

One-Year Enlistments of Companies D, F, and G Recruited in August and September 1862

When enlisting in the summer of 1862, a recruit to the 2nd West Tennessee Cavalry had the option of joining for either one or three years. Colonel Hurst of the 1st West Tennessee Cavalry (later 6th) felt that the one-year companies gave an unfair advantage to the 2nd and deprived him of some of his candidates.[45] A disadvantage of the one-year companies may have been that they provided no enlistment bounty, at least at first.

Company D enlisted its first two volunteers, John Ellis and Samuel Dodd, on July 4, 1862. Out of the eighty-eight men who served in the company, however, seventy-one joined in Carroll County in August of 1862. The majority mustered in a month later on September 24 at Trenton in Gibson County. The men lived generally in the Maple Creek area, now a part of the Natchez Trace State Park. This area in the southeast corner of Carroll County borders northeast Henderson and southwest Benton. The largest number of men lived in Carroll County, with a few residents of Henderson and Benton Counties.

Original officers of Company D were:
Captain John Alexander Miller (age 28)
Lieutenant Henry C. Butler (age 30)
Lieutenant Joseph C. Miller (age 29)
Sergeant James Riley Hall (age 19)
Sergeant Andrew B. Hampton (age 27)
Sergeant Stephen Hollowell (age 32)

45. Kevin D. McCann, *Hurst's Wurst, A History of the 6th Tennessee (U.S.) Cavalry* (Self published, Ashland City, Tennessee, 1995), 10.

Sergeant James F. Rogers (age 20)
Sergeant Wilie Dewitt Robinson (age 29)
Sergeant Ferman C. Sanders (age 25)

Company F proved a bit unusual in that it received its largest number of recruits in September rather than August. The earlier recruits enlisted in Carroll County but the September men signed up in both Carroll County and at Trenton in Gibson County. Most mustered in at Trenton on either August 11 or September 24. Also, unlike most of the other companies of the 2nd, this one oversubscribed, having one hundred fifteen men by the end of 1862. Many came from the area near Liberty All Methodist Church in Carroll County. Two physicians signed up in this group, Captain Ashton W. Hawkins and Lieutenant William W. Murray, although neither served officially as a doctor. Others who listed an occupation, other than farmer, were two laborers, one shoemaker, a clerk, a merchant, and a pilot, presumably of a riverboat.

Original Officers of Company F were:
Captain Ashton W. Hawkins (age 37)
Lieutenant Samuel W. Hawkins (age 18)
Lieutenant John Terrell Robeson (age 24)
Sergeant Elijah Freeman (age 35)
Sergeant John Sims Laycook (age 22)
Sergeant Josephus McCracken (age 18)
Sergeant John A. McLoud (age 35)
Sergeant John Orr (age 28)
Sergeant Franklin Travis (age 29)

Company G enlisted its first eight men on the first four days of August 1862. The 5th of August, however, proved to be the big day for Company G at the Huntingdon and Clarksburg recruitment stations. Sixty-six men volunteered that day making this group the largest in the 2nd West Tennessee to enlist in a single day. The total by the end of the year reached eighty-four. Slightly over half of the men resided in Carroll County, with men from northern Henderson County the second largest group. About one fourth furnished their horses and equipment. The rolls contain no mention of a bounty and give descriptions for only half the men. The men were farmers, with the exception of two carpenters.

Three-fifths were twenty-five or under, one-fourth still teenagers. The clerk failed to record the muster-in dates in most cases but other evidence indicates they reported for duty from September-November at Trenton in Gibson County.

The first officers of Company G were:

Captain Thomas Belew (age 39)
1st Lieutenant Milton W. Hardy (age 25)
2nd Lieutenant Joel W. Chambers (age 24)
Quarter Master Sergeant Allen Pinckley (34)
1st Sergeant Scott Pinckley (age 23)
1st Duty Sergeant Ren Springer (age 25)
3rd Duty Sergeant Henry Marion Roark (age 34)
4th Duty Sergeant Hosea Springer (age 23)

All the officers lived around Clarksburg in Carroll County. Several had families connected to the Roan's Creek Christian Church (Church of Christ). Many could claim kinship by blood or marriage.

Non-Existent Companies

Although one occasionally finds a soldier said to be in Company J, no such company existed. Most likely transcribers misread the letter I for a J. The Union Army normally skipped the letter J when naming companies. The muster rolls also list four men as having been in Company L. Two of them died at Andersonville Prison. No information exists on their enlistment, muster, etc. in the rolls except their deaths in prison. On Adam Finch's records, a notation says "no evidence of Company L or Finch.[46] No Company L ever organized. Most likely an "I" has been misread again or the men served in some other regiment.

Mustering In the 1862 Companies

On August 14, 1862, Andrew Johnson, the military governor of Tennessee, telegraphed Captain J. Morris Young of the 5th Iowa to muster in all the Tennessee troops gathered at Humboldt. On the day of the

---

46. "Adam Finch," *Compiled Service Records* 7th Tennessee, Roll 395-65, #595.

telegraph, however, Young had gone to Huntingdon to a "war meeting" at Colonel Hawkins' home. In the meantime, scouts from Humboldt captured some Kentuckians thought to be from a large group headed south toward Young and Hawkins.[47] Colonel Hawkins also heard about the Kentuckians and reported to his superior that "400 or more Kentuckians dressed in citizens' clothes were near Huntingdon" the night before (14th) and planned to capture Captain Young and his party of thirty.[48] Young, however, escaped the Kentucky threat, if it ever existed[49] and returned safely to Humboldt.

Someone had already mustered fifty-four volunteers into Company E on August 11, 1862. Another group of twenty-five from Company B mustered on August 26 and a few men continued to muster in at Humboldt until the 24th of September 1862.[50] Mustering took place in August and early September primarily in Benton County, Jackson, and Humboldt.

Summary of 1862 Recruitment and Muster plus Early Equipage

The recruitment of the 2nd West Tennessee Cavalry began in June 1862 only two months after the battle of Shiloh. Six companies awaited muster by August and a seventh one month later.[51] At the end of September, the 2nd contained about 675 enlisted men and officers. Companies A, B, C, H, (three-year enlistments) and D, F, G (one-year enlistments) mustered into the army by order of Major General U. S. Grant.[52] With the mustering of the original companies completed, the 2nd West Tennessee volunteers became a regulation unit within the Union Army.

On September 4, 1862, the 12th Wisconsin newspaper gave an account of the equipment of what appears to be members of the 2nd West Tennessee stationed in Humboldt. "The loyal Tennesseans have been armed with rifles and bayonets with plenty of ball cartridge, so they will be able to give a good account of themselves when the foe makes his

47. George E. Bryant to John A. McClernand, August 15, 1862, *OR*, 1, XVII, (2), 168.

48. *Ibid*, 174.

49. Young rose in the ranks and made colonel in the east by 1864. *OR*, 1, XLIX, (2), 873.

50. *Compiled Service Records 7th Tennessee*, M395 RG094 rolls 63–69.

51. "Isaac R. Hawkins," *Compiled Service Records 7th Tennessee*, Roll 395-65, #790.

52. *Ibid.*

appearance. This is only temporary until their regular cavalry armament and equipments arrive."[53] The 2nd remained ill equipped, however, in late December 1862.[54]

53. *Soldiers' Budget Newspaper*, July–September 1862, Vol. 1, No. 4, August–September 4, 1862. G.M. Dodge to M. Rochester, September 2, 1862, *OR*, 1, XVII, (2): 194–195.

54. Robert Ingersoll, report, December 27, 1862, *OR*, 1, XVII, (1), 554.

CHAPTER TWO

THE 2nd WEST TENNESSEE JOINS UNION FORCES AND FIGHTS FOUR BATTLES

The Regiment Assigned Occupation Force Duties Within the Union Army

In the late summer and fall of 1862 the regiment began its service in the 16th Army Corps, District of West Tennessee, the Army of the Tennessee, under the command of Major General Ulysses S. Grant. It served occupation duty at Trenton in Midwest Tennessee near General Grant's Jackson, Tennessee headquarters. Earlier Union successes in the spring and summer of 1862 resulted in an ever-increasing need for occupation forces in recently subdued areas. As Grant prepared to move the major part of his invasion troops deeper into the South, the danger to supply lines and communications from Confederate cavalry raids, guerillas and irate citizens increased. The area behind the advancing Union forces could be as treacherous as the unconquered terrain ahead. Some have estimated that the Union needed as many as one-third of its troops serving in the rear at any given time. Two of the main duties of these forces involved railroads and telegraph lines.[1]

During the Civil War, and for the first time in American history, railroads played an important part in military strategy. The South had about 9,280 miles of track.[2] Both sides tried to deprive the other of the use of those lines. In addition to moving troops quickly, a single-track railroad could supply sixty to seventy thousand soldiers,[3] an especially important statistic for an invading army in hostile territory. Although two water routes, the Tennessee and the Mississippi, bounded West Tennessee, the Tennessee River often became too shallow for boat traffic in summer[4] and much of the Mississippi was under Confederate control.

The railway lines that crossed West Tennessee went from Memphis to Bowling Green, Kentucky, from Mobile, Alabama to the Ohio River near Cairo, Illinois, from Memphis to Chattanooga, and from Grenada, Mississippi to Jackson, Tennessee. The main junctions occurred at Memphis, Grand Junction, Humboldt, and Jackson.[5] The West Tennessee rail lines fell under nominal control of the Union after Grant's 1862 campaign. Southern guerillas and cavalry troops, however, destroyed bridges and tore up sections of the tracks whenever possible, attempting to thwart Union usage. The men of the 2nd were assigned to Humboldt and Trenton, both on the Mobile & Ohio Railroad to begin their service in West Tennessee.

The telegraph also became a new factor in military strategy. The first telegraph message had been sent less than twenty years before the Civil War began. As a result of this new technology commanders on both sides had more information, and more up to date information, than in previous wars. That is, they did until the other side cut the wires or spliced into the system to gather intelligence. Occasionally both sides transmit-

---

1. William W. Freehling, *The South vs. the South: How Anti-Confederate Southerners Shaped the Course of the Civil War* (New York: Oxford University Press, 2001), 4.

2. James L. Roark, Michael P. Johnson, Patricia Cline Cohen, Sarah Stage, Alan Lawson and Susan M. Hartmann, *The American Promise, Volume I: to 1877* (Boston: Bedford St. Martin's, 2000), 385.

3. H.C.B. Rogers, *The Confederates and Federals at War*, 102.

4. QM Meigs to QM Easton, January 15, 1864, *OR*, 1, XXXII, (2), 104.

5. H.C.B. Rogers, *The Confederates and Federals at War*, 92.

ted false information, as well.[6] The advantages of the telegraph, however, far outweighed the disadvantages.

In addition to guarding railroads and telegraph lines, other duties included protecting loyal citizens, fighting guerillas, keeping Confederate recruiters from operating in the occupied zones, and protecting stockpiles of war equipment. Troops also commandeered supplies from the civilian population for their own needs. Although both the Union and Confederate armies took private resources without permission, citizens most resented having goods taken from them by the side they opposed.

Since the federal authorities stationed the 2nd West Tennessee in its home territory, the soldiers knew exactly which rebel citizens had the most provisions. For example, on September 14, 1862, six men led by Lieutenant Newton Cox appeared at the Carroll County home of Williamson Younger, a wealthy planter whose sons fought for the Confederacy. According to Younger's diary, the men took "a fine horse worth $200, and a good leather halter." Younger recognized Cox and Private Jacob Barnhart, both Carroll County natives, and accused Cox of threatening to burn his house. Later when Confederates took a horse, Younger only complained that the receipt for Tennessee currency lacked much value.[7]

In another diary teenager Annie Cole of McKenzie complained that local soldiers, most likely from either the 1st or 2nd West Tennessee Cavalries, took her school horse. She described the men as "homemade Yankees" and accused them of "fighting against their own country and committing ravages in their native state."[8]

Troops on horseback had an especially important role in occupied areas due to their ability to respond more quickly to problems within the large area under surveillance. Cavalry scouted the area constantly and also provided the first response when the enemy, usually also on horseback, came on raids. Some detachments from mounted units served as scouts for infantry regiments at other locations.

Most soldiers considered the cavalry to be an elite assignment. The men of the 2nd, and also the 1st, West Tennessee Cavalry would most

6. *OR*, XVII, (1), 44. *OR*, 1, XVII, (2), 674.

7. Williamson Younger, "The Diary of Williamson Younger, 1817-1876," *West Tennessee Historical Society Papers* 13 (Memphis: West Tennessee Historical Society, 1959): 60, 62.

8. Annie Cole Hawkins, "War Leaflets," on line at <www.rootsweb.com/~tncarrol/civilwar/warleaflets1.htm> and at Gordon Browning Library, McKenzie, TN.

likely have been assigned to the infantry except for their usefulness as spies and scouts in their home territory.

Experiences of 2nd West Tennessee in the Fall and Winter of 1862

In the fall of 1862 all members of the 2nd had yet to assemble in one place. General Dodge, in command at Trenton, Tennessee mentioned the need for arms and muskets for three companies of Tennesseans still at Humboldt, Tennessee in September.[9] When finally assembled, the regiment began its first real assignment at Trenton in Gibson County. This site had been a Confederate post in 1861 but fell to General Dodge's troops in June of 1862. As the 2nd assembled, the post came under the command of Colonel Rinaker of the 122nd Illinois Infantry who relieved Colonel George W. Deitzler of the 1st Kansas Infantry. In addition to the 122nd Illinois and the 2nd West Tennessee, the fort also held the 4th Illinois Cavalry, and a battery of the 2nd Illinois Artillery. In November the 122nd left Trenton[10] and Colonel Jacob Fry of the 61st Illinois Infantry took command. He also commanded the Union troops at the junction of the Mobile & Ohio and the Memphis to Bowling Green railroad lines at Humboldt. Colonel Fry, a veteran of the Black Hawk War and a participant in the battle of Shiloh,[11] outranked Hawkins, as did the two previous commanders at Trenton. Hawkins mustered in on November 14, 1862, as only a lieutenant colonel even though he had originally been commissioned a colonel.[12]

The late fall of 1862 must have been used for equipping and training the new recruits. According to the muster rolls, at least 310 men brought horses and equipment into the army with them. This must have left half the men without mounts and firearms. Apparently the part of the regi-

9. G.M. Dodge to M. Rochester, September 5, 1862, *OR*, 1, XVII, (2), 194–195. *Soldiers Budget Newspaper*, published by 12th Wisconsin. S.J. Mundy of the 12th Wisconsin set up a "picture gallery" near the camp and did a good business taking pictures of the soldiers. Some of the pictures of the 7th in uniform may be the work of Mundy.

10. *Report of the Adjutant General of the State of Illinois* (Springfield: Phillips Bros. State Printers, 1900), http://www.rootsweb.com/~ilcivilw/history/122.htm.

11. Thomas L Crittenden, report, April 15, 1862, *OR*, 1, X, (1), 354.

12. "Isaac R. Hawkins," Muster Roll 7th Tennessee, Roll 395-65, #790.

ment without horses acted with the infantry and the part with mounts, called "Hawkins' Horse," with the cavalry.[13]

Outfitting the regiment with necessities of various kinds constituted a problem. In December, Captain Ashton Hawkins finally obtained some needed supplies from the stores at Jackson, Tennessee. The list included 500 pairs of drawers, 500 stockings, 200 cavalry boots, 400 cavalry hats, plus 19 army wagons, and 114 sets of mule harnesses. Hawkins applied further to St. Louis, Missouri for 270 cavalry horses, 114 mules and 500 great coats—all "sadly needed."[14] No record shows if the regiment ever received them.

Health issues became a problem as well when the weather grew colder. November of 1862 proved especially hard on the new recruits. Two men died of pneumonia and two more of unknown causes.

The 2nd West Tennessee spent at least some of the fall and early winter scouting the familiar countryside. Small groups of guerillas and rebel cavalry kept the occupation forces and Unionist citizens constantly under threat of attack. On the evening of December 8, 1862, however, peace prevailed. Col Hawkins, riding with 150 men near Huntingdon and Lexington, Tennessee reported that the scouting group found no militant rebels in those neighborhoods up to 7 P.M.[15] In a few days, however, the situation changed dramatically.

The 2nd West Tennessee Participates in Four Battles December 1862

Prelude to the Battle at Lexington, Tennessee

On or about the 12th of December 1862, Colonel Jacob Fry at Trenton received a telegram from General Grant warning that surveillance suggested Brigadier General Nathan Bedford Forrest and a large cavalry force would soon cross the Tennessee River into West Tennessee behind Union lines.[16] Presumably all federal posts guarding West Tennessee's

13. "Command District of Columbus, Kentucky," *OR*, 1, XVII, (2), 341-342.

14. "Ashton W. Hawkins," Muster Roll 7th Tennessee, Roll 395-65, #789.

15. Jacob Fry to J. C. Sullivan, December 8, 1862, *OR*, 1, XVII, 394.

16. Jacob Fry, report, January 17, 1863, *OR*, XVII, (1), 560.

occupied areas received this unwelcome news. Riders on horseback could strike in unexpected places and leave before occupation forces, usually infantry, could congregate. In addition, the raiders would have the support of the majority of the populace. Such forays involved little risk and great rewards for the invaders but major headaches for the occupiers.

The Confederacy needed desperately to do something diversionary in the west. Grant's army seemed poised to strike deep into Mississippi. A cavalry raid on railroads and telegraph lines could create confusion behind Union lines. Cutting off supplies and communication to Grant's troops would, at the very least, delay his advance further south. Forrest could also expect to gain recruits to his regiment from the largely sympathetic population and capture badly needed military supplies from scattered Union depots such as Trenton.

Upon hearing the possibility of a raid, Colonel Fry immediately sent a fifty member 2nd West Tennessee scouting party toward Lexington to look for Forrest. Fry described them as "men who were raised in the country" and as "excellent scouts."[17] Their familiarity with the terrain and populace made them far more useful for scouting than northern soldiers. In an effort to secure Trenton, Fry ordered the remaining soldiers to throw up earthworks sufficient to enclose 1,500 men. The men also dug rifle-pits "on an elevation completely commanding the depot and other public property." The colonel felt certain that the number of troops then at his disposal could hold Trenton against a cavalry assault.[18]

Forrest's raiders crossed the Tennessee River at Clifton in Wayne County, Tennessee on the 15th of December 1862. The site of their crossing led Grant and others to believe that Forrest intended to attack Jackson in Madison County, Tennessee,[19] a post then commanded by Brigadier General Jeremiah C. Sullivan, Grant having moved on to La Grange, Tennessee in early November. The Union, therefore, dispatched troops from all over the area to Jackson,[20] an important depot and railroad junction.

17. Jacob Fry to J.C. Sullivan, December 15, 1862, OR, 1, XVII, (2), 414.

18. Jacob Fry, report, January 17, 1863, OR, 1, XVII, (1), 560.

19. U.S. Grant to H. W. Halleck, December 21, 1862, OR, 1, XVII, (1), 477.

20. Jacob Fry, report, January 17, 1863, OR, 1, XVII, (1), 560. Fry to Sullivan, December 15, 1862, OR, 1, XVII, (2), 414.

Colonel Robert Ingersoll[21] of the 11th Illinois Cavalry, who commanded the cavalry for General Sullivan, gathered a force to counter Forrest's advance. On the 16th of December Ingersoll left Jackson with 200 men of 11th Illinois under Lieutenant Colonel Meek, plus one section of the 14th Indiana battery under Lieutenant McGuire. He sent orders to Colonel Hawkins at Trenton to meet him with all his effective men. Ingersoll reported that Hawkins and 272 men joined him at Lexington on December 17.[22] Ingersoll's force then numbered 450.[23] Later in the day 200 raw recruits from the 5th Ohio Cavalry arrived raising the total to 700 men.[24] They would face Forrest's command of at least 2,100-2,500,[25] outnumbered three to one.[26] In this battle, Forrest definitely arrived with the "mostest."

Near the end of the day Union pickets[27] encountered the pickets for Forrest's cavalry near Beech Creek, about five or six miles east of Lexington. The Union troops[28] fell back across the creek toward the town and prepared to fight on the 18th.

21. Robert Ingersoll, currently patron saint of American Atheists, Inc., was the most famous atheist of the late 19th century. At the time of the battle of Lexington, however, he had not declared himself publicly.

22. Robert Ingersoll, report, December 27, 1862, *OR*, 1, XVII, (1), 553. This seems a very small number of effective men for the 2nd West Tennessee since it had over 600 men at the time. Some may have been detached to Sullivan's forces at Jackson, and 50 left earlier to look for Forrest.

23. Robert Ingersoll to U.S. Grant via Sullivan, December 18, 1862, 2 A.M., *OR*, 1, XVII, (2), 429. Forrest estimated the Union forces at about 800.

24. Robert Ingersoll, report, December 27, 1862, *OR*, 1, XVII, (1), 553. The 5th Ohio was under the command of Adjutant Harrison.

25. John Allan Wyeth, *That Devil Forrest* (Baton Rouge, Louisiana State University Press, 1959), 92.

26. Ingersoll had 672 men plus "one section" of artillery. Forrest crossed the Tennessee with about 2,500.

27. Robert Ingersoll, report, December 27, 1862, *OR*, 1, XVII, (1), 554.

28. Ingersoll's command: one section of 14th Indiana, 200 men 11th Illinois, 272 men 2nd West Tennessee Cavalry, plus 200 new recruits of the 5th Ohio who arrived the night of the 17th.

The Battle of Lexington , December 18, 1862

Sometime before 2 A.M. on the 18th, Colonel Ingersoll sent two companies of the 2nd West Tennessee to reconnoiter.[29] At some point after dark on the 17th and before dawn on the 18th, he ordered Lieutenant Newton Cox[30] of the 2nd to destroy the lower bridge over Beech Creek and picket the road from the bridge. Two roads crossed over this creek, the old Stage Road on the right and the lower road on the left. Both roads had bridges. Northern troops destroyed the bridge on the Stage Road but the 2nd proved unable to destroy the lower bridge beyond repair before the advancing rebel troops arrived.[31]

Colonel Ingersoll admitted in his report that he thought Forrest would advance over the Stage Road, not the lower road. He sent a battalion (usually two companies or about 200 men) under Major Funke of the 11th Illinois (Ingersoll's own regiment) to cover the Stage Road crossing. Funke fended off the smaller portion of the Confederate troops advancing on the Union position by the Stage Road. Colonel Hawkins, with about the same number of men defended the lower road.[32] The main Confederate force, with Colonel George G. Dibrell and the 4th Alabama Cavalry in advance, charged unexpectedly over the lower road straight into Hawkins' companies.[33] When Ingersoll determined that the main thrust came on the lower road he moved more men to that position but discovered the enemy "pouring in on all directions." He withdrew the reinforcements to the position of his artillery and sent Captain Hays of the 2nd to hold "the point," which he said Hayes failed to do. Left alone to face the brunt of the attack, the 2nd West Tennessee reportedly retreated "in confusion and on the full run, pursued by the enemy."

After Ingersoll managed to establish a defensive position beside his artillery, Forrest's troops arrived and threatened the right end. At this vulnerable spot, the colonel placed an ill equipped, and as yet unengaged,

29. Robert Ingersoll to U.S. Grant via J.C. Sullivan, December 17, 1862, *OR*, 1, XVII, (2), 429.

30. Ingersoll's report accuses Lieutenant Fox but there was no Fox in the 2nd only Cox. *OR*, 1, XVII, (1), 554.

31. Robert Ingersoll, report, December 27, 1862, *OR*, 1, XVII, (1), 554.

32. *Ibid.*

33. George G. Dibrell, report, January 6, 1863, *OR*, 1, XVII, (1) 598. Dibrell was a Unionist before the war began.

company of the 2nd West Tennessee. Although they rallied three times, this company eventually failed to hold the position. When Forrest broke through on the right, he surrounded the artillery site and forced Ingersoll and around 100 men to surrender. The remainder of the approximately 600 Union troops, northern and southern, fled the field. Union casualties of the Lexington battle included 11 Union men dead plus 124 taken prisoner, either during the battle or during the retreat.[34] No member of the 2nd West Tennessee died but the rebels captured fifteen of the men, some at the battle site and some while attempting flight.[35]

Colonel Ingersoll Blamed the 2nd West Tennessee Cavalry for the Loss at Lexington

In Jackson, Tennessee on December 27, slightly over a week after his defeat and parole by Forrest, Colonel Ingersoll wrote a report defending the loss to his superiors. He laid a major part of the blame on the 2nd West Tennessee. Ingersoll's own decisions, however, contributed heavily to the loss.

1. He placed too few men on the lower road when he wrongly assumed the main thrust would be on the Stage Road. He then blamed the 2nd for retreating in the face of overwhelming numbers even though he, and the reinforcements he sent, did the same.

2. He accused Lieutenant Cox of failing to destroy the bridge on the lower road as though Cox (or the 2nd) forgot or disobeyed orders.[36] Confederate Colonel Dibrell, however, in his report to Forrest, said Hawkins' men attempted to destroy the bridge but an advance guard of the 4th Alabama arrived and drove them back.[37] This indicates that Ingersoll's orders to Cox came too late to accomplish the task.

34. Robert Ingersoll, report, December 27, 1862, *OR*, 1, XVII, (1), 555.

35. *Compiled Service Records 7th Tennessee*, Rolls 395-65. Wm. B. Harris, Zacharias Lewis, Wm G. Palmer, Ira Powers, John H. Rogers, Andrew J. Small, and Wm. Stone, Jr. were captured at Lexington; Matthew Vaughn wounded at Lexington; Cornelius Brewer captured at Farmville with a severely wounded thigh; John C. Dodd captured at Kenton Station, TN. A few stragglers were picked up at Spring Creek, Pleasant Exchange, and Parker's Cross Roads, December 18–21, 1862.

36. Robert Ingersoll, report, December 27, 1862, *OR*, 1, XVII, (1), 554.

37. George G. Dibrell, report, January 6, 1863, *OR*, 1, XVII, (1) 598. Dibrell thought Colonel Hawkins commanded the Union troops at Lexington rather than Ingersoll. Dibrell, a Tennessean, was perhaps more familiar with Hawkins, who had been active in Tennessee politics.

3. He accused the 2nd of hardly firing at all on the lower road and Captain Hayes of "not firing a single gun."[38] Confederate Colonel Dibrell, however, reported that the 4th Alabama "drove" Hawkins' men back, which assumes at least some resistance of their part [39] and probably included the firing of guns.

4. He makes it sound as though the 2nd West Tennessee left the battle at a "full run" that proved "impossible to stop."[40] That the men hurriedly left the lower road does not mean that they left the field. Some men attempted to hold the right, and some remained to retreat with Colonel Meek of the 11th Illinois.[41] Even the men who left for Trenton might have done so after the surrender became inevitable. Northern men left the field as well.

5. He chose to blame one company of the 2nd for ultimately losing the battle. He wrote, "Had they held the right for only a minute or two the guns could have been brought off." By his own admission, he sent a group of poorly equipped and untried men to hold a critical area. Even with these disadvantages, the men rallied three times which surely took longer than a minute. Given the miscalculations Ingersoll made earlier and Forrest's superior numbers, it defies reason that the Union troops would have won except for a particular "minute or two."

6. He accused Colonel Hawkins of being "missing," as though he deserted his men. Hawkins, however, turned up the next day at Trenton along with his men. Ingersoll neglected to mention the northern officers who also fled and turned up in Jackson, Tennessee.

If blame needed to be placed in this fairly hopeless situation, the question arises as to why Ingersoll chose to vilify Hawkins and the men of the 2nd West Tennessee as if they alone deserved blame. Perhaps they presented a convenient scapegoat. All the other troops under Ingersoll came from his own Midwest area. He had recruited and trained many of them.

The Union authorities appear to have blamed Ingersoll for the loss rather than Hawkins. Ingersoll could have been exchanged and returned

---

38. Robert Ingersoll, report, December 27, 1862, *OR*, 1, XVII, (1), 554.

39. George G. Dibrell, report, January 6, 1863, *OR*, 1, XVII, (1) 598.

40. Robert Ingersoll, report, December 27, 1862, *OR*, 1, XVII, (1), 554.

41. *Ibid.*

to active duty but he was placed in charge of the parole camp at St. Louis, Missouri. Reading the writing on the wall, he resigned from the military six months later. (June 30, 1863) [42] Hawkins, however, retained his command.

The Battle on the Outskirts of Jackson, Tennessee
December 19, 1862

After the defeat at Lexington, the members of the Union Army fled toward Trenton and Jackson, the stations from which they deployed. General Forrest followed the part of the army retreating toward Jackson.[43] A major rail crossing for West Tennessee, Jackson served as a concentration point for troop carrier railroad cars, and contained a "large amount of government stores."[44] It functioned as Grant's headquarters during October and early November 1862, only a little over a month earlier. If it could be captured, it would have been a real "plum" for the Confederacy and for Forrest.

The U.S. military authorities heard of the defeat of Colonel Ingersoll by the afternoon of the Lexington battle. Colonel Englemann led a force out of Jackson, comprised of the 43rd and 61st Illinois Infantries, to pick up any of Ingersoll's retreating cavalry and make a stand. It encountered about 300 men from the 11th Illinois, 5th Ohio, and 2nd West Tennessee cavalries (all regiments that had been at Lexington) about three and a half miles outside Jackson.[45]

Even if members of the 2nd made up a third of the retreating cavalry there would have been only about 100 men. A Sergeant Doss led the 2nd.[46] That a sergeant ranked highest among the refugees must indicate that most of Hawkins officers and men fled toward Trenton rather than

42. "Adjutant General's Report," 11th Illinois Cavalry.

43. N.B. Forrest, report, December 24, 1862, *OR*, 1, XVII, 593. George G. Dibrell, report, January 6, 1863, *OR*, 1, XVII, 598.

44. J.T. Coulter, report, October 2, 1862–January 7, 1863, *OR*, 1, XVII, 301.

45. Mason Brayman, report, December 31, 1862, *OR*, 1, XVII, (1), 482.

46. *Ibid.*

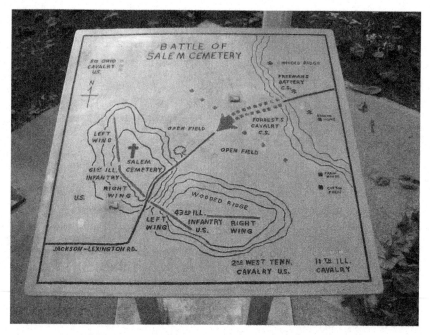

Marker at the site of the Battle of Salem Cemetery

Jackson. A colonel and a major[47] led the other two retreating detachments. No known records exist, however, for a Sergeant Doss in the 2nd or in any other Tennessee regiment. General Brayman may have been mistaken.[48]

Englemann's combined Union infantry and cavalry force found Forrest's men camped at dark about five miles east of Jackson. The Union forces dropped back about a half mile to a defensive position on Salem Cemetery Ridge, and prepared to fight at dawn on the 19th of December. The commander assigned the 2nd West Tennessee detachment to the right flank and ordered it to patrol to the Lexington Road.

Unbeknownst to the Union forces, a portion of Forrest's Cavalry (8th Tennessee) under Colonel Dibrell left at 10 P.M. under cover of night, moving to the north of Jackson. They purposed to capture Carroll Station and tear up track to prevent more Union reinforcements from entering

47. Colonel Meek of 11th Illinois Cavalry and Major Hayes of the 5th Ohio Cavalry. Colonel Meek was mentioned in Ingersoll's December 27, 1862, account as a participant in the battle at Lexington. *OR*, 1, XVII, (1), 555.

48. Colonel Engelmann failed to mention a leader for the 2nd West Tennessee. Adolph Engelmann, report, December 29, 1862, *OR*, 1, XVII, (1), 555.

Jackson by rail.[49] At 10 P.M. on the 18th, therefore, Forrest still planned to attack Jackson. His later report says that on the 18th he "advanced on Jackson"[50] rather than he made "a feint" in that direction. If he intended "a feint"[51] around the town from the beginning, he would have wanted Jackson fully re-enforced. Any Union soldiers entering Jackson would deplete the guards at the isolated outposts Forrest would later attack.

On the morning of the 19th, Union forces faced the Confederate troops on the Lexington to Jackson Stage Road. The U.S. Cavalry continued to fall back toward Jackson leading the Confederate troops into an infantry and cavalry ambush near Salem Cemetery. Here, at what became known as the Oak Tree Massacre, Forrest lost a number of men.[52] Under increasing artillery fire, Union troops withdrew further, hoping to retreat until they drew the Confederates within range of the guns at Jackson.[53]

Forrest partisans often claim Salem Cemetery as a Confederate victory and label it as a useless attempt to keep Forrest from attacking Jackson, which in their opinion he never intended to do.[54] In his report Forrest treated the skirmish as a rout of Union troops. He failed to mention that he lost about 60 dead or wounded, had three men taken prisoner, including one lieutenant, or that the Union lost only five men.[55]

Colonel Coulter, with the troops in Jackson, believed that the rebels had to be "satisfied with the feint upon Jackson."[56] Forrest explained later that he "withdrew"[57] because he believed the town re-enforced to 9,000 defenders. The Union troop buildup and the battle at Salem Cemetery contributed to a change in plans. On the evening of the 19th, Forrest ordered his forces north of town toward less well-manned installations.[58] Capture of Jackson, Tennessee would have been a major coup if Forrest could have managed it. He opted, however, for easier targets.

49. George G. Dibrell, report, January 6, 1963, *OR*, 1, XVII, (1), 598.
50. N.B. Forrest, report to Braxton Bragg, December 24, 1862, *OR*, 1, XVII, (1), 593.
51. Forrest's "feint against Jackson" is repeated in innumerable books.
52. Adolph Dengler, report, December 28, 1862, *OR*, 1, XVII, (1), 558-60.
53. Adolph Englemann, report, December 29, 1862, *OR*, 1, XVII, (1), 555.
54. http://www.nps.gov/vick/camptrail/sites/Tennessee-sites/Forrest%2.
55. Adolph Englemann, report, December 29, 1862, *OR*, 1, XVII, (1), 557.
56. J.P. Coulter, report on operations, October 2, 1862–January 7, 1863, *OR*, 1, XVII, (1), 301.
57. N.B. Forrest, report to Braxton Bragg, December 24, 1862, *OR*, 1, XVII, (1), 593.
58. *Ibid.*

The Attack on Trenton, Tennessee
December 20, 1862

Even after the 2nd West Tennessee left Trenton for Lexington on December 17, Colonel Fry felt the 500 men and three pieces of artillery remaining could hold the place if attacked. He had earthworks in place and rifle pits dug on an elevation above the depot. Late on the 18th (Thursday) two men of the 2nd West Tennessee returned to Trenton bringing news of Ingersoll's defeat at Lexington. On the 19th General Sullivan, believing correctly that Jackson would be Forrest's next target, ordered the 500 men left at Trenton to Jackson. This left Trenton guarded by only a few men, some of them convalescents. With an area far too great to defend, Fry abandoned the larger area and concentrated his remaining men around the train depot, which housed various military necessities. He barricaded the depot platform (about 150 by 40 feet) with "stores" including hogsheads of tobacco, barrels of pork and bales of cotton.[59]

The federal government confiscated cotton as contraband from rebels and also bought it from locals. The approximately 600 bales on hand at Trenton awaited shipment north.[60] Some Carroll and Henderson County men unluckily arrived in Trenton with cotton to sell while Fry re-enforced the breastworks. He confiscated that as well and used it at the depot.[61]

The railroad depot sat in the western edge of town on low ground easily commanded from two higher points about 200 yards distant. After the battle Colonel Ihrie of General Grant's staff visited Trenton and vehemently criticized Colonel Fry's choice of site to defend. Ihrie felt Fry should have fortified the courthouse in the middle of town. This, he thought, would have kept Forrest from using artillery since the citizens of Trenton generally supported the Confederacy.[62] Ihrie neglected to recall that Fry determined his plan of defense when he had sufficient troops to defend a larger area.

59. Jacob Fry, report, January 17, 1863, *OR*, 1, XVII, (1), 560.

60. N.B. Forrest, report, December 24, 1862, *OR*, 1, XVII, (1), 594.

61. The Carroll County men included Washington Enochs, Mr. Smith, Alexander Williams, E J. Kyle, and Atlas J. Butler according to Butler's *Southern Claims Commission* application. Eli Taylor McGill of Henderson County said he lost six bales. Sam Crockett, who sold his cotton a day earlier, is said to have received 52 cents per pound.

62. George P. Ihrie to John Rawlings, December 31, 1862, *OR*, 1, XVII, (1), 566.

Colonel Fry telegraphed for reinforcements by rail from Columbus, Kentucky on Friday morning (the 19th) when it seemed obvious to everyone that Forrest would attack Trenton. His plea went unheeded. Friday evening, however, Colonel Hawkins and some of his men returned from Lexington. As would be expected, it had taken time to travel the 40 miles on horseback.[63] On Saturday morning (the 20th), Fry again attempted to gain reinforcements. This time he tried to contact Jackson but rebels had cut the telegraph lines, and it became obvious that the force at Trenton would have to go it alone.[64]

Fry estimated about 250 men available to fight. This included "convalescents, stragglers, fugitives" and the men of the 2nd who returned from the battle at Lexington.[65] Hawkins told Fry he believed that Forrest's troops consisted of only about 800 men.[66] A Negro came in on the 20th and reported 700 or 800 Confederate cavalry at Spring Creek in northern Madison County, Tennessee the night before.[67] Fry believed that Trenton could hold out against a detachment of Forrest's command if they lacked artillery. He placed twenty-five sharpshooters, under the command of Lieutenant William Francis Allender of the 2nd, on the roof of a brick building across from the train depot. A three foot high parapet gave them some protection. Another six men manned windows in an adjacent building. The remaining men entered the stockade. Scouts came in sometime after noon and reported Confederates within a few miles of the camp.[68]

At about 3 P.M. on Sunday, December 20, Forrest's cavalry arrived.[69] Colonel Biffle, Major Cox, Freeman of the Tennessee battery, Captain M. Little, head of Forrest bodyguard and Forrest led the contingents. They charged in two columns and ran into the fire from the 2nd West

63. Forrest reported few of the horses captured at Trenton to be of "any value." Forrest, report, December 24, 1862, *OR*, 1, XVII, (1), 593. These would have been the mounts for the 2nd West Tennessee as no other cavalry unit was there.

64. Jacob Fry, report, January 17, 1863, *OR*, 1, XVII, (1), 560–561.

65. N.B. Forrest, report, December 24, 1862, *OR*, 1, XVII, (1), 593. Forrest reported that he captured a total of 700 men, a discrepancy of 450.

66. Jacob Fry, report, January 17, 1863, *OR*, 1, XVII, (1), 561.

67. I.R. Hawkins to J.C. Sullivan, December 20, 1862, *OR*, 1, XVII, (2), 444.

68. Jacob Fry, report, January 17, 1863, *OR*, 1, XVII, (1), 560-1.

69. *Ibid*, 561.

Tennessee sharpshooters and the men in the stockade. This resulted in seven rebels wounded and two killed.[70] The Confederate cavalry withdrew out of the range of the defenders' fire. The rebels completely surrounded the depot but ceased fighting while they set up artillery on an elevated position. They placed two of the guns within the earthworks Fry had built earlier but had been forced to abandon due to insufficient manpower. The artillery shelled the defenders while the rebel cavalry sat and watched.[71] One of the sixteen shells fired came particularly close to hitting ammunition stored within the depot. It seemed obvious to Fry that Trenton would be unable to hold out more than 30 more minutes, if that long. The officers unanimously agreed to surrender in order to save lives. The terms were unconditional.[72]

The reports of the battle by Forrest and Fry differ somewhat, as expected. Forrest said his forces killed two men; Fry said he had one killed and none wounded.[73] Forrest reported his losses as seven men wounded and two killed.[74] Fry thought from talking to his captors that the attackers suffered 50 wounded and 17 killed.[75] A non-military eyewitness reported "several saddles" emptied.[76] Given sharpshooters on buildings and rounds of artillery fire aimed at "sitting ducks" in the depot, the loss of only eight wounded and three men killed in the battle seems improbable.

The Aftermath of the Battle of Trenton

Forrest reported taking over 700 prisoners at Trenton.[77] Fry insisted that the fort held only 250 men available to fight but that may be too low. The muster roll records of the 2nd West Tennessee show about 300 men captured at Trenton and Lexington. No major part of any other

70. N.B. Forrest, report, December 24, 1862, *OR*, 1, XVII, (1), 593.

71. The brochure at Trenton calls this battle a "brilliant affair" and says only 275 of Forrest's men were engaged. Since one side had artillery and the other did not, even 275 men were not needed.

72. Jacob Fry, report, January 17, 1863, *OR*, 1, XVII, (1), 562.

73. *Ibid.* The man was from the 122nd Illinois.

74. N.B. Forrest, report, December 24, 1862, *OR*, 1, XVII, (1), 593.

75. Jacob Fry, report, January 17, 1863, *OR*, 1, XVII, (1), 562.

76. "The Capture of Trenton, Tennessee by the Rebels—A Cavalry Force Badly Cut Up—General Sherman Leaving Memphis With a Large Force," *New York Times*, December 24, 1862.

77. N.B. Forrest, report, December 24, 1862, *OR*, 1, XVII, (1), 593.

regiment participated in the battle since the majority of the men previously at the fort had been sent to defend Jackson.[78] Perhaps Forrest's estimate of 700 prisoners included men captured previously on the way north from Jackson.

The Confederates spent the night of the 20th of December 1862 paroling the prisoners and selecting what they wanted from the depot. Not wishing to be encumbered with supplies and lacking any way to transport them, Forrest's troops went through the stores and chose needed items. They destroyed the rest of the stores, which included arms, ammunition, provisions, plus 600 bales of cotton, 200 barrels of pork,[79] and several hogsheads of tobacco. The Union recaptured some of the ammunition Forrest took from Trenton and Lexington at the battle of Parker's Cross Roads a few days later on December 31st.[80]

In his report to his superiors Forrest commented that several hundred horses captured at Trenton had little value. This indicates that the 2nd West Tennessee rode poor mounts. The bulk of the horses would have been theirs. According to Forrest, the raiders donated the horses to rebel citizens in the neighborhood of the fort.[81]

Colonel Fry's report on the behavior of the 2nd West Tennessee at Trenton contrasted greatly with the account of Colonel Ingersoll on their performance at Lexington. Not only did Fry fail to blame the Tennessee troops for the loss but he testified "to the efficiency and bearing" of Colonel Hawkins, Captain Aston W. Hawkins, Captain Thomas Belew, Lieutenants William Francis Allender, Samuel W. Hawkins, and John T.C. Robinson.[82] If one believes both reports, the 2nd went from cowardice and "confusion" to "efficiency and bearing" in two days time.

The battles at Lexington and Trenton made the *New York Times* on December 22 and 24, 1862. A telegrapher sent the first report of the surrender on the 20th to Cairo, Illinois. This made its way to New York by the 22nd. On the 24th the paper reported the 5th Ohio and "Colonel Hawkins' Tennessee Regiment" as "badly cut up" at Lexington by a

---

78. Jacob Fry, report, January 17, 1863, *OR*, 1, XVII, (1), 562.

79. Did they stop to count cotton and pork they were about to set on fire, or just guess?

80. N.B. Forrest, report, January 3, 1863, *OR*, 1, XVII, (1), 597.

81. N.B. Forrest, report, December 24, 1862, *OR*, 1, XVII, (1), 593–594.

82. Jacob Fry, report, January 17, 1863, *OR*, 1, XVII, (1), 562.

large rebel force. The paper neglected to mention the presence of Colonel Ingersoll or the Illinois troops. It also printed an eyewitness account of the Trenton engagement which mentioned the small number of men in the fort, the cotton bales, Forrest's use of artillery, and the thirty rounds of ammunition fired before the fort surrendered.[83]

Experience of Tennessee and Northern Parolees from Trenton

Colonel Fry reported that Forrest told the Tennessee troops to return immediately to their homes. In addition to being extremely dangerous, this violated Union regulations. Standing orders existed for parolees in the western theater of the war to make their way to Benton Barracks in Missouri. Most of the men of the 2nd headed north as instructed. A few did return to their homes, however, as evidenced by AWOLs on the muster rolls during this time period.

An unknown number of northern parolees from Trenton marched north under Forrest's escort.[84] They arrived at Union City, Tennessee on December 21st at the same time as a 94-member company of the 54th Illinois. According to the Union commander, the Confederates carried a flag of truce. While the Union company accepted the parolees, General Forrest and his troops rode up, surrounded them all and demanded the surrender of the company. The Union commander believed Forrest sent the flag of truce so the company would be unprepared to fight.[85] Forrest bragged he had captured 106 Federals[86] at Union City "without firing a gun."[87] If he did demand surrender under a flag of truce it would explain the lack of gunfire. Federals consistently claimed Forrest's troops violated the rules connected with truces.[88]

83. "The War in the Southwest," *New York Times*, December 22 and 24, 1862. The "empty saddles" most likely resulted from sharp shooting by the 2nd West Tennessee.

84. Jacob Fry, report, January 17, 1863, *OR*, 1, XVII, (1), 562.

85. Samuel B. Logan, report, December 27, 1862, *OR*, 1, XVII, 567–568. Thomas A. Davies report, January 9, 1863, *OR*, 1, XVII, (1) 548.

86. Apparently he added in five civilians he captured as well. *OR*, 1, XVII, (1), 568.

87. N.B. Forrest, report, December 24, 1862, *OR*, 1, XVII, (1), 594.

88. For example, at Columbus, Fort Pillow, and Paducah in 1864. "From Chicago," *New York Times*, May 22, 1864.

The Battle at Parker's Cross Roads
December 31, 1862

The federal government had planned an election in the occupied areas of West Tennessee for December 29, 1862 to choose representatives to the 37th U.S. Congress. In the 9th Congressional District, Alvin Hawkins, first cousin and former law partner of Colonel Hawkins ran against W. W. Freeman.[89] General Stephen A. Hurlbut, who commanded the 16th Army Corps, had to postpone the election since Forrest remained on the loose in the area.[90] General Sullivan's Union troops at Jackson, Tennessee set out to intercept the raiders.

On the 31st of December 1862, General Forrest's troops swung to the south intending to attack Bethel Station, an outpost guarding the Mobile and Ohio Railroad between Corinth, Mississippi and Jackson, Tennessee. He, however, encountered General Sullivan's troops at Parker's Cross Roads about 10 miles north of Lexington. At first the Confederates dominated the field but four of their companies left in the rear at Clarksburg, Tennessee failed to alert them of the arrival of Union reinforcements. Forrest barely managed to disengage his men and run for the Tennessee River, giving up his plans for a raid on Bethel Station. He left behind much needed ammunition, the forage he had stashed below Lexington for the Bethel raid, his dead and wounded plus many of his men as prisoners.[91]

Even though Forrest failed in his objective of attacking Bethel Station, had twice as many causalities as the Union forces, lost half of his artillery,[92] and had to retreat from the field in great personal danger, Forrest worship continues to be so strong that even the National Park Service lists Parker's Cross Roads as a Confederate victory.[93] A re-enactment

89. 37th Congress, House of Representatives, Report Number 46. The 9th District included Carroll, Henderson, Weakley, Gibson, Henry, Dyer, Lauderdale, Obion, and Tipton Counties.

90. S.A. Hurlbut to John A. Rawlins, December 30, 1862, *OR*, 1, XVII, (2), 508. Carroll County had a partial vote. The 2nd West Tennessee Cavalry was part of the 16th Army Corps under Hurlbut.

91. N.B. Forrest, report, January 3, 1863, *OR*, 1, XVII, (1), 595-7.

92. Estimated Union casualities were 237, Confederate 500. Forrest reported that his men killed and wounded from 800 to 1,000 men. N.B. Forrest, report, January 3, 1863, *OR*, 1, XVII, (1), 596.

93. http://www.cr.nps.gov/hps/abpp/battles/tn011.htm.

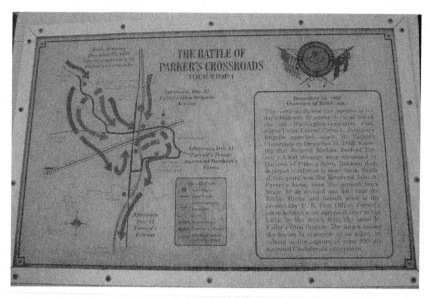

Marker at the Site of the Battle of Parker's Cross Roads

the author witnessed at the site some years ago stopped the show before Union reinforcements arrived, leaving the jubilant pro-Confederate audience with the impression that the Union troops abandoned the field in defeat. Although Forrest's entire 1862–63 raid may be declared a success, the battle at Parker's Cross Roads hardly qualifies as a victory.[94] It stopped Forrest from attacking Bethel Station and from further raiding in West Tennessee for the time being. He scurried across the Tennessee River into safer territory.

The *Huntsville* (Alabama) *Confederate* in January 1863 considered the battle at Parker's Cross Roads a defeat even if the National Park Service thinks otherwise. It reported that Forrest and his men had to fight their way out and that Forrest barely escaped by "riding at full speed along a ravine and leaping his horse over a ten rail fence." The paper blamed the defeat on Union soldiers who it said raised a white flag in surrender then took up arms when reinforcements arrived. It also estimated that Forrest

---

94. Forrest's best-known biographer admits Parker's Cross Roads was a defeat, but insists Forrest showed "remarkable genius." Wyeth, *That Devil Forrest*, 113.

began the raid into West Tennessee with 4,500 men and ended with only 3,000, losing 1,500 men, 500 in this battle.[95]

Some members of the 2nd West Tennessee participated in the battle at Parker's Cross Roads. These men had either been on scout or had escaped at the battle of Lexington, ending up at Jackson rather than Trenton. They came to the field with Sullivan's troops. Captains Martin, Parsons and Hays, who remained free, may have led them. Forrest's troops managed to capture Private Andrew D. Massey and Sergeant William P. Bolton but paroled them very quickly.[96]

A strange incident at this battle involved two officers of the 2nd West Tennessee. The muster rolls indicate that Lieutenant Alexander T. Hart, who commanded Company A after Captain Smith became a major, ordered Sergeant James W. Harris of Company I shot, for some undisclosed reason. Perhaps Harris disobeyed orders at a crucial point or caused others to do so. Hart faced court martial charges in January 1863 but he retained his commission until his resignation in March 1864 [97] so he must have been cleared of the charges.

95. *Huntsville* (AL) *Confederate*, January 9, 1863, as reprinted in "The Fight at Parker's Cross-roads," *New York Times*, February 8, 1863.

96. "William P. Bolton," Muster Roll 7th Tennessee, Roll 395-63 #776, and "Andrew D. Massey," Roll 395-65 #1084.

97. "James W. Harris," #776 and "Alex T. Hart," #782, Muster Rolls 7th Tennessee, Roll 395-65.

CHAPTER THREE

———◆———

THE REGIMENT DIVIDED

Experiences of the Men Paroled at Lexington and Trenton

The Transfer of the Trenton Parolees to Missouri then to Ohio

All paroled prisoners from General Grant's Army had orders to report to Benton Barracks, a huge Union encampment near St. Louis, Missouri.[1] The parolees, though sworn to cease fighting, remained in the military and needed to be available for exchange. How men made it to Missouri poses something of a problem. They most likely walked to a train line undamaged by Forrest or caught a Union gunboat patrolling the Tennessee or Mississippi River. Colonel Fry, Colonel Hawkins and at least some of the men from the 2nd West Tennessee arrived at Benton Barracks during January 1863. Colonel Fry wrote his report on Trenton from there on January 17, about a month after the battle. Colonel Hawkins arrived on January 30. Private Bond, who escaped capture,

1. Hoffman correspondence, December 15, 1862, *OR*, 2, V, 85. General Fremont built Benton Barracks in September 1861 to house 20,000 men. It is lost to city expansion.

wrote to his wife in early February that the "parole boys" had "gone up to the Benton Barracks" and that he could not tell when "their would be x changing [sic]."[2]

Hawkins and some of his men transferred from Benton Barracks to Camp Wallace, Ohio on the 6th of February 1863.[3] On February 24th Adjutant Hardy led more men from Missouri to Ohio, five of whom deserted en route. The 2nd West Tennessee parolees remained at Camp Wallace only a short time before being transferred about eight miles away to Camp Chase, a new facility near Columbus, Ohio.[4]

It appears that some men reported directly to Camp Chase without going through Missouri. By some method and route, at least 306 men and nine officers of the 2nd managed to arrive.[5] All eight companies raised in 1862 had men in parole camp:

Company A, 36
Company B, 56
Company C, 30
Company D, 36 plus Captain John Miller, Lieutenant Henry C. Butler
Company E, 31
Company F, 67 plus Captain A.W. Hawkins and Lieutenant
    S.W. Hawkins
Company G, 37 plus Captain Thomas Belew
Company H, 13

The Field and Staff captured officers included Colonel Hawkins, Adjutant Milton Hardy, Major Thomas Smith, and Quartermaster Sergeant Franklin Travis. The Captains were John Miller, A.W. Hawkins, and Thomas Belew, and the Lieutenants were Henry C. Butler and Samuel W. Hawkins.

---

2. Andrew J. Bond, letter to wife Elizabeth Bond, February 9, 1863. Gordon Browning Library, McKenzie, Tennessee.

3. "Isaac R. Hawkins." Muster Roll 7th Tennessee Cavalry USA, Roll 395-65, #790.

4. Ohio Historical Marker 27-25 at the site of the former camp in Columbus, Ohio.

5. Andrew Johnson to Abraham Lincoln, August 9, 1863, *OR*, 1, XXIII, (2), 603.

The Paroled Prisoners of the 2nd West Tennessee
in Parole Camp in Ohio

Camp Chase, at the time about 4 miles west of Columbus, Ohio on the old National Road, lies "under" Columbus at present. Named for Salmon P. Chase, Lincoln's Secretary of the Treasury, it served four functions for the U.S. military. (1) Ohio soldiers trained there upon entering the military. (2) Soldiers who had served their enlistment, or became ill, mustered out from the camp. (3) U.S. soldiers captured and paroled by the Confederates awaited exchange. (4) Some Confederate POWs held for exchange spent the time there, as well. It functioned primarily, however, as a facility for Union soldiers. During its existence 150,000 Union troops domiciled there but only about 25,000 Confederates.[6]

At the time the 2nd West Tennessee entered Camp Chase, Union parolees numbered about 2,000 and included men from most of the western states.[7] The 2nd made up about one-sixth of the total. General James Cooper served as commandant of the camp.[8] The administrators made every effort to keep incoming parolees from the same regiment together during the wait. They assigned Hawkins' men to Companies A and B of the 1st and 2nd Battalion Paroled Cavalry. The muster rolls indicate that Hawkins took "charge of the paroled forces in camp" soon after his arrival. Whether this command included other parolees than those of the 2nd remains unclear. Lieutenant Allender also had camp responsibilities.[9]

Most articles on Camp Chase describe the section of the camp that housed the Confederate prisoners rather than the Union parolees. At first the rebel prison camp had a good reputation, later however, as the war drug on, conditions worsened.[10] It never, however, gained the bad reputation of some of the other Civil War prisons. Over two thousand Confederates, nevertheless, died there and lie buried in the cemetery formerly attached to the camp. A number of these died in a smallpox epidemic.

6. Ohio Historical Marker 27-25 at the site of the former camp in Columbus, Ohio.

7. *Ibid.*

8. *Democratic Standard* (Delaware, Ohio), April 2, 1863, page 2, column 2.

9. "Isaac R. Hawkins." Roll 394-65, #790, Muster Roll 7th Tennessee Cavalry USA. "Wm. F. Allender." Roll 395-64, #38.

10. Camp Chase defense against article in the newspaper "Crisis," December 1862, gives one view. *OR*, 2, V, 139–145.

Better conditions should be envisioned for the paroled Union soldiers awaiting exchange. The U.S. government provided good basic shelter, clothing and food. Corporal James M. Smith of Company G remembered that the 2nd West Tennessee "fared all right there and had plenty of good clothes." They "slept on bunks in houses" and remained "warm and comfortable. Plenty to eat of ordinary food." Private Irvin Hampton remembered that they had "plenty provision most of the time."[11]

Occasionally food supply became a problem. When this happened the camp went on half rations. Since the men received pay, they could always supplement their diet from the vendors who entered the Union side of camp. In a letter written from Camp Chase Captain Ashton W. Hawkins of Company F mentioned how much the men enjoyed seeing the children who sold nuts, apples and oranges because they reminded the soldiers of home. He also described the beggars from town who went through the camp daily asking for anything the soldiers might give away.[12] One of the men of the 2nd who escaped capture wrote his wife that the detachment at La Grange, Tennessee heard from Camp Chase every week and the "boys up there" reported being "fat and saucy."[13] Since life in parole camps had the reputation of being easier than regular duty, military authorities worried that some soldiers might surrender in order to sit out their enlistment in comparative comfort.[14]

Union parolees could leave Camp Chase when off duty. They had liberty to go into the surrounding area or even further with permission. The diary of Zelotes Musgrave, a parolee in another regiment, mentions fishing trips to the Scioto River several days in a row.[15] Men could also

11. *Tennessee Civil War Veterans' Questionnaires*, 62, 119.

12. A.W. Hawkins, letter to daughter Flora, April 13, 1863, *Ansearchin' News* (Memphis: Tennessee Genealogical Society, Winter 1995): 150–151.

13. Andrew J. Bonds, letter to wife Elizabeth. May 16, 1863. Gordon Browning Library, McKenzie, TN.

14. Edwin M. Stanton to David Tod, Columbus, Ohio, September 9, 1862, *OR*, 2, IV, 499.

15. Diary of Zelotes Musgrave of the Ohio 45th. Unpublished excerpt at http://www.homestead.com/ohio45/musgrave.html.

visit a large inn near their quarters called the "Four Mile House," reportedly a "favorite resort of both officers and soldiers."[16]

Sometimes parolees even left the general area. Captain Ashton W. Hawkins visited Olney, Illinois on private business. Colonel Hawkins spoke "at some length and with special effect" at a home front unity rally in Toledo, Ohio on the 18th of March 1863.[17] Lieutenant Milton W. Hardy left for Memphis to have the muster rolls of Company G signed.[18] James Riley Hall carried his relation, Pumphrey W. Gooch who died at camp of pneumonia, home to Carroll County for burial in March 1863.[19] Thirty men on the muster rolls of the 2nd left Camp Chase without permission and never returned.

Illness in the Civil War camps often resulted from crowded conditions, contaminated water, extreme weather and communicable diseases. The 2nd West Tennessee found it necessary to discharge fifteen men at Camp Chase as no longer fit for service. Lung diseases such as pneumonia, TB, pulmonalia, and bronchitis caused the most dismissals. Officers Thomas Belew and Henry C. Butler both resigned due to poor health. Thirteen soldiers died, five of them with pneumonia and the others from typhoid, diarrhea, dysentery, brain fever, hernia, and general disability.[20] Fortunately for the 2nd the regiment left the camp before the smallpox epidemic in 1864 which proved disastrous, especially for the Confederate detainees.[21]

Boredom proved to be another downside of parole camp. Some felt they signed up to fight and contribute to the cause but ended up sitting around doing nothing. Captain Hawkins wrote home that although most

16. *The Story of Columbus: Past, Present and Future of the Metropolis of Central Ohio, Practical Demonstration of its Development by the Reproduction of Rare Historical Photographs*, 2nd edition (Columbus, Ohio: np, 1900), 30–31.

17. Clark Waggoner, *History of the City of Toledo and Lucas County, Ohio* (New York: Mussell and Co., 1888), 93. Perhaps Hawkins was a bit "long-winded."

18. Lieutenant Hardy to Lewis Richmond, Camp Chase, Ohio, July 31, 1863.

19. "James R. Hall," Muster Roll 395-65, #742. Gooch is buried in New Hope Cemetery, Carroll County, TN. Hall became ill and did not return to Camp Chase.

20. *Compiled Service Records 7th Tennessee*. M395 RG094 rolls 63–69.

21. http://columbusoh.about.com/library/weekly/aa020503c.htm.

of the men behaved well, some became drunk and had "to be sent to the guardhouse."[22]

Perhaps a major reason for discouragement centered on the delay in exchanges. Soldiers from other regiments left before those of the 2nd West Tennessee although they arrived at a later date.[23] Bias against southerners might be suspected. A more probable reason concerned the number of men in the one-year companies whose enlistment would end within a few months. At least 135 of the 300 men at Camp Chase would be eligible to muster out in the period from August through October of 1863.[24] Exchanging men with more time left on their enlistments would be more advantageous to the military.

The Men of the 2nd West Tennessee Who Escaped Capture at Lexington and Trenton

The Detachment at Jackson, Tennessee January–April 1863

When Forrest captured approximately 300 men of the 2nd at Lexington and Trenton, it left about 300 of the 600 men in the regiment in need of placement. By 31 January 1863, this remnant had been assigned to the Cavalry Brigade, District of Jackson, Department of Tennessee in Jackson, Tennessee under General Jeremiah C. Sullivan, who had a reputation for strictness. An Illinois soldier stationed there at the same time described Jackson as a "delightful little town" and bemoaned Sullivan's strict orders to stay out of downtown.[25] Most of the 2nd, however, lived so near Jackson all their lives that visiting downtown would be of little interest. Sneaking off home would be more enticing, as the numerous AWOLs on the records testify.

On the 20th of February, the 3rd Michigan Cavalry, also stationed at Jackson, mounted a surprise attack on Clifton, Tennessee and captured Captain Newsom and the men with him. The records show fourteen men from the "Second Tennessee" accompanying the 3rd Michigan. Writers

22. *Compiled Service Records 7th Tennessee*, M395 RG094 rolls 63–69.

23. Andrew Johnson to Abraham Lincoln, August 9, 1863, *OR*, 1, XXIII, (2), 603.

24. *Compiled Service Records 7th Tennessee*. M395 RG094 rolls 63–69.

25. Charles Wright Wills, *Army Life of an Illinois Soldier* (Globe Printing Company, 1906), 145.

usually identify these men as from the 2nd West Tennessee. A Sergeant Mize led them but neither the muster rolls of the 2nd West Tennessee nor the 3rd Michigan contain a person by this name. The 2nd East Tennessee, however, does have a Sergeant Mize.[26] The men on the Clifton raid might have been from East Tennessee.

In the period from March 31 to April 3, 1863, some members of the 2nd West Tennessee definitely rode with the 3rd Michigan Cavalry. They scouted toward the Duck River to ascertain if any large Confederate forces operated in that vicinity. Embarrassingly, while on this scout the 3rd Michigan captured three men AWOL from the 2nd West Tennessee. Captain Asa N. Hays of Company C took them back to Jackson,[27] presumably for trial.

While stationed at Jackson, several men of the detachment died, some in camp and some at their nearby homes. In Henderson County, two succumbed to pneumonia, one to congestive fever, and two to undetermined diseases. Another returned to Decatur County where he died of chronic disease and another to Carroll County where he succumbed to brain fever. Including one more death from pneumonia at Jackson, eight men died of disease during the period from the battle of Lexington in December 1862 to the end of March 1863.[28]

The detachment of the 2nd West Tennessee remained in Jackson for three months. On April 9, 1863, however, Private Andrew J. Bonds sent a letter to his wife from Camp Jackson sorrowfully informing her that the regiment would embark south for "La Grange, Mississippi [sic]" the next day or two.[29] Bonds seemed to feel that a move south placed him in greater danger. He told his wife that if he fell in the war he hoped to meet her in heaven.[30] The regiment most likely made the entire trip by rail since the Mississippi Central Railroad went from Jackson through Bolivar to the site of the new assignment at La Grange, Tennessee.

26. Frederick Adamson, report, February 21, 1863, *OR*, 1, XXIV, (1), 357.

27. Thomas Saylor, report, April 3, 1863, *OR*, 1, XXIV (1): 487-488.

28. *Compiled Service Records 7th Tennessee*, M395 RG094 rolls 63-69.

29. La Grange is actually in Tennessee near the Mississippi line.

30. Andrew J. Bond to his wife Elizabeth, April 9, 1863. Gordon Browning Library, McKenzie, TN.

The Detachment at La Grange, Tennessee April–May 1863

The military importance of La Grange stemmed primarily from its position at the junction of the Memphis & Charleston Railroad with the Mississippi Central Railroad. At the beginning of the war, La Grange contained about 2000 people and enjoyed the reputation as a wealthy and cultured town.[31] In late 1862, after the invasion of West Tennessee, General Sherman made his headquarters at "Woodlawn," one of the local antebellum mansions. When Grant pushed toward Vicksburg in 1863, La Grange housed supplies and part of the guard to his rear. It also contained over 750 runaway slaves, some of whom joined the Union Army when the federal government began accepting African-Americans in the military.[32] The convergence of Union troops, contrabands and refugees wrecked havoc on the town. Many residents fled further south. Buildings became hospitals for Union soldiers and fences served as firewood.[33] The town never fully recovered and now contains less than 200 residents.[34]

The detachment of the 2nd West Tennessee arrived at La Grange about ten months after the occupation. The purpose for the move from Jackson, Tennessee appears to have been to replace troops who were leaving to participate in the Vicksburg campaign. The 16th Army Corps, of which the 2nd constituted a part, guarded supplies, protected railroads and scouted the area for guerilla and Confederate raiders. They also made frequent forays into northern Mississippi. The area between the southern Tennessee line and the Confederate forts along the Yalobusha River near Grenada, Mississippi remained a "no man's land," where frequent skirmishes took place. Private Bond of the 2nd wrote his wife from La Grange about "fighting going on" in the vicinity "every day."[35] Captain Asa N. ("Black Hawk") Hayes of Company C commanded the

31. Fayette County Chamber of Commerce, P.O. Box 411, Somerville, TN 38068.

32. John Cimprich, *Slavery's End in Tennessee, 1861-1865* (Tuscaloosa, AL: The University of Alabama Press, 1985), 53, 82. Figure from March 1863.

33. Aletha Sayers, "La Grange, Tennessee," quoting Captain Forbes, 7th Illinois Cavalry, http://ehistory.osu.edu/.

34. U.S. Census, 2000.

35. Andrew Bond to Elizabeth Bond, La Grange, May 16, 1863.

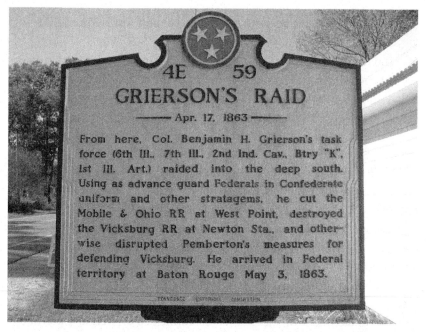

Grierson's Raid Historical Marker at La Grange, Tennessee

detachment, Colonel Hawkins still remaining at Camp Chase, Ohio under parole.[36]

Seven days after the arrival of the 2nd West Tennessee, Colonel Benjamin H. Grierson left La Grange with 1,700 federal cavalry on a fifteen-day, 600-mile cavalry raid from southern Tennessee through Mississippi and into Louisiana.[37] This daring exploit inspired a movie entitled "The Horse Soldiers," with John Wayne portraying Grierson.[38] Reminiscent of what happened on Forrest's earlier raid into West Tennessee, attempts by the Confederates to find and stop Grierson proved as much a comedy of errors as the Union efforts to stop Forrest. It demonstrated once again how cavalry raiders, from either side, could sweep across the countryside wrecking havoc without being caught. Grierson's

36. District of Jackson regiments, *OR*, 1, XXIV, (3), 254. 16th Army Corps, 3rd Division, unassigned.

37. Henry Steele Commager, ed., *Illustrated History of the Civil War* (New York: Promontory Press, 1976), 170.

38. Director John Ford made the 1959 motion picture "The Horse Soldiers," which was about Grierson's raid.

cavalry managed even the added difficulty of crossing terrain with very few Union sympathizers; Forrest depended on willing help from numerous Confederates in the area he traversed. Although not on the raid per se, the 2nd participated in the diversionary raids from La Grange that helped confuse Grierson's pursuers.[39] These forays also drew Confederate forces into northern Mississippi which aided Grant in his campaign toward Vicksburg.

The 2nd West Tennessee remained in La Grange from April 12 through May 1863. During these two months, one man died of congestion, one of pneumonia and another of an unknown cause. No one died in battle while stationed at La Grange but one man obtained a discharge with "a suspicious gunshot wound to his right foot."[40]

Around the time the 2nd arrived at La Grange, someone produced a puzzling list of 125 deserters from duty.[41] The muster rolls, however, show most of these men present at the time they reportedly left without permission. Over fifty of them received honorable discharges at the end of their enlistment, and another thirty or so died of imprisonment or disease while on duty. Fifteen of the men never seem to have been members of the regiment. Only twenty men on the list went AWOL never to return. Being on this particular list gave men little difficulty when applying for pensions in later years since the clerk failed to record the supposed desertions on the muster rolls.[42]

The Recruitment of Company K

In April of 1863, the military authorities authorized recruitment of another company for the 2nd West Tennessee. Sergeants John W. Beatty and John J. Wallace of the 3rd Michigan Cavalry, a northern unit also stationed at La Grange, recruited the majority of the men and became their officers. By May the new Company K contained 66 volunteers and

39. S.A. Hurlbut to H.W. Halleck, April 29, 1863, *OR*, 1, XXIV, (3), 247. Edward Hatch, report, May 5, 1863, *OR*, 1, XXIV, (1), 579. The 80 men of the West Tennessee Cavalry were more likely the 1st instead of the 2nd West Tennessee.

40. *Compiled Service Records 7th Tennessee*, M395 RG094 rolls 63–69.

41. 7th Tennessee Cavalry. Index to names in Regimental Papers. Memphis City Library.

42. *Compiled Service Records 7th Tennessee*, M395 RG094 rolls 63–69, and individual pension applications.

by February of 1864 had a total of 109 or a full company. Beatty and Wallace received promotions to captain and lieutenant in June 1863.

Only sixteen men in the new company furnished their own horses, reflecting no doubt the depletion of mounts in the countryside by 1863. Visualize the men as overwhelming blue or light eyed, over half born in Henderson County, median age 25.[43] Everyone described himself as a farmer except for three mechanics, one engineer, one blacksmith, one miller, one clerk, one musician and one saddler.

The original officers were:

Captain John W. Beatty (age 29), transfer from 3rd Michigan
1st Lieutenant Robert W. Helmer (age 35), transfer from 3rd Michigan
2nd Lieutenant John J. Wallace (age 28), transfer from 3rd Michigan
1st Sergeant John Madison (age 23)
Sergeant Graves Carter (age 26)
Sergeant Thomas J. Hoosier (age 20)
Sergeant Aaron Powell (age 44)
Sergeant Levi Stewart (age 19)[44]

Removal of the Detachment to Grand Junction, Tennessee June 1863

By June 10, 1863, the 200 men of the 2nd West Tennessee formerly at La Grange now guarded the crossing of the Mississippi Central and the Memphis & Charleston Railroads at Grand Junction, Tennessee.[45] They served out of Fort McDowell, an installation in the shape of an eight-pointed star. Although an owner of the land destroyed the walls, the outline for the fort persisted in an aerial view taken in 1987.[46] Men stationed in garrisons such as Fort McDowell also protected the railway from blockhouses built at strategic points along the tracks.[47]

43. *Ibid.*

44. *Ibid.*

45. R.J. Oglesby to Henry Binmore, June 10, 1863, *OR*, 1, XXIV, (3), 398.

46. Douglas W. Cupples, "Silent Sentinels: A Photographic Documentation of Existing Civil War Fortification in West Tennessee." *West Tennessee Historical Society Papers* 51 (Memphis: West Tennessee Historical Society, 1987): 35, 39, 44–45.

47. U.S. Grant to J.E. Smith, December 26, 1862, *OR*, 1, XVII, (2), 492–493.

Orders for the detachment still came from La Grange, about 10 miles to the east and from northern officers. When John Bonds wrote to his sister-in-law to inform her of her husband's death, he complained of "a new commander" over the 2nd "as tight as he cain bee [*sic*]." This reorganization resulted from Grant's need for troops in his campaign against Vicksburg. General Richard J. Ogelsby organized a new division of cavalry and placed Colonel John K. Mizner of the 3rd Michigan temporarily in command.[48] The 2nd West Tennessee became part of the Fourth Brigade, led by Colonel Basil Meek of the 11th Illinois Cavalry.[49] Most likely one of these officers made the men "all down on him," feeling they had "no way to help themselves" according to Bonds.[50] Mizner received a commendation in late June because his command had done a lot of damage in Mississippi.[51] Perhaps he pushed his command very hard during this period. Mizner also seems more likely to have been the offender since the men fought alongside Meek in the actions around Jackson, Tennessee without known complaints. The West Tennessee troops, however, were never known for taking orders very well.

On June 10, 1863, twelve men of the 2nd West Tennessee went AWOL or, at the very least, left without the knowledge of the officer in charge. Confederates captured eight of them at Ripley, Tennessee on the same day[52] and later two more in Decatur County. Union forces caught one. On the 13th of June, twenty-four more men left Grand Junction. Guerillas caught one and paroled him on the 14th. On the 19th of June, the detachment lost nineteen more men. The next day, an additional twenty left. The 10th Tennessee Cavalry CSA captured twenty-one men near Mount Pinson and Jacks Creek, Tennessee on June 19th and 20th.[53] On the 21st seven more left camp and on the 22nd, four more joined the unauthorized exodus. The number of men who went AWOL in June of

48. R.J. Oglesby to Henry Binmore, June 10, 1863, *OR*, 1, XXIV, (3), 398.

49. General orders from S. Wait, June 9, 1863, *OR*, 1, XXIV, (3), 396.

50. John Bonds letter to sister-in-law Elisabeth Bonds, June 12, 1863. Gordon Browning Library, McKenzie, Tennessee.

51. S.A. Hurlbut to John A. Rawlings, June 28, 1863, *OR*, 1, XXIV, (3), 448.

52. Some have suggested this was Ripley, Mississippi, but the records state it was Ripley, Tennessee.

53. This may refer to members of Napier's older group since the 10th is not known to have been in West Tennessee at the time.

1863 totaled at least 100,[54] or about half the detachment. Among these was John Bonds, who complained about the new commander. Most of the absentees cooled off, however, and returned within a few months. These even included men captured by the rebels and imprisoned in Richmond, Virginia. Some received exchanges rather quickly and returned to the unit in a very short time.[55]

These June 1863 AWOLs recorded on muster rolls gave members of the 2nd West Tennessee a lot of difficulty when they applied for pensions in later years. If the veteran persisted he could usually "explain" his absence, often with the aid of a former officer. Excuses, or perhaps occasionally real reasons, included being on a spying mission, being ill, or on the way back to camp when caught. Most could point to their presence on the rolls after the AWOL, thereby proving a return to duty. Having been paroled from prison seems to have forgiven their indiscretion, as well. Several of the widows of the men who died in Richmond received pensions.[56]

Experiences of the Men Imprisoned at Richmond, Virginia 1863

Sixty-three men of the 2nd West Tennessee captured by the Confederates in 1863 entered prisons in Richmond, Virginia. This group included those caught AWOL from Grand Junction, Saulsbury, and La Grange plus anyone caught spying, on cavalry raids, or at home on leave. The sites of capture given in the muster rolls included Bolivar (3), Carroll County (2), Como (6),[57] Corinth (1), Decatur County (2), Grand Junction (1), Jackson (1) Henderson County (3), Mt. Pinson/Jacks Creek (21), and Ripley (11) in Tennessee, but also in Pontotoc, Mississippi (1), Rodgersville, Alabama (2), West Tennessee (5), on scout (1), on way to regiment (1) and eight unknown places.[58] Their imprisonment, rather than immediate parole, reflected the decreasing number of paroles given in the field

54. *Compiled Service Records 7th Tennessee*, M395 RG094 rolls 63–69.

55. *Ibid.*

56. Individual pension applications.

57. The Como captives were in the 3rd West Tennessee Cavalry. They were taken to Danville, Virginia, then to Richmond, Virginia. Some ended in Andersonville Prison. Their records were included in the muster rolls of the 2nd West Tennessee.

58. *Compiled Service Records 7th Tennessee*, M395 RG094 rolls 63–69.

as the war dragged on. Too many men on both sides gave their word to cease fighting until exchanged, but immediately rejoined their units.

It took only a month or two for the West Tennessee prisoners to arrive in Richmond. Their captors probably walked them to the nearest train within Confederate-held territory. The records show that at least one prisoner went through Atlanta, Georgia and another through Knoxville, Tennessee en route.[59] The men captured at Mt. Pinson/Jacks Creek made the trip in exactly one month. The Ripley men took one to three months.[60]

Enlisted men usually spent their imprisonment on Bell Island, a camp of a few tents and shacks on land in the James River, or in warehouses and other sites around the city.[61] Officers usually domiciled in Libby Prison within the city limits of Richmond.

The twenty-one men captured at Mt. Pinson/Jacks Creek spent very little time in Virginia prisons. They arrived in Richmond on the 10th of July 1863 and exchanged four days later at City Point, Virginia about 20 miles south of Richmond on the James River in an area now part of the town of Hopewell, Virginia. The next day, they returned to Union lines at Camp Parole, Maryland. They removed to Camp Chase, Ohio two days later where they joined their comrades who had surrendered at Trenton, Tennessee in December 1862.[62]

The Mt. Pinson/Jacks Creek captives had remarkable good fortune compared to the others. None of the Ripley group received parole before October 1863. Some men remained in Virginia into 1864 when exchanges ended. Thirteen men of the 2nd West Tennessee died in Richmond prisons. A few appear to have been transferred to Andersonville Prison in Georgia.

The only commissioned officer among the Richmond captives, Lieutenant Robert Young Bradford of Company E, escaped from Libby Prison. On the night and morning of February 9 and 10, 1863, he participated in one of the most amazing prison breaks of the war. Over a period of a few weeks, a small group of the officers secretly dug a 60 foot tunnel.

59. "David M. Hodgins," Roll 395-66 #859. "John P. Hicks," Roll 395-65, #847. *Compiled Service Records 7th Tennessee.*

60. *Compiled Service Records 7th Tennessee*, M395 RG094 rolls 63–69.

61. *Ibid.*

62. *Ibid.*

One hundred and nine men out of about 1,200 at Libby made their escape. The men formed groups of three or four. Lieutenant Bradford went out with Captain David Jones of the 1st Kentucky Infantry and Colonel William P. Kendrick of the 3rd West Tennessee Cavalry, the only other southerners among the escapees. They emerged from the tunnel at 2 A.M. and headed southeast toward Norfolk, Virginia. Union Cavalry on the lookout for the Libby escapees found them about 10 miles from Williamsburg on February 27, 1864, and took them to federal lines.[63] Bradford lived to rejoin the regiment, be captured again, and escape once more.

The enlisted men of the 2nd West Tennessee who had not been exchanged desperately needed Bradford's skill or luck. When the Union Army threatened Richmond, the Confederate authorities transferred the remaining prisoners from Virginia to Georgia.[64] The move seems to have included members of the 2nd,[65] at least three of whom died in Andersonville Prison.

63. "Robert Bradford," *Compiled Service Records 7th Tennessee*. Rolls 395-63 #225. Linus Pierpont Brockett, *The Camp, the Battle Field, and the Hospital: or, Lights and Shadows of the Great Rebellion. Including adventures of spies and scouts, thrilling incidents, daring exploits, heroic deeds, wonderful escapes, sanitary and hospital scenes, prison scenes, etc., etc., etc.* (Philadelphia: National Publishing Company, c. 1866), 285–292, http://www.mdgorman.com/Prisons/john_f_porter_account.htm.

64. S. Cooper to H. Cobb, February 7, 1864, *OR*, 2, VI, 925. John Winder to H. Cobb, February 7, 1864, *OR*, 2, VI, 925-926.

65. David Altom, John K. Browning, George W. Cooper, Henry K. Johnson, and William H. Smith.

CHAPTER FOUR

———•———

THE PAROLEES RELEASED AND
THE REGIMENT REUNITED

Men from Camp Chase Rejoin the Detachment
June–October 1863

The Officers at Camp Chase Exchanged in June 1863

Exchanges for the men captured at Trenton and Lexington, Tennessee began after a stay of about four months at Camp Chase. Officers left first, beginning on June 1, 1863. Colonel Hawkins, Lieutenant Allender, Captain Smith, and Captain Miller embarked for Grand Junction, Tennessee where the detachment was stationed. Several problems faced the officers upon arrival. These included a morale problem due to the reorganization and the manpower shortage, resulting when about 100 men walked off earlier in the month. In addition, the officers arrived on June 21 and a Confederate force threatened Grand Junction at 8 p.m. on June 23rd. The fort held, however, and the rebels fell back during the night.[1]

———

1. R.J. Oglesby to S.A. Hurlbut, June 23, 1863, *OR*, 1, XXIV, (3), 433. R.J. Oglesby to Colonel Binmore, June 24, 1863, *OR*, 1, XXIV, (3), 436. The 2nd Iowa was also there. Charles C. Horton, report, July 31, 1864, *OR*, 1, XXXIX, (1), 318.

On July 4, 1863, General Grant accepted the surrender of Vicksburg opening the Mississippi River to Union water traffic. His assignment accomplished, Grant left the western front with his combat troops and proceeded east. The continuous removal of manpower threatened the security of the already sparsely guarded western front. Major General Hurlbut, who commanded the 16th Army Corps, kept the small cavalry still under his command, including the 2nd West Tennessee, in "motion all the time" in an effort to be "advised in time to prevent serious disasters."[2] The remaining troops in the west spread out. Sometime in July 1863, Colonel Hawkins and his men left Grand Junction and moved about 10 miles east to Saulsbury, Tennessee.[3] The 2nd/7th Tennessee[4] joined the 122nd Illinois stationed there since June 25, 1863. As at Trenton, Colonel Rinaker of the 122nd, rather than Lieutenant Colonel Hawkins, commanded the post. The two regiments served together previously in the fall of 1862.

The Move to Saulsbury, Tennessee

Saulsbury, a small town then and now (only 81 residents in the 2010 census), owed its existence to the Memphis and Charleston Railroad (presently the Norfolk Southern Railway). The town pleased at least one soldier in the regiment. Soon after his arrival Private Richard Morris, in a letter to his wife, called it "a healthy place,"[5] an important consideration given the frequent number of camp deaths in many other places.

The exact type of fortifications at Camp Saulsbury remains unknown but by inference may have been minimal. Confederate troops from the south often chose to enter West Tennessee near Saulsbury rather than by the large installations at La Grange and Grand Junction. Some evidence of Union occupation at Saulsbury remains, however. The owner of a wooded area to the south of town discovered some 30–40 rifle pit rows while clear-cutting land in 2005. The artifacts at the site indicate

2. S.A. Hurlbut to J.B. McPherson, November 1, 1863, *OR*, 1, XXXI, (3), 12.

3. I.R. Hawkins to August Mersy, July 31, 1863, *OR*, 1, XXIV, (3), 566.

4. The 2nd West Tennessee was officially the 7th Tennessee by this time, but the old name was still in use.

5. R.H. Morris, letter to wife from Saulsbury, August 10, 1863. Unpublished letters with Morris family.

Route of the old Memphis & Charleston Railroad at Saulsbury, Tennessee, located on the Mississippi border

federal use.[6] Since the 2nd West Tennessee and the 122nd Illinois seem to have been stationed at Saulsbury for several months, they most likely dug at least some of the rifle pits.

Recruitment of Company M

Due to the impending discharge date for the one-year enlistees, recruitment began in earnest for another company. Only fifty-three men volunteered, however. Most (thirty-three) enrolled in McNairy County. The second highest number (ten) enlisted at Clarksburg. Men resided mainly in Henderson, Hardin, Carroll, and McNairy counties, a recruitment area larger than for earlier companies but still in Tennessee. Descriptions survive for twenty-eight of the men. Seventeen had dark hair; twenty had blue or light eyes. Everyone listed himself as a farmer except for one blacksmith. The records never list a captain, due undoubtedly to low enlistment.

6. Betty Daniel, letter to author, February 25, 2005. Pits are on Daniel land.

The original officers were:

1st Lieutenant James Matt Neely (age 24), transfer from the 5th Iowa[7]
Sergeant James T. Barnes (age 26)
Sergeant Richard L. Quick (age 28)
2nd Sergeant Moses Gamble (age 46)
3rd Sergeant George W. Pickens (age 19)[8]

Military Life at Saulsbury, Tennessee, Fall 1863

Scouting parties frequently went out from Saulsbury into southern West Tennessee and northern Mississippi. On July 31, 1863, Colonel Hawkins reported his men unable to catch up with a Confederate force estimated about 700 strong.[9] A scout toward Bolivar on August 4, 1863, found 150 to 200 Confederates there.[10] On August 5, the colonel reported a detachment of the 2nd West Tennessee sent out on the Ripley, Mississippi road had "been badly cut up five miles out and scattered" by a force of about 150 to 200 rebels.[11] The next day, however, Hawkins sheepishly admitted that two detachments of his command mistakenly fought each other on the 5th with no particular damage done. That the two detachments failed to recognize each other as Union soldiers may indicate that neither set wore Union uniforms. Hawkins sent a disguised member of this same group to spy ten miles further south. This man obtained information concerning two Confederate generals and a colonel, plus their troop locations, numbers of men, and equipment.[12] A genuine southern accent must have been extremely helpful when posing as a rebel.

On the 2nd of September 1863, fifty men from the regiment kept watch for a Confederate group who reportedly entered West Tennessee 12 miles to the east.[13] On September 25, Colonel Hawkins reported to his superior that Colonel Hurst of the 1st West Tennessee sent a force to

7. Neely was a native of Carroll County, Tennessee.

8. *Compiled Service Records 7th Tennessee Cavalry USA.* M395 RG094 rolls 63–69.

9. I.R. Hawkins to August Mersy, July 31, 1863, *OR*, 1, XXIV, (3), 566.

10. I.R. Hawkins to August Mersy, August 4, 1863, *OR*, 1, XXIV, (3), 576.

11. I.R. Hawkins to August Mersy, August 5, 1863, *OR*, 1, XXIV, (3), 577.

12. I.R. Hawkins to August Mersy, August 6, 1863, *OR*, 1, XXIV, (3), 579.

13. I.R. Hawkins to John I. Rinaker, September 2, 1863, *OR*, 1, XXX, (3), 295.

Ripley.[14] General Hurlbut obviously kept his much-diminished cavalry busy along the railroad. Undoubtedly many other forays failed to be recorded.

Although Hawkins and some of the officers had rejoined the regiment, many of the enlisted men still remained at Camp Chase in August of 1863. One-year enlistments would end in October so the government most likely chose to exchange men with longer service time remaining. Andrew Johnson, the military governor of Tennessee, took note of these three hundred Tennesseans still in camp and wrote a letter on August 9 to President Lincoln on their behalf. He characterized the men as good soldiers, anxious to rejoin their regiment.[15] Johnson's appeal may have helped. In early September, Lieutenant Milton W. Hardy escorted 113 men from Camp Chase to Memphis, Tennessee.[16] Some men, however, remained at the camp into September and October 1863.

Charles Pierson, a Confederate sent to spy on the regiments stationed along the Tennessee line above Mississippi and Alabama, arrived at Saulsbury on October 20, 1863. He reported that the 122nd Illinois Infantry and the 7th Tennessee at Saulsbury totaled 800 men. Less than 300 of this number would have been from the 2nd/7th Tennessee. Strangely, the Confederate spy used the new designation, 7th Tennessee Cavalry, for the 2nd West Tennessee Cavalry before Colonel Hawkins used it in his surviving dispatches from the same period.[17]

Mustering Out the One-Year Companies, October 1863

On the 25th and 26th of October 1863, at least 134 men from companies D, F, and G mustered out from Camp Saulsbury.[18] A few, however, received their pay and discharge at Memphis. Private Albert Birdwell of Company D remembered that after his discharge at Saulsbury he boarded a boat on the Mississippi River at Memphis, then went up the

14. J.F. Drish to August Mersy, September 25, 1863, *OR*, 1, XXX, (3), 845.

15. Johnson to Abraham Lincoln, August 9, 1863, *OR*, XXIII, (2), 603.

16. "Milton W. Hardy." *Compiled Service Records 7th Tennessee Cavalry USA*. Roll 395-65 768. Order #17, Cairo Illinois, September 8, 1863.

17. Charles Pierson, report, forwarded October 25, 1863, *OR*, 1, 31, (3), 592.

18. Morris was anxious for the one-year men to return home so someone could carry by hand a letter to his wife. R.H. Morris, letter to his wife, August 10, 1863.

Tennessee River to Bomans' Landing and walked the 25 miles home. Private Wesley Carter of Company F (age 20) went to Memphis, took a boat to Hickman, Kentucky, a train to Union City, Tennessee, and walked home through the woods, accompanied by fellow company member Joseph Branch (age 19). Private Irvin Hampton of Company G (age 19) walked to Carroll County, Tennessee from Columbus, Kentucky. Although suffering from hunger and exposure, Hampton later recalled it as an exciting time. Once at home Hampton went back to farming. He described his life as "lying out every night and plowing in the day time" in order to "keep from being mistreated, perhaps killed by Guerrillas."[19]

The one-year men had several choices. They could go north into Union territory, hide out in the woods near home, or re-enlist in another company of the 7th or a different regiment. Their discharges left the 7th Tennessee desperately in need of new recruits and re-enlistments. On October 24, General Hurlbut told General Sherman that he planned to send the regiment out to recruit.[20] Twenty-one new men signed up at Union City in November and December 1863 and eleven more enlisted in other places.[21]

The Recruitment of Company I

Most of the new recruits in late 1863 joined Company I. A few men had served in the recently discharged one-year companies. Company D contributed six veterans; Company G, one; and Company F, nine, resulting in a total of sixteen, a dismal percentage of those who mustered out. Men signed up primarily at Huntingdon, Buena Vista, and Union City, Tennessee. By the end of 1863, Company I contained only about 50 volunteers. The majority mustered in on December 15, 1863, at Union City in Obion County, Tennessee, where the regiment relocated in late 1863. Like Company M, the new group failed to merit a captain due to low enlistment.

19. *Tennessee Civil War Veterans Questionnaires*, 1:15, 32, 63.

20. S.A. Hurlbut to W.T. Sherman, October 24, 1863, *OR*, 1, XXXI, (1), 720.

21. *Compiled Service Records 7th Tennessee Cavalry USA*. Roll 395-64–69. Ten members of the 7th Tennessee filled out questionnaires.

The original officers for Company I:
1st Lieutenant William W. Murray (age 24)
2nd Lieutenant Samuel W. Hawkins (age 22)
Sergeant Benjamin Elinor (age 23)
Sergeant Hampton Finch (age 35)
Sergeant James W. Harris
Sergeant James Riley Haywood (age 25)
Sergeant John H. Moore

One reason for low re-enlistments in Company I involved Lieutenant Milton W. Hardy, formerly of Company G. He left the Hawkins' command and transferred to the 15th Tennessee Cavalry in order to raise a new unit for that regiment called "Hardy's Battalion." At least 40 men from the one-year companies re-enlisted in that unit. After Hardy's death in battle[22] his recruits transferred to companies G and K of the Second Tennessee Mounted Infantry and some returned to the 7th Tennessee.

The 2nd West Tennessee Cavalry
Becomes the 7th Tennessee Cavalry

When Tennessee first raised its Union regiments no state adjutant general existed to assign numerical designations, which led to confusing duplication. For example, six regiments used 1st Tennessee somewhere in their names. By June of 1863, the Adjutant General had renumbered the units.[23] Confusion, however, continued to reign for some time. Apparently the directive failed to reach Colonel Hawkins until after the 5th of August 1863, as he signed "Colonel Second West Tennessee Cavalry" to a letter on that date.[24] In November General Grierson referred to Hawkins as commanding the 7th West Tennessee, a combination of the old and new names.[25] In January 1864, Colonel Hawkins referred to

22. Hardy died near Paris, Tennessee attempting to kidnap or assassinate Tennessee Governor Isham Harris.

23. Richard Nelson Current, *Lincoln's Loyalists* (New York: Oxford University Press, 1992), 59.

24. I.R. Hawkins to August Mersy, August 5, 1863, *OR*, 1, XXIV, (3), 12.

25. Benjamin Grierson to I.R. Hawkins, November 15, 1863, *OR*, 1, XXXI, (3), 189. West was incorrect.

the 7th Tennessee Cavalry using the correct designation.[26] Some soldiers continued for years to refer to the unit by its original designation. This proved especially true of those who served for only 12 months and left before the number change became well established.

The 7th Tennessee Returns to La Grange, Tennessee Fall 1863

General Hurlbut at Memphis, Tennessee expected Confederate troops in Mississippi and Alabama to take advantage of the continuing removal of Union troops to the eastern front. When General Dodge abandoned Iuka and Corinth, Mississippi to join General Sherman, the use of the railway from Memphis to Corinth would be lost to the Union sometime within the week. On November 1, General Dodge telegraphed General Hurlbut to ask that the 6th (formerly 1st West Tennessee) and 7th Tennessee Cavalries remain guarding the railroad until he could send some of the rolling stock back to Memphis to keep communication open with Hurlbut a while longer. On these cars Dodge planned to send over 600 sick men, as well as anything at Iuka and Corinth that might prove useful to the Confederates after his departure.[27]

Stephen A. Hurlbut

General Hurlbut agreed to Dodge's proposal, but sent orders to the 6th and 7th to join Colonel Mizner at La Grange rather than remain at Saulsbury. He thought some Confederate troops currently north of the railroad planned to cross into Mississippi near Saulsbury. He believed they could be better resisted with a concentration of troops stationed at

26. I.R. Hawkins, report, January 11, 1864, *OR*, 1, XXXII (1): 69.

27. G.M. Dodge to S.A. Hurlbut, November 1, 1863, *OR*, 1, XXXI, (3), 13.

La Grange who could deploy east or west as needed along the railroad tracks.[28]

The Confederate attacks on the weakened Union positions in West Tennessee began immediately as predicted. Skirmishes all along the Memphis and Charleston Railroad took place from November 3 to November 5. One of the larger confrontations took place southeast of Memphis at Collierville, a post guarded by the 7th Illinois. Confederates attacked a little before 11 A.M. Around noon, however, reinforcements which included a battalion of the "2nd Tennessee" arrived from Germantown. Most likely, the writer intended the 2nd (native colored) Tennessee rather than the 2nd/7th Tennessee. Both, however, remained in the general area. One or the other helped the Union forces repulse the attack in a three-hour battle.[29]

Sometime during this period, both the 6th and the 7th Tennessee Cavalries greatly aggravated General Hurlbut. On November 7, he accused them of having "behaved badly." The offense of the 6th Cavalry concerned abandonment of its post along the railroad and loss of contact with headquarters.[30] Hurlbut gave no explanation for his displeasure with the 7th. He at least knew their location as he ordered them to Memphis where he planned to "make something of them or break them."[31]

Later in November, General Hurlbut attempted to convince Andrew Johnson, military governor of Tennessee, to relieve both Colonel Hawkins and Colonel Hurst of the 6th. Johnson, however, felt that to relieve them "from their commands without their consent" would be harsh and unjust treatment for two men who recruited the earliest regiments in West Tennessee at considerable risk and sacrifice to themselves. In addition, the Union needed "their influence in raising troops."[32] Hurst and Hawkins kept their commands. Hurlbut continued to dislike them.

28. S.A. Hurlbut to G.M. Dodge, November 1, 1863, *OR*, XXXI, (3), 13.

29. George W. Trafton, report, November 5, 1863, *OR*, 1, XXXI, (1), 246. Charles Pierson, report, *OR*, 1, XXXI, (3), 592. Pierson lists the 2nd Tennessee Colored at Moscow on November 19.

30. J.D. Stevenson to S.A. Hurlbut, November 7, 1863, *OR*, XXXI, (3), 82.

31. S.A. Hurlbut to J.D. Stevenson, November 7, 1863, *OR*, 1, XXXI, (3), 189.

32. Andrew Johnson to Stephen A. Hurlbut, November 29, 1863, in Graf and Haskins, eds., *The Papers of Johnson* 6:496, quoted in *Hurst's Wurst*, 29. After the war, U.S. Representative Isaac R. Hawkins voted against "impeaching" President Johnson.

The 7th Moves to Memphis, Tennessee, November 1863

The Scout to Hernando, Mississippi

On November 18, 1863, General Grierson, by then returned from his famous raid, ordered the 7th to leave Memphis with one day's ration and proceed on a reconnaissance mission toward Hernando, Mississippi, about 30 miles due south. He warned Hawkins to hold his troops "well in hand, and allow no pillaging or marauding," an order indicating the regiment had a reputation for such behavior. Colonel Hawkins also received instructions to "immediately" report in person to Grierson when he returned.[33] Presumably, this insured that the 7th Tennessee would leave northern Mississippi quickly without wandering around causing problems. Hawkins' men found no rebel force until it arrived at Hernando. The twenty Confederate pickets fled, leaving behind one dead and one prisoner. Colonel Hawkins saw no other forces on the mission but mentioned "a great many people upon the roads, especially ladies." On November 19, 1863, Hawkins reported back to Grierson as instructed,[34] apparently without his troops having "pillaged or marauded."

Reputation Among Confederates

West Tennessee Unionist troops sometimes deserved their reputation for destruction of property and violence against Confederate citizens. Occasionally they did so with specific instructions from their northern superiors, as in the situation where General Smith ordered the 6th Tennessee to "grub up" West Tennessee.[35] But in addition to the usual cruelty practiced in war, West Tennessee Unionist and Confederate troops often added personal vengeance. Both sides had troops operating on home territory that included partisans of each army. Men heard about the persecutions of their families by soldiers and civilians of the other side and wanted revenge. A lot of the complaints about West Tennessee Union troops came from Forrest's men, a group Unionists felt to be especially cruel. The 7th Tennessee never developed as unsavory reputation with

33. S.L. Woodward to I.R. Hawkins, November 18, 1863, *OR*, 1, XXXI, (3), 189.

34. Benjamin Grierson, report, November 19, 1863, *OR*, 1, XXXI, (1), 571.

35. William Sooy Smith to U.S. Grant, January 17, 1864, *OR*, 1, XXXII, (2), 124.

Confederates as did the 6th Tennessee Cavalry and 2nd Mounted Infantry regiments. Perhaps Colonel Hawkins' "southern gentleman" convictions helped to somewhat temper the 7th Tennessee's actions.

The 7th Tennessee Transferred to Union City, Tennessee 1864

At the beginning of the war Union City, a small settlement at the junction of the Mobile & Ohio Railroad with the Nashville & Northwestern Railroad, had been in existence for about seven years. In 1861, the Confederates established a training base a little north of the town[36] in a swampy wooded area. It had two camps, one of tents and one of wooden huts, with a forty acre parade ground between them. It remained an important post until March 1862 when Union Colonel N.B. Buford attacked, routed the defenders, then burned and sacked the camp.[37] The town came behind Union lines after the fall of Island No. 10 and Grant's successes in West Tennessee in 1862.

By January 1864, the 7th Tennessee had removed to Union City from Memphis. Colonel Hawkins commanded the majority of the regiment at the new post while Lieutenant Milton Hardy led a detachment stationed at Paducah, Kentucky. Both Paducah and Union City came under the District of Cairo (Illinois) and received most orders from General Hugh T. Reid instead of General Hurlbut at Memphis.[38] Given Hurlbut's unfavorable opinion of Hawkins and the 7th, a new command and some distance from Hurlbut must have been very welcome change.

Beginning in late December 1863 and continuing into January 1864, scouts from the 7th Tennessee rode with Brigadier General Andrew Jackson Smith's troops in a search for General Nathan Bedford Forrest. Smith occupied Jackson, Tennessee for three days and combed the area. When he determined Forrest had crossed the railroad into Mississippi on the 28th of December, Smith returned to Columbus, Kentucky by way of Union City leaving Colonel Hawkins at Huntingdon on the 3rd of January 1864.[39]

36. Lists of CSA Musters, *OR*, 4, I, 629.

37. N.B. Buford, report, March 31, 1862, *OR*, 1, VIII, 116–118.

38. District of Cairo regiments, January 31, 1864, *OR*, 1, XXXII, (2), 302.

39. A.J. Smith to S.A. Hurlbut, January 8, 1864, *OR*, 1, XXXII, (2), 50. Smith defeated Forrest later in 1864 at the battle of Tupelo, Mississippi.

Hawkins, taking advantage of being in his home territory without much organized rebel opposition, pursued other matters. He recruited 102 more men to add to the 262 men he had when he left on scout from Union City. He also detached 100 men to Lexington, Tennessee where they took some prisoners and killed one guerrilla in the act of robbing. In a bit of luck, about 70 reluctant Confederate conscripts from that area surrendered to Colonel Hawkins in order to obtain paroles, some of whom even brought in their horses and equipment.[40]

Although General Smith believed he had searched the area carefully for signs of rebel activity and found none, Captain Beatty of Company K noticed and reported the beginning of a Confederate buildup at Jackson, Tennessee. Hawkins also thought he detected signs of a concentration there as well.[41] Both observed correctly, as later events would prove.

The men returned to Union City on the 11th of January 1864. On the 15th, Colonel Hawkins and Colonel J.K. Mills of the 24th Missouri at Paris, Tennessee received orders to immediately march their commands to Dresden, Tennessee where they would receive further instruction.[42] The order seems to have resulted from concern about a possible attack on Memphis. Adjutant Woodward advised Colonel Mizner on the same day that he had ordered several cavalry units to Memphis from Union City."[43] The orders may have been rescinded since no evidence exists that the 7th actually arrived in Memphis.

In early February, the regiment provided cover for the transfer of Colonel Bradford's 13th (14th) Tennessee Cavalry[44] to Fort Pillow, an installation on the Mississippi River in West Tennessee. Sixty men scoured the area east and west of Dresden and others furnished a guard for the troop train.[45] The 13th, a new and as yet incomplete West Tennessee Unionist regiment, consisted of men raised over a broad area, generally more north and west, than the 6th and 7th. Many of these men and their colonel perished two months later (April 12, 1864), along with the

40. I.R. Hawkins, report, January 14, 1864, *OR*, 1, XXXII, (1), 69–70.

41. *Ibid.*

42. A.J. Smith to I.R. Hawkins, January 15, 1864, *OR*, 1, XXXII, (2), 107.

43. S.L. Woodward to J.K. Mizner, January 15, 1864, *OR*, 1, XXXII, (2), 108.

44. S.A. Hurlbut, report, April 15, 1864, *OR*, 1, XXXII, (1), 554. Although called the 13th, it was officially the 14th.

45. I.R. Hawkins to Hugh T. Reid, *OR*, 1, XXXII, (2), 321.

colored troops, defending the fort in what became known as the Fort Pillow Massacre. General Forrest and his men harbored a special dislike for southern Unionists and colored troops, which helps explain the viciousness of the battle.[46]

At Union City, scouting trips of the 7th Tennessee took on a more northerly circuit. Forays now included western Kentucky and northern West Tennessee. On February 27, 1864, a detachment left Union City in search of guerillas operating along the railroad to Paducah. On the 28th, it found a "squad of rebels" at Dukedom, Tennessee on the Kentucky line. The detachment "dispersed them, capturing 1 prisoner, 4 horses, 4 loaded revolvers, 1 carbine, and the hats of perhaps the entire party." General Reid at the Cairo headquarters thought the action important enough to include the details, hats and all, in one of his reports.[47]

Interaction Between Union City and the Folks at Home
January–March 1864

While stationed at Union City, members of the 7th Tennessee were only 50–75 miles from their families to the southeast. Evidence for varied and frequent communication abounds.

Letters and Visitors

On the 20th of February, Mr. Coleman, a civilian, arrived at camp with news for Private Richard H. Morris. He had seen Morris' wife Margaret and reported that she did "as well as expected." Coleman returned home the next morning, so Morris sent word to his wife that he might soon go on a scout near Huntingdon and if so, Colonel Hawkins might allow the men to visit their homes. Morris also sent his wife updates on various kinsmen and neighbors to be conveyed to their families.[48] Information was also relayed from Lieutenant Bradford about Private

---

46. N.B. Forrest to Jefferson Davis, April 15, 1864, *OR*, 1, XXXII, (1), 612. James R. Chalmers, report, April 20, 1864, *OR*, 1, XXXII, (1), 623.

47. Hugh T. Reid , report, March 1, 1864, *OR*, 1, XXXII, (1), 485.

48. Richard H. Morris letter to wife Margaret, February 20, 1864. Others mentioned: James Harris, Benjamin Duke, Mart Morris, C.N. Hale, A. Carey, Felise Carey, and Jessie McCord, all members of the 7th Tennessee.

Private Richard H. Morris and wife

William D. Prichard, a prisoner in Richmond and gossip about Alexander Gibson's stay in the guardhouse.[49] News and letters seem to have moved mostly through private channels.

Confederate civilians from home occasionally visited the fort as well. In February 1864, Williamson Younger of Carroll County dropped by Union City on his way home from Paducah to complain to Colonel Hawkins about gangs of robbers in the area he thought received Federal protection. The visit proved unproductive for Younger, however, who felt he received "no satisfaction"[50] from the colonel.

Visiting Home Territory

In addition to the mail and visitors, men of the 7th Tennessee also kept up with family and community concerns by going home on leave and going home without official leave. They also entered their home counties

49. Richard H. Morris letter to wife Margaret, February 20, 1864.

50. Williamson Younger, "The Diary of Williamson Younger," *West Tennessee Historical Society Papers* (Memphis: West Tennessee Historical Society, 1959) 13: 64.

on scouting expeditions.[51] In February 1864, Lieutenant Robinson and six of his men captured eight rebels in Carroll County, Tennessee.[52] Sometime in early March 1864, the regiment went out into the countryside in order to insure voters' safety during the coming election. Scouts penetrated to thirteen miles south of Lexington, Tennessee and eight miles above Jackson, Tennessee. On the 12th of March, Lieutenant Bradford and Lieutenant Hawkins' commands had a ten-mile "running fight" with about the same number of men from Captain Bolen's[53] command.

The 7th killed two men, wounded one, captured one, and took six horses without a loss to themselves. The regiment returned to Union City on March 14th with thirty prisoners. Colonel Hawkins reported his men to be in excellent health but failed to mention whether he allowed any visits to families.[54]

Henry M. Powers

Henry M. Powers, one of the men who failed to go on the March scout due to the lack of a horse, assumed the men would be able to at least contact home folks. He sent a letter along for his wife Perriller since he no longer knew when he would "get to come." He wanted her to write him her first chance and let him know how she made out with the old cows and whether she had feed for them or not. He reported his own rations as crout, pickles, Irish potatoes, and souse in abundance, especially when part of the regiment decamped. Clearly the men of the 7th Tennessee

51. As evidenced by the numerous children born in soldiers' families, 1863–1866.

52. *Nashville Daily Union*, February 16, 1864.

53. Probably Captain James N. Bolen of Bolen's Independent Company of Kentucky Cavalry.

54. I.R. Hawkins to H.T. Reid, March 14, 1864, *OR*, 1, XXXII, (1), 495–496.

communicated with their families more often than the average Civil War soldier,[55] even when stuck at the fort with no horse.[56]

Political Information

Even political information from home reached Union City. When the regiment returned from its successful March scout,[57] Colonel Hawkins brought the results of the federal elections held in the Western District the first Saturday in March 1864.[58] He proudly reported to General Reid that the Unionists in his home territory voted even though postings everywhere warned that voters would be severely punished.[59] Confederate General Polk's plan to use Forrest's raid to frighten voters failed, at least in Carroll County.[60]

Trade and Provisions

Goods as well as men and information traveled between Union City and the folks at home. Richard Morris mentioned sending a book to his father and promised books to his children. He ordered two pounds of coffee and eight pounds of sugar from Paducah, Kentucky and somehow had it delivered to his wife.[61] Henry Powers' wife wrote about salt she "sent for" but failed to receive. Powers promised to send more when opportunity presented.[62] These Union soldiers apparently had access through

55. Henry M. Powers letter to wife Perriller, 14 March 1864. Powers starved to death in prison seven months later.

56. Mason Brayman, report, May 2, 1864, *OR*, 1, XXXII, (1), 508. Mason Brayman, report, March 24, 1864, *OR*, 1, XXXII, (1), 502. The 479 men at Union City shared about 300 horses. Forrest said he only captured 200 at Union City on March 24. N.B. Forrest to President Davis, April 5, 1864, *OR*, 1, XXXII, (1), 611.

57. I. R. Hawkins to H.T. Reid, March 14, 1864, *OR*, 1, 32 (1), 495.

58. A. Lincoln to E.H. East, February 27, 1864, *OR*, 3, IV, 141.

59. I.R. Hawkins to H.T. Reid, March 14, 1864, *OR*, 1, XXXII, (1), 495. 1,326 brave souls voted in Carroll, 564 in Henderson, and over 1,100 in Weakley.

60. Leonidas Polk, report, March 4, 1864, *OR*, 1, XXXII, (1), 342–343. Polk had hoped Forrest could "break up" the elections.

61. R.H. Morris, letter to his wife Margaret Morris, March 1864.

62. Henry M. Powers to his wife Perriller W. Powers, March 14, 1864.

Paducah to northern goods virtually unknown in the Confederacy by 1864. They shared these luxuries with their families as opportunities arose.

Some Unionist Families Moved to be Near Federal Troops

After the exit of the majority of Union troops to the eastern theater by the fall of 1863, the skeleton federal troops left in West Tennessee failed to keep order. Bushwhackers and guerillas, many of whom no longer supported the war effort for either side, formed lawless gangs roaming the countryside, terrorizing both Union and Confederate sympathizers.[63] By 1864, the situation in West Tennessee became increasingly difficult. Some refugees walked to Paducah, Kentucky and others stood on the banks of the Tennessee River hoping for Union boats to take them north.[64] A few 7th Tennessee family members fled to live near Union garrisons.

The federal soldiers stationed closest to eastern West Tennessee, where most 7th family members lived, guarded a depot at Johnsonville across the Tennessee River in Humphreys County. Supplies to support the campaigns on the east coast went by ship up the river to Johnsonville, then traveled by rail to the armies in the east. About 4,000 troops, including many African-Americans, occupied the depot in 1864 and some civilian Unionists found employment there.[65]

A West Tennessee refugee remembered Johnsonville as having "a few stragling [sic] houses all occupied by more than one family and children playing and soldiers going around in groups; and mud mud everywhere."[66] Most likely the families who went to Union City, Tennessee and Paducah, Kentucky to be near their 7th Tennessee relatives found similar circumstances. Sergeant Richard Morris at Union City advised his wife if at all possible not "to move to soldiers."[67] The numbers who came to the 7th at Union City posed such a problem that the authorities eventually

63. N.B. Forrest to T. M. Jack, March 21, 1864, *OR*, 1, XXXII, (3), 664.

64. A.W. Ellett, report, April 30, 1863, *OR*, 1, XXIII, (1), 279. A. Asboth to H.W. Halleck, June 23, 1863, *OR*, 1, XXIV, (3), 434. Some built rafts or commandeered boats. Molly Neely Owen, *Memoir.*

65. Johnsonville State Historic Park in Humphreys County, TN contains remains of ramparts and rifle pits which protected the depot during the war.

66. Molly Neely Owen, *Memoir.* Neely had family members in the 7th Tennessee.

67. R.H. Morris, letter to wife Margaret, March 1864.

appointed James Wyley Morgan as lieutenant in charge of distributing aid to destitute refugees.

Depot at Johnsonville, Tennessee (Library of Congress)

———•———

CHAPTER FIVE

THE ATTACK ON UNION CITY, TENNESSEE
MARCH 1864

Prelude to the Attack

Forrest's Movements Precipitate Rumors and Preparations

Bad news began filtering into Union City on March 22, 1864. Ten men from Major Milton W. Hardy's command arrived unexpectedly. They reported that Confederates attacked Hardy and about twenty of his men the previous day and most likely captured them.[1] Hardy, previously a popular 26-year old lieutenant in the 7th Tennessee, departed in December 1863 to raise what became known as "Hardy's Battalion," a part of the 15th Cavalry. Many of his recruits re-enlisted from the recently discharged one-year men of the 7th. Colonel Hawkins advised his superior by telegraph that he felt "apprehensive for the fate of the major." His fears proved well-founded. Confederate troops killed Hardy near Paris, Tennessee on the 21st of March 1864 when Hardy and his men tried to either kidnap or assassinate Isham Harris, former governor of

---

1. I.R. Hawkins to Mason Brayman, March 22, 1864, in *OR*, 1, XXXII, (1), 624.

Tennessee now aide-de-camp at the headquarters of the Confederate Army of the West.[2]

On the same day Hardy's survivors arrived, Union officers in North Alabama and West Tennessee produced a flurry of telegraph correspondence concerning the whereabouts of General Forrest and his command. Most believed Forrest planned another of his raids, but the question re-

mained whether it would be in Alabama, Middle, or West Tennessee.[3] Forrest, however, had already reached Jackson, Tennessee by the 21st of March. Scouts reported his troops near Trenton on the 22nd and estimated the force around 7,000–8,000 strong.[4] By March 23, Union headquarters surmised that Forrest planned to attack Union City Tennessee and/or Columbus, Kentucky, perhaps continuing

Major Milton W. Hardy

on to Paducah, Kentucky.[5] Colonel Hawkins determined from his own sources that Forrest planned an attack on Union City even before receiving official word.[6] His scouts reported forty rebels near Gardner's Station, Tennessee, plus increased rebel activity in the surrounding counties. A scout came in at 8 A.M. on the 23rd and reported Forrest had been through Jackson, Tennessee with six or seven thousand men and was headed north.[7]

Hawkins anxiously sent telegrams at 8, 9, and 10 A.M. to Brigadier General Mason Brayman, the new commander at Cairo, Illinois, giving

2. "Milton W. Hardy." *Compiled Service Records 7th Tennessee*, Rolls 395-65 #768. Also Hardy's records in 2nd Mounted Infantry papers.

3. Correspondence Sherman, Everts, Dodge, Fox, Grierson, Sawyer, etc., March 22, 1864. *OR*, 1, XXXII (3): 110–117.

4. James H. Odlin to Mason Brayman, March 23, 1864. *OR*, 1, XXXII (3): 128. Forrest reported about 5,000. N.B. Forrest, report, April 15, 1864. *OR*, 1, XXXII: 611. General Bragg thought there should have been more given the number Forrest bragged he had recruited. Bragg to President Davis, April 28, 1864. *OR*, 1, XXXII: 614.

5. Mason Brayman to Captain Pennock, March 23, 1863. *OR*, 1, XXXII (3): 127.

6. James H. Odlin to Mason Brayman, March 23, 1864. *OR*, 1, XXXII (3): 128.

7. I.R. Hawkins to Mason Brayman, March 23, 1864. *OR*, 1, XXXII (3): 129–130.

what information he could gather about the situation and advising that, on the basis of his information, Union City should be "immediately abandoned or largely re-enforced."[8] He received no response of any kind to his telegrams until sometime before 4:15 P.M. in the afternoon. Instead of instructions for dealing with the dangerous situation at Union City, Brayman's adjutant, Captain James H. Odlin, sent an almost unbelievable request that troops from the 7th go into Graves County, Kentucky on an errand. He also wanted information about whether the men could subsist on the land or must carry rations. Hawkins, who expected to be attacked within hours by at least ten times his numbers, felt surely his earlier dispatches had never reached Cairo, Illinois or went unread.[9]

General Brayman, who arrived in Cairo only five days earlier, replaced General Reid as head of the Department of Cairo. Although he had been on active duty at the beginning of the war, he left the war zone seven months earlier due to illness. His last assignment had been as commander of Camp Dennison in Ohio.[10] Hawkins had little, if any, knowledge of Brayman's administrative efficiency or lack thereof. He decided to send another telegram at 4:15 P.M., repeating the same information given in the three telegrams sent earlier in the day.[11]

Finally, at least eight hours after Hawkins' first plea for help, Brayman replied sometime after 4:15 P.M. that he had read all the previous dispatches. He assured Hawkins that he would "receive sufficient aid and definite instructions." Hawkins should "fortify," "keep well prepared," "send out scouts," and keep headquarters "advised."[12] These generalities seem vague and unreassuring given the desperate situation.

Even before receiving the general instructions above, Hawkins had complied. He sent scouts under Lieutenant Robeson, Captain Parsons, and Lieutenant Royall to areas surrounding the camp with instructions

8. I.R. Hawkins to James H. Odlin, March 23, 1864. *OR*, 1, XXXII (3): 129. Charles L. Lufkin. "West Tennessee Unionists in the Civil War: A Hawkins Family Letter," *Tennessee Historical Quarterly* (Spring 1987) #1, 46: 37. Hereafter, Hawkins Family Letter. Lufkin obtained access to the letter from Anne E. Quigley of Huntingdon, the great granddaughter of Hawkins.

9. I.R. Hawkins to James H. Odlin, March 23, 1864, 4:15 P.M., in *OR*, 1, XXXII, (3), 129.

10. "Affairs in the West," *New York Times*, June 28, 1863. "List of General Officers Without Commands," *New York Times*, January 15, 1864.

11. I.R. Hawkins to James H. Odlin, March 23, 1864, 4:15 P.M., in *OR*, 1, XXXII, (3), 129. It seemed as though Brayman did not understand Union City was in danger.

12. Mason Brayman to I.R. Hawkins, March 23, 1864, in *OR*, 1, XXXII, (3), 130.

to stay out till midnight. He telegraphed nearby Columbus, Kentucky for a train car and shipped out his sick, baggage, extra guns, and tents.[13] About 8 P.M., he moved the telegraph office and troops inside the fort.[14] Sometime during the night, he and his men captured a spy within the fort.[15] Hawkins sent out more patrols to stay out all night, doing all he could do on his own initiative.

Headquarters finally sent some definite instructions. It issued orders for the 7th Tennessee to have its "baggage ready to load on cars."[16] General Brayman sent another train to Union City from Columbus, Kentucky 26 miles away under the supervision of Captain James H. Odlin, with Lieutenant Thomas C. Moore as an observer.[17] It arrived around dark on the 23rd.[18] The arrival of the train with only a train guard greatly disappointed Colonel Hawkins. He expected the train to bring the "sufficient aid" he had been promised earlier in the day.[19] Odlin later admitted that Brayman only sent him "to find out if reinforcements were necessary."[20]

The train crew loaded the stores belonging to the government and the railroad company on the cars. They also took on 150 contrabands employed as railroad workers in the area.[21] A captain with the 7th later testified that after the surrender, Duckworth's troops indicated they had hoped to find colored troops at Union City.[22] These 150 workers barely escaped a return to slavery, or perhaps a massacre on the order of that at Fort Pillow, which happened a little over two weeks later.

One African American apparently remained in the area but evaded capture. He gave one of the earliest accounts of the battle to the authorities at Cairo, Illinois. The *Chicago Times* quoted him, but then qualified

---

13. Hawkins Family Letter, *Tennessee Historical Quarterly* (Spring 1987): 37.

14. James H. Odlin to Mason Brayman, March 23, 1863, in *OR*, 1, XXXII, (3), 130.

15. James H. Odlin to Mason Brayman, March 24, 1863, in *OR*, 1, XXXII, (1), 540.

16. James H. Odlin to I.R. Hawkins, March 23, 1864, in *OR*, 1, XXXII, (3), 128.

17. "Capture and Escape of a United States Telegrapher," *Missouri Democrat*, July 18, 1864, reprinted in *New York Times*, July 26, 1864.

18. I.H. Williams to Mason Brayman, March 23, 1864, in *OR*, 1, XXXII, (3), 128.

19. Hawkins Family Letter, *Tennessee Historical Quarterly* (Spring 1987): 37.

20. James H. Odlin, *Joint Committee on the Conduct of the War Report*, May 5, 1864, 38th Congress, Representative Committee #63: 76. Hereafter *Joint Committee of 38th Congress*.

21. James H. Odlin, *Joint Committee of 38th Congress*, May 5, 1864, Representative Committee #63: 77.

22. *Ibid*, 71. Gray testified that the soldiers intended to kill any Negroes found at Union City, but he might have told a committee interested in Fort Pillow what they wanted to hear.

its endorsement by saying that no reliable information about the capitulation had been received. Although short, the account later proved to be accurate.[23]

At 3 A.M. on the morning of the 24th,[24] communication by telegraph ceased in the middle of an attempt by Captain Odlin to send information to General Brayman in Cairo, Illinois about the situation. This interruption indicated a rebel presence along the track between Union City and Columbus, Kentucky. Union City found itself in the process of being surrounded. In order to save the train, contrabands, and stores, Captain Oldin left almost immediately for Columbus.[25] The train barely made it across a burning bridge at the state line between Tennessee and Kentucky. Union troops who unsuccessfully guarded the bridge tried to find a way back to the fort at Union City. The occupation of the area between the bridge and the fort by rebels prevented their passage.[26]

When the train arrived in Columbus, Kentucky, Captain Odlin warned General Brayman by telegraph that Colonel Hawkins would be unable to hold out for long and that troops must be sent quickly.[27] When Odlin left Union City, he still assumed Forrest's whole command would attack. In his report after the battle, however, Brayman wrote that Odlin advised him that Hawkins could hold out until aid would reach him.[28] A copy of the telegram, however, trumps a memory after the fact.

The advance Confederate troops began arriving immediately after the train departed. Lieutenant Royall of Company B, leading one of the scouting missions looking for Forrest, sent in a messenger who reported that a heavy force, two miles long or more, approached Union City on all roads from the east. He thought they had artillery.[29] Lieutenant John Robeson of Company C reported Colonel Faulkner's regiment on the road from the southwest. Rebels drove Captain Parsons' scouts in from the north. Lieutenant Robeson's men came in, but the advancing

23. "Forrest's Raid: The Capture of Union City—The Repulse at Paducah," *Chicago Times*, March 27, 1864, reprinted in *New York Times*, April 1, 1864.

24. J.H. Munroe to Captain Pennock, March 24, 1864, in *OR*, 1, XXXII, (3), 142.

25. Mason Brayman, report, March 24, 1864, in *OR*, 1, XXXII, (1), 503.

26. James H. Oldin to Mason Brayman, March 24, 1864, 10:20 A.M., in *OR*, 1, XXXII, (1), 541.

27. *Ibid.* Hawkins was by this time about to begin negotiations on surrender.

28. Mason Brayman, report, March 24, 1864, in *OR*, 1, XXXII, (1), 503.

29. Hawkins Family Letter, *Tennessee Historical Quarterly* (Spring 1987): 37. Royall was probably correct. Forrest's main troops were to the east of Union City and had artillery.

Confederates cut off Lieutenant Royall of Company B and his men from returning.[30] Some of the pickets from Company K also failed to return.[31]

Information Available to Colonel Hawkins
When Communication Ended

At 3 A.M. on March 24, when all communication to and from Union City ceased,[32] the only incoming information arrived with returning scouts. An earlier telegraph message from General Brayman said wait for reinforcements but Captain Odlin, Brayman's representative, had given new instructions before he left to hold the fort for reinforcements or fall back on Columbus, Kentucky. He wanted Hawkins to at least skirmish some with the enemy to keep up appearances.[33]

When the battle began at around 5 A.M. on March 24, Hawkins had been asking for reinforcements for at least 14 or 15 hours. He also knew none had been sent at 3 A.M. when the telegraph communication ceased.

Therefore, at the time the battle began:

1. Hawkins and all his superiors believed that the main force of Forrest's troops, thought to be 5,000–8,000 men, occupied the area around Union City, some of them unseen from the fort (i.e. the men who cut the telegraph line to Columbus, those who burned the railroad bridge six miles to the north, and the men who kept the scouts from returning to the fort.)[34] A possibility also existed that troops and artillery might be hidden in the deeply wooded, swampy areas that surrounded the camp. Everyone agreed that Forrest possessed artillery, while Hawkins had none. Both Hawkins and the higher command assumed the 7th Tennessee would be unable to resist very long against Forrest without reinforcements and artillery.[35]

---

30. Hawkins Family Letter, *Tennessee Historical Quarterly* (Spring 1987): 37.

31. John Beattie, *Joint Committee of 38th Congress*, May 5, 1864, Representative Committee #63: 72.

32. Munroe to Pennock, March 24, 1864, in *OR*, 1, XXXII, (3), 142.

33. James H. Odlin, *Joint Committee of 38th Congress*, May 5, 1864, Representative Committee #63: 77.

34. Hawkins Family Letter, *Tennessee Historical Quarterly* (Spring 1987): 38.

35. James H. Odlin to Mason Brayman, March 24, 1864, 10:10 A.M., in *OR*, 1, XXXII, (1), 541. Hawkins to Odlin, March 23, 1864, in *OR*, 1, XXXII, (3), 129.

2. Although Hawkins was told to wait for reinforcements, General Brayman's assurance of "sufficient aid" came when he had no troops at his disposal.[36] This must have been well-known to both sides. Captain Odlin reported Forrest's troops as "taking their time," assuming the Union had "no force to send out."[37] The shortage of troops in the west and the low priority of the Union City post would have given Hawkins little hope. No evidence existed that help would ever arrive.

The Fort at Union City

When the 7th Tennessee moved to Union City, Colonel Hawkins ordered a fort, or more accurately a square redoubt, built for defense of the post.[38] A description of the fort written by a former soldier of the 7th about a month after the battle described it as "a rude structure, composed of a sort of long wall, four feet high against which an embankment of earth had been thrown from a shallow ditch outside the wall." It enclosed some acres of ground and "was made more for the protection of the horses of the command than to resist an attack."[39]

Years after the fort no longer existed, one of Forrest's men remembered the installation as being "an enclosure with walls of dirt thrown up about ten feet high, with logs placed upon top and small portholes underneath the log, every few yards apart. It was probably seventy yards square, the timber cut down, felled from the stockade with the limbs

36. Mason Brayman, report, March 24, 1864, *OR*, 1, XXXII, (1), 503. He finally borrowed some troops in transit to the east. They were there by accident since their transport had not arrived.

37. James H. Odlin to Mason Brayman, March 24, 1864, *OR*, 1, XXXII, (3), 541. N.B. Forrest to Thomas M. Jack, March 21, 1864, *OR*, 1, XXXII, (3), 664.

38. Robert W. Helmer, report, March 31, 1864, *OR*, 1, XXXII, (1), 545. Richard Ramsey Hancock. *Hancock's Diary: A History of the Second Tennessee Confederate Cavalry: with Sketches of First and Seventh Battalions.* (Nashville, TN: Brandon Printing Co., 1887): 346. Hereafter Hancock, *Hancock's Diary.*

39. "The Facts Relative to the Surrender of Union City," *Nashville Daily Union*, April 26, 1864, 2, reprinted from the *Olney Illinois Journal.* Apparently written by Aston W. Hawkins, cousin to Colonel Hawkins.

and branches trimmed to a sharp point."[40] The fort seems to have grown taller and stronger in postwar memory.

Stumps and fallen timber from the building of the stockade lay on the ground near the enclosure.[41] Shanties stood outside the camp until the early hours of the 24th when Hawkins' men set them on fire. This prevented their use by the enemy as shelter and threw light on the attackers in the early morning hours.[42]

The Mobile & Ohio Railroad ran to the west of the stockade. A depot existed and may have stood south of the southwest corner of the fort on the east side of the track near the modern depot.[43] Currently an old railroad car parked on a side track serves as a reminder of times past. Union City contains little evidence of the former fort or any significant structures from the era. It does, however, have a small privately maintained museum with a model of the fort and some Civil War memorabilia.[44]

The Attack on Union City, March 24, 1864

The Action Began at Dawn

About 4 A.M., the Confederates drove the 7th Tennessee's pickets into the fort. By sunrise a portion of Forrest's cavalry under Colonel William L. Duckworth surrounded the fort with between 500 and 1,800 men, depending on the person counting.[45] According to several reports, the Confederate forces included Duckworth's own regiment, the Confederate 7th Tennessee Cavalry, Faulkner's Kentucky regiment, and McDonald's

40. William Witherspoon, "7th Tennessee CSA vs. 7th Tennessee USA," in Robert Selph Henry, ed., *As They Saw Forrest* (Jackson, TN: McCowat-Mercer Press, Inc., 1956), 104. Hereafter: Witherspoon, *As They Saw Forrest*. This memoir was written nearly fifty years after the events took place.

41. Hawkins Family Letter, *Tennessee Historical Quarterly* (Spring 1987): 38.

42. *Ibid*, 38. Hancock, *Hancock's Diary*, 346.

43. John Johnston, *Personal Reminiscences of the Civil War*, 1861–1865, Published 1900. Map on microfilm, Civil War Collection, Tennessee State Archives, Box 13, Folder 9, roll 586.

44. In 2004, this small private museum was run by John Bell and was open by appointment.

45. John W. Beatty, report, April 12, 1864, and Thomas P. Gray, report, April 4, 1864, *OR*, 1, XXXII, (1), 542, 544. Estimated 1,500. Hawkins Family Letter, *Tennessee Historical Quarterly* (Spring 1987): 38. Estimated 1,800. Witherspoon, *As They Saw Forrest*, 106. Estimated 475. Hubbard said 500.

Railroad car at the Union City, Tennessee depot

Model of the fort at Union City, Tennessee

battalion.[46] The attackers took up positions behind fallen timber and the railroad embankment, then began firing small arms.

In Hawkins' account, the rebels charged the fort four times during the morning.[47] Duckworth's first assault came when Faulkner's cavalry attacked the southwest corner of the fort about 5 or 6 A.M. They failed to make much progress, "were easily repulsed," and fell back. The same men dismounted for a second attempt and came close to the breastworks but again failed.[48] Colonel Hawkins thought this attempt "amounted to nothing more than to carry away their dead and wounded." On the third charge a regiment moved down the railroad from the north and hit the western side of the camp but retired, returning again to pick up the dead and wounded. A fourth charge on the northeastern wall failed as well with more losses for the attackers, at least according to Union sources.[49] About an hour and a half of sharpshooting followed the attempted assaults, then the firing ceased.[50]

Confederate casualty statistics for the battle at Union City are unavailable, but Forrest reported his losses at Union City and Paducah together as at least twenty-five and most likely more. The Union reportedly buried 300 rebels left behind by Forrest at Paducah, so a large discrepancy exists.[51] The higher mortality numbers for the two battles seem more likely since Forrest reported four colonels killed or wounded.[52] One of these officers, Lieutenant Colonel W.D. Lannom of Faulkner's regiment, suffered severe wounds in the fighting at Union City.[53] The graves of twenty-nine unknown Confederate soldiers in the Confederate Cemetery at Union City might contain the rebel battle casualties.

46. John Allan Wyeth, *That Devil Forrest: Life of General Nathan Bedford Forrest* (Baton Rouge: Louisiana State University Press, 1989; reprint from 1959, first published 1899), 301. Hancock, *Hancock's Diary*: 340.

47. Hawkins Family Letter, *Tennessee Historical Quarterly* (Spring 1987): 37–38.

48. Thomas P. Gray, *Joint Committee of 38th Congress*, May 5, 1864, Representative Committee #63: 69.

49. Hawkins Family Letter, *Tennessee Historical Quarterly* (Spring 1987): 37.

50. Thomas P. Gray, *Joint Committee of 38th Congress*, 69.

51. "Forrest's Raid," *Chicago Times*, March 27, 1864, reprinted in *New York Times* April 1, 1864.

52. N.B. Forrest, report, March 27, 1864, *OR*, 1, XXXII, (1), 607.

53. James D. Porter and Gen. Clement A. Evans, ed., *Confederate Military History: A Library of Confederate States History* (Atlanta: The Confederate Publishing Company, 1899) 8:288. Colonel Lannom survived the war, but was shot and killed in Paris, Tennessee in 1872. *Weekly Intelligencer*, Paris, Tennessee, March 7, 1872.

The Highly Questionable—but Frequently Cited—Witherspoon Memoir

In a very late memoir written in 1906 and republished in *As They Saw Forrest* in 1956, Lieutenant William Witherspoon of the 7th Tennessee Cavalry CSA praises the sharpshooting ability of his fellow attackers during the Union City assaults and pokes fun at the men in the fort for popping "up their heads above the logs," thereby receiving shots to their heads from "a dozen or more rifles." He brags that sharpshooters killed five men in this manner, all of whom died instantly.[54] The muster rolls of the 7th Tennessee record no deaths at Union City. A report filed by a Union captain about a week later mentions one man dead and two men wounded.[55] The pension application of the widow of Private Thomas Herndon says that Herndon received a shot in the head at Union City. He may be the one casualty but even he could have died of a wound after the battle. His 6' 6" height, rather than his curiosity, may have been his disadvantage.[56]

The Confederate sharpshooters' aim turns out to be less accurate and the men of the 7th Tennessee less foolish than the old veteran from Jackson, Tennessee remembered in his declining years.[57] Of the six men of the 7th Tennessee (U.S.) known killed in battle during the entire war, Forrest's troops killed only two: one at Union City and one the day after when Forrest's main body of troops attacked Paducah, Kentucky.[58]

Confederates Send in Flag of Truce Demanding Surrender

The shooting at Union City ended about 11 A.M. when a truce escort from the Confederate line asked to talk to Colonel Hawkins. They brought a surrender demand, supposedly signed by Forrest. If the 7th

54. Witherspoon, *As They Saw Forrest*, 103.
55. Thomas P. Gray, report to Mason Brayman, April 4, 1864, *OR*, 1, XXXII, (1), 545.
56. "Thomas D. Herndon," Muster Roll 7th Tennessee Cavalry USA, Roll 395-66 #831. Widow's pension #109,825.
57. At the battle at Paducah, Kentucky, eleven men from a colored regiment were shot in the head. "Forrest's Raid," *Chicago Times*, March 27, 1864, reprinted in *New York Times* April 1, 1864. Although he was not at Paducah, perhaps Witherspoon confused this event with the Union City fighting in his later years.
58. "Richard E. French," Muster Roll 7th Tennessee Cavalry USA, Roll 395-65 #615.

surrendered at once, then it would receive treatment due to "prisoners of war," the implication being that failure to surrender meant they would be killed even if they tried to surrender later."[59] Eighteen days after this battle, African-American troops and the 13th/14th Tennessee Cavalry, another West Tennessee Unionist regiment, declined the invitation to surrender at Fort Pillow and suffered the consequences threatened at Union City.

The same Lieutenant Witherspoon who exaggerated the sharpshooting casualties wrote that Duckworth told Hawkins that Forrest "didn't care if they did not surrender" and "wanted to wipe such traitors to their State and the South off the face of the earth." He wanted to "blow them to hell and not leave a greasy spot."[60] The quotations might convey Forrest's general opinion but are too late to be taken literally.

General Forrest considered both Hawkins and Hurst as renegades.[61] He sent demands that the Union authorities try Colonel Hurst and certain of his men. They declined to do so, therefore Forrest declared the 6th Tennessee Cavalry to be "outlaws, and not entitled to be treated as prisoners of war."[62] The "Wizard of the Saddle," with thousands under his command, spent an inordinate amount of time complaining about the small West Tennessee Unionist regiments.[63] He labeled them "a terror to the whole land."[64] All this attention most likely indicates their effectiveness, at least as a constant irritant.

Many men in Forrest's and Hawkins' commands knew each other. The primary Unionist regiments and many in Forrest's command came from the same areas of West Tennessee.[65] While detachments from the two groups skirmished almost constantly in West Tennessee, Kentucky, and northern Mississippi, their families battled each other on the home front.[66]

Given the bitterness between the groups, it seems understandable that Hawkins would ask to speak to Forrest personally for clarification

59. Hawkins Family Letter, *Tennessee Historical Quarterly* (Spring 1987): 38.
60. Witherspoon, *As They Saw Forrest*, 104.
61. N.B. Forrest, report, March 27, 1864, *OR*, 1, XXXII, (1), 607.
62. N.B. Forrest to Whom It May Concern, March 22, 1864, *OR*, 1, XXXII, (3), 119.
63. N.B. Forrest reports, March 21–22, 1864, *OR*, 1, XXXII, (3), 117, 663–665.
64. N.B. Forrest to Jefferson Davis, April 15, 1864, *OR*, 1, XXXII, (1), 612.
65. Witherspoon, *As They Saw Forrest*, 102.
66. Hancock, *Hancock's Diary*, 351. Hancock says Forrest's men wanted to go home to protect their families from the 13th Cavalry at Fort Pillow.

of terms before agreeing to surrender. Duckworth refused by claiming Forrest declined to meet with officers of inferior rank, a plausible reply. As for the surrender demand, Hawkins said later that he told the other officers he "did not believe it was Forrest's handwriting."[67] Most biographies of Forrest imply that he had little education, so perhaps the note seemed too literate. There remained, however, the possibility that Forrest had dictated the note.

Colonel Hawkins asked for time and obtained fifteen minutes to confer with his officers.[68] Whether the fort could hold out hinged on whether the attackers had artillery within reach. All previous Union intelligence confirmed that Forrest's troops, numbering in the thousands, overran northwestern Tennessee and had artillery with them on the raid.[69] Whether artillery was close enough to Union City to be used before reinforcements arrived remained to be seen. The men inside the fort generally agreed that the fort would be unable to hold out against artillery and the men would be slaughtered.[70] Hawkins (and his superiors) believed from their own reconnaissance that Forrest and artillery were present in the general area.[71] Duckworth used that belief to his own advantage.

Witherspoon's Influential "Memory" Again

Witherspoon claimed in his often quoted reminiscences that Hawkins and his men surrendered because the attackers made logs into fake artillery and yelled bogus firing instructions that fooled the 7th Tennessee into thinking they saw artillery present at the fort.[72] According to Captain Beatty, however, only the telegraph operator (a civilian)[73] thought

67. Hawkins Family Letter, *Tennessee Historical Quarterly* (Spring 1987): 38. Not confirmed elsewhere.

68. *Ibid.*

69. *Ibid*, 37. J.H. Odlin to Brayman, *OR*, 1, XXXII, (1), 541. Wm. H. Lawrence to J.H. Odlin, March 5, 1864, *OR*, 1, XXXII, (3), 153. Forrest brought artillery on the 1862–63 raid.

70. John W. Beatty, report, April 12, 1864, *OR*, 1, XXXII, (1), 542–544. Hawkins Family Letter, *Tennessee Historical Quarterly* (Spring 1987): 38.

71. Hawkins Family Letter, *Tennessee Historical Quarterly* (Spring 1987): 37. Lieutenant Royall thought he saw artillery about eight miles out from Union City while he was scouting.

72. Witherspoon, *As They Saw Forrest*, 105. Witherspoon, 7th Tennessee Cavalry CSA—Company D, 1910, http://pages.prodigy.net/rebel7tn/History.html.

73. Civilians belonging to private telegraph companies operated the United States Military Telegraph Corps. H.B.C. Rogers, *The Confederates and Federals at War*, 80.

he actually saw artillery.[74] Captain Parsons said he saw no artillery. Sergeant Gray, immediately after the battle, reported artillery not "seen or used" before the surrender.[75] Witherspoon contradicted himself when he reported in the same memoir that Captain Hays "did not believe Forrest had any artillery there" and advised Hawkins "to hold out until that was shown." Hawkins supposedly answered Hayes that waiting to actually see artillery would "be too late."[76] Such inconsistencies cast grave doubts on Witherspoon's memory.

Surely in a seven-hour battle the men inside the fort would have noticed the lack of action from artillery, especially in a situation where the defenders repulsed the attackers four times. The regiment had experienced Forrest's use of artillery previously at the battle of Trenton and knew how it looked and sounded. Perhaps the buglers and the cannon fakers only imagined their ruse effective or maybe this teller of old war stories exercised the right of all storytellers to "never leave a good story unimproved." Colleagues of Witherspoon had less fanciful explanations.

Fellow Lieutenant John Milton Hubbard, who actually went in with the flag of truce and thereby observed the negotiations firsthand, wrote in his account that Duckworth told Hawkins that Forrest was "near at hand with his artillery," not that artillery could obviously be seen and heard. Hubbard said nothing of fake cannons or artillery calls.[77]

Richard Ramsey Hancock, another of Forrest's men, attributed the surrender to Duckworth's assertion of Forrest's presence.[78] Confederate General Chalmers believed "a ruse" caused Hawkins to surrender, but it was Duckworth having "made the enemy believe that Forrest was present."[79] His presence in the vicinity implied artillery nearby.

Duckworth's ruse worked because Hawkins believed information obtained earlier when the Union command and his own scouts thought

74. John W. Beatty to Mason Brayman, April 12, 1864, *OR*, 1, XXXII, (1), 543. Beatty says Hawkins was "satisfied" the enemy had artillery, not that he had actually seen any.

75. John W. Beatty to Mason Brayman, April 12, 1864, *OR*, 1, XXXII, (1), 543. Thomas P. Gray to Mason Brayman, April 4, 1864, *OR*, 1, XXXII, (1), 545. Hawkins called Gray a sergeant, but Gray lists himself as a captain.

76. Witherspoon, *As They Saw Forrest*, 104.

77. John Milton Hubbard, "Attack at Union City," in Robert Selph Henry, ed. *As They Saw Forrest*. (Jackson, TN: McCowat-Mercer Press, Inc., 1956), 154. This is also a very late account, but the information seems less fanciful than Witherspoon's writing.

78. Hancock, *Hancock's Diary*, 346.

79. James R. Chalmers to his men, April 20, 1864, *OR*, 1, XXXII, (1), 623.

Union City would be the destination of Forrest's main troops. No contemporary, or even late writing, mentions yells or fake cannon except Witherspoon. He alone suggests that the surrender had anything to do with the 7th Tennessee having seen logs on wagon wheels pretending in broad daylight to be cannon or hearing men yelling orders to artillery that failed to fire for seven hours. If the men in the fort had actually seen what they believed to be artillery, there would have been no discussion whatever about the need to surrender. They believed Forrest to be somewhere nearby with artillery, not within eyesight.

Was Forrest "Near At Hand With Artillery?"

From various sources, Forrest's movements can be traced on the 23rd and 24th of March. After sending Duckworth's command toward Union City, Forrest left Jackson, Tennessee in the late morning of March 23[80] and traveled 37 miles, making camp at 10:30 P.M. about 15 miles northeast of Trenton, Tennessee on the Dresden Road.[81] Assuming he resumed travel around dawn, he left his camp some twenty-five miles south of Union City at about the time Duckworth's detachment began the attack at sunrise on the 24th. Forrest's main troops took the Dresden Road to Dresden, Tennessee and then on to Dukedom on the Tennessee state line. They camped near midnight about four miles south of Mayfield, Kentucky,[82] having covered some 42 miles in about 18 hours. Assuming departure from the Trenton area at dawn, time and distance wise they could have been near Dresden at 11 P.M. when Hawkins surrendered some 12 miles away. Although nothing indicates Forrest would have diverted artillery to Union City if Hawkins had refused to surrender, Duckworth's assertion that Forrest was "near at hand with artillery" might indeed have been true.

Captain Beatty testified before a congressional committee that the rebels told him after the surrender that they actually had artillery "in supporting distance" on the Dresden to Paducah road and could have called

---

80. N.B. Forrest, report, March 27, 1864, *OR*, 1, XXXII, (1), 607.
81. Hancock, *Hancock's Diary*, 340–341.
82. *Ibid*, 341.

it in.[83] In his diary, Richard R. Hancock of the 2nd Tennessee Cavalry (CSA) mentions four pieces of artillery on the road between Mayfield and Paducah on the 25th,[84] which means it had been near Dresden on the 24th. Theoretically at least, artillery might have been dispatched to Union City before Union reinforcements arrived since reinforcements had barely left Cairo, Illinois at the time of the surrender.

Differences of Opinion About the Officers' Agreement to Surrender

After Colonel Hawkins returned inside the fort from the flag of truce meeting, he called his officers together to discuss the situation. The meeting most likely included Major Smith and Captains Beatty, Hayes, Parsons, and Harris. Some, but not all, of the lieutenants attended.

Contemporary information about how and why the decision to surrender was made in the officer's meeting comes from three major sources: 1) Officers Beatty, Helmer and Gray, who escaped from Duckworth, wrote reports to General Brayman within two and a half weeks after the surrender, Colonel Hawkins being unavailable to do so; 2) the testimony of Captains Gray, Beatty, and Parsons, Adjutant Odlin, General Brayman, and General Hurlbut given to a joint committee of the U.S. Congress in May 1864; and 3) Colonel Hawkins, who wrote about the battle in a personal letter to his cousin six months after the surrender when he returned from prison to active duty. These accounts differ in numerous details. The earliest reports by the escapees and the testimonies to Congress figure most prominently in how the Union authorities at the time viewed the surrender. The Hawkins' letter only surfaced in 1987[85] and has had little influence so far in later accounts.[86]

In his report of the meeting of the officers to discuss surrender, Lieutenant Robert Helmer, a transfer from the 3rd Michigan, said Hawkins failed to give the lieutenants the vote and that out of the four captains in

83. John W. Beatty, *Joint Committee of 38th Congress*, May 5, 1864, Representative Committee #63: 72.

84. Hancock, *Hancock's Diary*, 341.

85. Hawkins Family Letter, *Tennessee Historical Quarterly* (Spring 1987): 33–42.

86. The 1906 memoir by Confederate soldier William Witherspoon in *As They Saw Forrest* has had great influence on general works since its publication in 1956.

attendance, only two wanted to surrender.[87] He thought all the lieutenants wanted to continue to fight.[88] His account casts the lieutenants in a brave and blameless light, but admits that at least two of the captains favored surrender.

Thomas P. Gray, a transfer from the 12th Illinois, said in his first report that "a large majority (of officers) violently opposed any capitulation whatever with the enemy."[89] He admitted in later testimony to Congress, however, that he monitored the flag of truce delegates during the meeting of the officers. He insisted that every man he heard say anything (after the fact) called the surrender "wholly unnecessary," a rather obvious observation by that point. Gray even intimated that some men thought Hawkins to be "half rebel."[90] Although acting with the regiment, Gray served without ever having been mustered in. Neither the regimental muster rolls nor the Day Book contain information on this man. The records of the 12th Illinois Infantry refer to him as a musician from Princeton, Illinois. Gray called himself the captain of Company C when he wrote his report. Six months later, however, Colonel Hawkins referred to him as a sergeant.[91]

Captain John W. Beatty, a transfer from the 3rd Michigan, reported all the officers at first wanted to fight except Major Thomas A. Smith.[92] Beatty said that Hawkins argued it would save lives to surrender and that if the 7th Tennessee renewed the fight, "they would kill every one that might fall into their hands." Beatty says the officers then agreed to a conditional surrender, the conditions being parole for officers and men, the men to keep private property, and the officers their firearms.[93] This more or less agrees with Hawkins' contention that all the officers met in council and after a few minutes of discussion, no dissenting voice arose against

87. Officers captured at Union City: Colonel Hawkins, Major Smith, Captains Hays, Parsons, and Beatty, Lieutenants Helmer, Hawkins, Allender, Bradford, Neely, Morgan, Jeptha, and John Robeson. Parsons, Beatty, Helmer, and Hawkins escaped from the captors almost immediately. Lieutenant Hawkins, however, was recaptured.

88. Robert Helmer to Mason Brayman, March 31, 1864, *OR*, 1, XXXII, (1), 544–545.

89. Thomas P. Gray to Mason Brayman, April 4, 1864, *OR*, 1, XXXII, (1), 544–545.

90. Thomas P. Gray, *Joint Committee of 38th Congress*, May 5, 1864, Representative Committee #63: 68-71.

91. Hawkins Family Letter, *Tennessee Historical Quarterly* (Spring 1987): 38.

92. John W. Beatty to Mason Brayman, April 12, 1864, *OR*, 1, XXXII, (1), 542–544.

93. *Ibid*, 543

surrender. It disagrees in that Beatty maintained that unless the attackers agreed to all conditions of parole, the officers wanted to fight on.[94]

Captain Pleasant K. Parsons, the only southerner who wrote an early account, mentioned that Colonel Hawkins asked Captain Harris, on provost duty with the 24th Missouri and the oldest officer at the fort, for his opinion on surrender. Parsons claimed Harris and all the other officers said "fight." This contradicts all the other accounts. Labeling the affair "one of the most cowardly surrenders there ever was," Parsons said he had personally preferred to fight and figured 300 men and officers out of 500 agreed with him.[95] His estimate leaves at least 200 men in agreement with Hawkins.

Colonel Hawkins' account of the conference between the officers reported much discussion among the officers as to the course of action to be taken. The colonel, however, claimed the officers eventually reached a unanimous agreement to surrender, seeking the best terms possible.[96]

General Hurlbut, commander of the 16th Army Corps, testified before the Joint Committee of Congress about Union City, although personally nowhere near the scene and badly misinformed. He insisted that Hawkins surrendered "contrary to the entreaties, prayers, and advice of all his officers and all his men" when reinforcements were "within six miles of him," and "from pure cowardice." He labeled the surrender as Hawkins' second to Forrest, neglecting to recall that Colonel Fry commanded at Trenton, Tennessee, rather than Lieutenant Colonel Hawkins.[97] Hurlbut's accusations and bad temper may be excused somewhat. He disliked the 7th from earlier experiences with it and the 6th Tennessee Cavalry at Memphis, and his superiors named his replacement five days earlier.

Events after the Surrender

Despite uncertainty over how many officers and men approved or disapproved the capitulation, all sources agree that Hawkins surrendered at

94. John W. Beattie, *Joint Committee of 38th Congress*, May 5, 1864, Representative Committee #63: 72–73.

95. Pleasant K. Parsons, *Joint Committee of 38th Congress*, May 5, 1864, Representative Committee #63: 74–75. The captain of the 24th Missouri was Wyatt Harris.

96. Hawkins Family Letter, *Tennessee Historical Quarterly* (Spring 1987): 38.

97. S.A. Hurlbut. *Joint Committee of 38th Congress*, May 5, 1864, Representative Committee #63: 68.

about 11 A.M. after only a few minutes deliberation.[98] A copy of the capitulation document survives. Although Duckworth failed to agree to all the terms Beatty said the officers wanted, the surrender was conditional.[99]

The document of surrender with original form, punctuation and spelling appears below:

> Terms of capitulation upon which the 7th Tennessee Cav US Army present surrender to the Confederate forces commanded by Major Gen N. B. Forrest.
> article 1st That all private property belonging to the officers, non com officers & men shall be respected and they permitted to retain the same, horses, horse equipments and arms excepted.
> 2d That all the officers included in the capitulation are to be allowed to retain all their private baggage.
> 3d. That all the officers included in the capitulation are to be allowed to retain all their private baggage,[100] retain all their private papers and such as relate to the settlement of their accounts with their government.
> 4th. That all privates non com officers and officers surrender as prisoners of war and are to be treated and respected as such according to the usages and customs of civilized nations.
> 5th That all public property is surrendered.
> signed in duplicate this 24th day of March 1864
> Isaac R. Hawkins col comdg 7th Tenn cav
> W. L. Duckworth Col Comd + Com C.S.A."[101]

The Myth of Rescue Troops Within Six Miles at the Time of the Surrender

A misconception arose that Hawkins surrendered with rescue troops very, very close by. This resulted from a message sent two days after the

98. John W. Beatty to Mason Brayman, April 12, 1864, *OR*, 1, XXXII, (1), 543.
99. *Ibid.*
100. The beginning of Article 3 is the same as Article 2 in Hawkins' copy of the surrender document.
101. *Tennessee Historical Quarterly* (Spring 1987) 46: 33. Photocopy of surrender document.

battle by General Hurlbut to his superior, General Sherman, at Nashville. Hurlbut, whose knowledge of the circumstances came secondhand, accused Hawkins of surrendering "when 2,000 infantry under Brayman was within 6 miles."[102] Apparently he either misunderstood Brayman's message to him or he attempted to deflect blame by ridiculing Hawkins.

General Brayman, lacking troops of his own to send as reinforcement for Hawkins, commandeered some soldiers waiting in Cairo, Illinois for boat transportation east. In a report dated the same day of the battle at Union City, Brayman said that about 2,000 borrowed troops under his command boarded water transportation at Cairo bound for Columbus, Kentucky between 9 and 10 A.M. on March 24.[103] He telegraphed General Sherman before he left Cairo that Forrest had attacked and probably occupied Union City.[104] These rescue troops left Cairo at least 16 hours after Brayman first promised "sufficient aid," some five hours after the attack on Union City began, and about an hour or so before the surrender of the fort. Brayman's borrowed troops arrived by boat at Columbus, Kentucky and boarded a train for Union City, Tennessee at 3 P.M.,[105] four hours after the surrender. It took another hour to entrain 2,000 men and cover the 20 miles from Columbus to the burned-out railroad bridge six miles from Union City where they arrived at 4 P.M.,[106] eleven hours after the battle began and five hours after the surrender. Brayman's report says he learned about the surrender at that point "with great pain and surprise,"[107] apparently forgetting he and Odlin assumed Union City was already occupied before he left.[108] If the troops had continued past the burned-out bridge on foot, it would have taken even more time to detrain the troops, cross the bridgeless Obion River, and walk 2,000 infantrymen the six miles to Union City.

102. S.A. Hurlbut to W.T. Sherman, March 25, 1864, *OR*, 1, XXXII, (3), 157.

103. Mason Brayman, report, March 24, 1864, *OR*, 1, XXXII, (1), 502. Mason Brayman, report, May 2, 1864, in *OR*, 1, XXXII, (1), 509. The ships from Cairo to Columbus were the "Empire City" and "Gladiator."

104. Mason Brayman to W.T. Sherman, March 24, 1864, *OR*, 1, XXXII, (3), 144.

105. Mason Brayman, report, March 24, 1864, *OR*, 1, XXXII, (1), 503. *Nashville Daily Union*, March 31, 1864, 2.

106. Mason Brayman, *Joint Committee of 38th Congress*, May 5, 1864, Representative Committee #63: 9.

107. Mason Brayman, report, March 24, 1864, *OR*, 1, XXXII, (1), 503.

108. Mason Brayman, report, May 2, 1864, *OR*, 1, XXXII (1), 509.

Therefore, it would have been five or six more hours after the surrender before troops could have arrived at Union City. Rather than Hurlbut's assertion of help only "six miles away" at the time of capitulation, a more accurate statement of the situation would be "borrowed infantry was about 50 miles away on two ships on the Mississippi River somewhere between Cairo, Illinois and Columbus, Kentucky" at the moment of surrender.

John Allan Wyeth, in his famous Forrest biography, *That Devil Forrest*, perpetuated the myth by saying that Brayman could have "marched away with" Duckworth's command if the 7th Tennessee had held out for Brayman to travel six more miles. Wyeth further misquotes Brayman's report by adding the phrase "At 11 A.M. on the morning of the 25th." If correct, Brayman would have been 24 hours late since the surrender took place on the 24th.[109]

Authors continue to blindly copy Hurlbut and Wyeth's accounts. The error has found its way into numerous books for nearly 150 years.[110] Two newer ones continue the myth. Andrew Ward's *River Run Red*, published in 2005, visualized the 7th tearing up their blankets to keep the rebels from using them and burying the regimental flag at Union City with the train six miles away.[111] A Forrest biography written two years later by Eddy W. Davidson and Nathan Foxx says, "the troop carrying train was six miles away when at 11 A.M. Hawkins" surrendered.[112] Somehow accounts of rescuers, who finally show up six miles away from an empty fort several hours after surrender, fail to have the same dramatic impact and literary appeal.

When Union authorities returned Hawkins to command after prison, he discovered that General Hurlbut had branded him a coward.[113] Hawkins vowed that he would see "full justice done to Hurlbut"[114] for his insult. Washburn had already replaced Hurlbut, however, without

109. Wyeth, *That Devil Forrest*, 303.

110. Including an article in the *West Tennessee Historical Society Papers* in 1988 by the author—who also did not do her homework—writing that rescue troops were "nearby" at the time of the surrender.

111. Andrew Ward, *River Run Red* (New York: Viking Penguin, 2005), 113. Ward accepts the old soldiers' stories in *As They Saw Forrest* without questioning their veracity in the least.

112. Eddy W. Davidson and Nathan Foxx, *Nathan Bedford Forrest: In Search of an Enigma* (Gretna, LA: Pelican Publishing Company, 2007), 218.

113. S. A. Hurlbut to W. T. Sherman, March 25, 1864, *OR*, 1, XXXII, (3), 157.

114. Hawkins Family Letter, *Tennessee Historical Quarterly* (Spring 1987): 41.

needing any input from Colonel Hawkins.[115] Major General C.C. Washburn became head of the 16th Army Corps in May 1864.[116]

An Evaluation of the Surrender

The 7th Tennessee most likely could have held out against Duckworth's troops since it had repelled them four times. Hawkins had little reason, however, to question the presence of Forrest's main troops in the neighborhood and their arrival if summoned. No real assurance existed that Union reinforcements would ever arrive. He erred on the side of safety for his men, believing the men would be paroled and the officers imprisoned.[117] In hindsight, his assumptions turned out to be disastrously incorrect. Once it became known that Forrest was on his way to Paducah, Kentucky with no intention of coming to Duckworth's assistance, many criticized Hawkins for his decision. Evaluations made with all the facts tend to be better than those made in isolation during a crisis without information. The harsh denunciation of Hawkins by Union authorities seems to have been one factor in Major Booth's and Colonel Bradford's refusal to surrender at Fort Pillow.[118]

Immediate Aftermath of the Surrender, March 24, 1864

The Confederates Take Charge at Union City

The escaped officers' accounts mostly agree that the surrender came as a surprise to the enlisted men. Gray said the surrendered troops became "very indignant on hearing of the surrender"[119] and denounced Colonel Hawkins "as a coward."[120] Lieutenant Helmer said, "The majority of the enlisted men were bitterly opposed to the surrender."[121] Captain Beatty reported that the men "cried like a whipped child," cursed the colonel,

---

115. "Farewell Address of General Hurlbut," *New York Times*, May 8, 1864.

116. "New Commander for West Tennessee," *New York Times*, April 19, 1864.

117. Hawkins Family Letter, *Tennessee Historical Quarterly* (Spring 1987): 38.

118. John T. Young, in *OR*, 1, XXXII, (1), 594-595.

119. Thomas P. Gray to Mason Brayman, April 4, 1864, *OR*, 1, XXXII, (1), 545.

120. Thomas P Gray, *Joint Committee of 38th Congress*, May 5, 1864, Representative Committee #63: 69.

121. Robert Helmer to Mason Brayman, March 31, 1864, *OR*, 1, XXXII, (1), 546.

called him "a traitor" and vowed, "they would never serve under him again."[122] The men's reaction may have been somewhat exaggerated by the officers. Parsons, after all, estimated that 200 of the men approved of surrender[123] and John Milton Hubbard, one of Forrest's men, remembered years later that the "men of the Seventh Tennessee, Federal, bore up manfully" at the surrender even though the Confederates jeered.[124]

The authors of the surrender accounts might be justifying their actions by painting the men's views of Hawkins' leadership in the worst possible light. Beatty, Parsons, and Gray wrote their accounts after having broken their parole oaths, defying Hawkins' orders. Parsons, the only southerner in the group, declined to call Hawkins a coward though he did call the surrender "cowardly."[125] Beatty, Parsons, and Helmer eventually had to face Hawkins when he returned to command after being released from prison.[126]

Once the 7th exited the fort enclosure, Duckworth's men proceeded to confiscate anything of use. Forrest claimed his forces acquired several hundred stands of arms and 200 horses.[127] The horses he branded as "very inferior,"[128] as he had after the battle of Trenton. The take at Union City must have been much less than expected. Hawkins sent the extra guns and tents[129] out on a train the previous day and Odlin took the government and railroad stores during the night so the fort contained fewer supplies than previously. Duckworth's men burned the fort and the supplies that proved difficult to be carted away.[130] The surrender document stated that officers would be allowed to keep papers related to the settlement of their accounts with the government. Many early records

122. John Beatty to Mason Brayman, April 12, 1864, *OR*, 1, XXXII, (1), 543.
123. Pleasant K. Parsons, *Joint Committee of 38th Congress*, May 5, 1864, Representative Committee #63: 74–75.
124. John Milton Hubbard, "Attack at Union City," in *As They Saw Forrest*, 104.
125. Pleasant K. Parsons, *Joint Committee of the 38th Congress,*, May 5, 1864, Representative Committee #63: 74.
126. Hawkins Family Letter, *Tennessee Historical Quarterly* (Spring 1987): 41.
127. N.B. Forrest to Jefferson Davis, April 15, 1864, *OR*, 1, XXXII, (1), 611. The fact that 500 cavalrymen had only 200 horses shows the regiment to be gravely in need of horses, even "very inferior" ones.
128. N.B. Forrest to Thomas M. Jack, April 15, 1864, *OR*, 1, XXXII, (1), 611.
129. Hawkins Family Letter, *Tennessee Historical Quarterly* (Spring 1987): 37.
130. William Witherspoon, *As They Saw Forrest*, 105.

failed to survive the war, however. They could have perished at this time or later on the trip south.

Witherspoon's Regimental Flag Story

Another of the widely mentioned stories of William Witherspoon involves the supposed discovery and acquisition of the regimental flag of the 7th Tennessee USA at Union City by a private in the 7th Tennessee CSA. Making slurs about the lack of bravery of the men defending it, Private Ab Estes[131] reportedly refused to sell it to an unnamed Union officer who offered to buy it because his sister made it. Estes was quoted as saying that the officer's sister, if she proved to be "good looking," could come to his home in Haywood County after the war and "make a trade." Witherspoon admitted that the family of Ab Estes and the members of the 7th Tennessee Cavalry CSA failed to locate the flag in question after the war when restoring of flags became popular.[132]

A story about an individual soldier who took home an important enemy flag warrants suspicion. Commanders bragged about the capture of flags, especially regimental ones. A lowly private who recovered even a company flag or pennant would be expected to surrender it to his commander. The glory of victory belonged to the group. Forrest's staff listed flags as being captured by units, not by individuals.[133]

Rather than hiding the flag from his superiors, Estes, the flag boy of Company D, 7th Tennessee CSA, supposedly flew it inverted under the regimental flag for all to see.[134] It would be extremely unlikely a private would have been able to keep such an important symbol when officers knew of its existence. It might be advisable to look for the flag elsewhere, if one actually survived from Union City.

On the 21st of April 1864, only a month after the battle at Union City, the provost marshal for Forrest's Cavalry in Okolona, Mississippi gave General Leonidas Polk a list of flags captured on the Spring 1864 West Tennessee raid. He mentioned one large and three smaller flags

131. Most likely Albert Carey Estes, Company D, 7th Cavalry CSA, 1849–1887. Albert Carey Estes would have been about 14 in 1864.
132. William Witherspoon, *As They Saw Forrest*, 106–107.
133. John Goodwin, report, April 21, 1864, *OR*, 1, XXXII, (1), 619–620.
134. William Witherspoon, *As They Saw Forrest*, 106–107.

from Fort Pillow and one guidon (pennant) captured from the 6th Tennessee by Colonel Neely near Bolivar.[135] This report failed to mention any flag taken at Union City, much less an important one.

On the 27th of May 1864, Major General S. D. Lee of Meridian, Mississippi sent several flags with Colonel T. J. White to the Confederate capital at Richmond, Virginia. Lee described these as "4 garrison flags and 8 guidons captured at Fort Pillow" and "one flag captured from the enemy at Union City" in April. The four garrison flags from Fort Pillow might be the same four mentioned earlier by the provost marshal in April 1864. Lee failed to designate the Union City acquisition as being as important as he did those from Fort Pillow.[136] A date in April rather than March was given for its capture and its grouping with the Fort Pillow flags probably means that Lee mistook the guidon of the 6th Tennessee captured at Bolivar in April as a 7th Tennessee flag. At the most, if Duckworth's troops captured a flag or pennant of any kind at Union City, this might be it, but it seems unlikely.

Reports in the Media Concerning the Battle at Union City

On the 27th of March 1864, the *Chicago Times* published an article from Cairo, Illinois about the Union City surrender. It reported Colonel Hawkins as being "very much censured for not maintaining the fight longer."[137] On March 31, the *Nashville Daily Union* published an article "to correct former reports, which, in some particulars, were incorrect." It mentions specifically that Brayman did not arrive at Columbus, Kentucky until 3 P.M., presumably one of the incorrect particulars, and places no specific blame on Hawkins. It implied incompetency, however, when it mentioned that the Confederates were only one-fourth the number reported and the fort had been assaulted unsuccessfully three times with only one man killed[138] at the time of the surrender. Nothing, however, stopped the rumors and blame.

A month later Dr. Aston W Hawkins, cousin of the colonel and a former captain in the 7th, wrote a long defense of Hawkins in the *Olney*

---

135. John Goodwin, report, April 21, 1864, *OR*, 1, XXXII, (1), 619–620.
136. S.D. Lee to S. Cooper, May 27, 1864, *OR*, 1, XXXII, (1), 606.
137. "Forrest's Raid," *Chicago Times*, March 27, 1864, reprinted in *New York Times*, April 1, 1864.
138. "The Raid on Union City," *Nashville Daily Union*, March 31, 1864, 2.

(Illinois) *Journal*. He said Colonel Hawkins was being denounced as a "coward and traitor" even though he was in prison and "could not be heard in his own defense." Dr. Hawkins' information varies little from other sources except he believed the men in the fort were running out of ammunition and that Lieutenant Helmer actually saw artillery. Helmer never mentions that he did, however, in his own account. Colonel Hawkins is described by his cousin as acting with extreme bravery and disregard for his own welfare during the assaults on the fort, walking about in plain view, while his officers begged him to "put himself under shelter." Dr. Hawkins says he gathered his information from officers at Cairo, Illinois who were present at Union City but escaped after the surrender.[139]

The *Chicago Times* quoted General Brayman immediately after the surrender as saying that Union City had "no value in a military point of view."[140] If Hawkins knew of this attitude among his superiors, it might be a reason he lost faith that rescue troops would arrive.

Men of the 7th Tennessee Who Evaded Capture at Union City

General Brayman estimated very quickly that at least 75 to 100 men assigned to Union City had evaded capture or escaped from their captors after the surrender.[141] These men came from several groups.

Hawkins sent the sick and their attendants on a train bound for Columbus, Kentucky on the 23rd of March when it became known that Union City might be attacked. The train also took a few men along with the extra baggage and arms stored in the town.[142]

Hawkins also sent out both pickets and scouts, some of both never made it back to the fort before being cut off by Duckworth's troops. About a half dozen of the scouts arrived in Columbus on Thursday the 24th in time to join Brayman's rescue troops aboard the train headed for Union City. Shortly after the train departed, another scouting party of about 30 men rode into Columbus. They had skirmished with the enemy for several hours near Jacksonville, Tennessee, a few miles from

139. "The Facts Relative to the Surrender of Union City," *Nashville Daily Union*, April 26, 1864, 2, reprinted from the *Olney Illinois Journal*.

140. "Forrest's Raid," *Chicago Times*, March 27, 1864, reprinted in *New York Times*, April 1, 1864.

141. Brayman, report, March 24, 1864, *OR*, 1, XXXII, (1), 503.

142. Hawkins Family Letter, *Tennessee Historical Quarterly* (Spring 1987): 37.

the fort. These would be the scouts from Company B under Lieutenant Elbert N. Royall.[143]

Men had detached several months earlier under Lieutenant Hardy to serve the infantry divisions at Paducah, Kentucky as cavalry scouts.[144] Some remained there in March 1864 since two men of the 7th died of disease earlier in the month and Private Richard E. French of Company B died in action[145] on March 25 when Forrest's main troops attacked Paducah the day after the surrender at Union City.

The acquisition of Union prisoners at Paducah and Union City gave Forrest the opportunity to consider an exchange for Confederate prisoners held in the fort at Paducah. This would have increased his army and freed him the necessity of escorting his captives south.

Forrest Offered to Exchange Prisoners at Paducah, Kentucky

Although Forrest's men failed in their attempt to take Fort Anderson at Paducah, they did sack much of the town. Unfortunately for two ailing men of the 7th Tennessee, the federal military hospital stood outside the fort. James Park and Henry Neighbors of Company E had the misfortune to be among the 30–40 men taken prisoner when Forrest's men took the hospital.[146] For a short time, a small chance existed that they might be freed.

Forrest sent in his last flag of truce before giving up on capturing Fort Anderson. He knew the federal guardhouse held Confederates and offered to "exchange man for man according to rank" for as many prisoners as the Union held

Nathan Bedford Forrest

143. "Forrest's Raid," *Chicago Times*, March 27, 1864, reprinted in *New York Times* April 1, 1864. Hawkins Family Letter, *Tennessee Historical Quarterly* (Spring 1987): 37.

144. See page 79.

145. "Richard E. French," Compiled Service Records 7th Tennessee Cavary USA, M395 RG094 roll 65, #615.

146. "Forrest's Raid," *Chicago Times*, March 27, 1864, reprinted in *New York Times* April 1, 1864. The hospital inside the fort burned in 1863. Both Park and Neighbors died in Andersonville Prison.

Confederates. He offered the 35–40 men he captured in the hospital outside the fort plus, most likely, some of the men of the 7th captured at Union City if needed. Colonel Hicks, however, replied that he had no authority to make the exchange.[147] Shortly thereafter on April 17, 1864, General Grant stopped all exchanges.[148] This ended any chance of a negotiated release for Union prisoners anywhere.

The Men Still Free Continued to Fight

While Paducah remained under attack, two telegrams involving Brigadier General Brayman and his staff mention "Hawkins' men." On March 26, 1864, William H. Lawrence, in command at Columbus, Kentucky, sent an appeal to Captain J. H. Odlin, aide to General Brayman, asking for "Hawkins' men." He thought they "would be invaluable" in countering Forrest's expected attack on Columbus.[149] Brayman replied that "Hawkins' men" went to Mound City, Illinois that night but that he would "try to have them back."[150]

The reason for the trip to Mound City proved to be some Confederate signal rockets between the Kentucky shore and the woods behind the town. The newspaper reported that General Brayman "having at Cairo some fifty experienced bushwhackers, a part of the garrison of Union City, which had escaped, sent them up to see what was going on." The men of the 7th Tennessee found the rebel camp and attacked it, killing two of the rebels and wounding others.[151] That a news release portrayed duly mustered southern soldiers in volunteer service to the Union for two years as bushwhackers shows some northern condescension.

On March 27, 1864, General Brayman reported to General Hurlbut that some more of "Hawkins' men" had escaped from Confederate Colonel Faulkner on the march and made their way to Columbus, Kentucky.[152] Several officers also escaped during the first few days after their

147. *Ibid.* "Raid on Paducah," *Chicago Journal*, March 28, 1864, reprinted in *New York Times*, April 2, 1864.

148. U. S. Grant to Benjamin F. Butler, April 20, 1864, *OR*, 2, VII, 76.

149. William H. Lawrence to J. H. Odlin, March 26, 1864, *OR*, 1, XXXII, (3), 396.

150. Mason Brayman to W. H. Lawrence, March 26, 1864, *OR*, 1, XXXII, (3), 160.

151. "From Chicago, 16 May 1864," *New York Times*, May 22, 1864.

152. Mason Brayman to S. A. Hurlbut, March 27, 1864, *OR*, 1, XXXII, (1), 506. Colonel W.W. Faulkner of 12th Kentucky.

capture.[153] Lieutenant Helmer's records show that he and most likely others also ended up in Columbus, as did perhaps the men from the Mound City raid. The 7th Tennessee, therefore, helped defend the fort at Columbus when Confederate General Buford demanded that the fort surrender or no quarter would be shown to the colored soldiers. Buford delivered this threat on the 13th of April 1864, one day after the massacre of black soldiers at Fort Pillow, Tennessee. Columbus contained a high percentage of colored troops. Buford offered to spare the white soldiers, treating them as prisoners of war. Fortunately for the men of the 7th, who had recently escaped capture and especially for the black soldiers, the Union commander knew the fort to be well fortified. He declared surrender to be "out of the question." Buford's men left the area.

On April 17, 1864, Brayman reported to General Sherman that about 60 "remnants of Hawkins command" in Cairo had orders to remove to Memphis. No record exists, however, of their having actually gone.[154] A requisition order does mention twenty-five men, led by Captain James M. Martin, who were under orders from General Brayman to report to Colonel Hicks, the commander of the post at Paducah, Kentucky.[155] At that time, the Union command feared Paducah would come under attack again.[156]

The constant shifting of soldiers resulted from the continued presence of Forrest's forces in the area. At least 150 men, or about one-fourth of the regiment on the rolls before March 24, 1864, can be identified as having escaped or never captured. Union occupation forces being so thin, even this small number of men were in demand.

Accounts of the battles at Paducah and Columbus compare unfavorably the bravery and success of the commanders at those posts as opposed to that of Hawkins at Union City. They neglect to point out that both

153. Hawkins Family Letter, *Tennessee Historical Quarterly* (Spring 1987): 38. Hawkins' son Samuel and Lieutenant Helmer made their escape before parole. Captains Beatty, Parsons, and Gray plus Lieutenants Bradford, Allender, and Morgan all violated parole when they escaped, according to Colonel Hawkins.

154. Mason Brayman to W. T. Sherman, April 17, 1864, *OR*, 1, XXXII, (3), 396. Three members of 7th Tennessee died in Cairo of pneumonia in the last half of April.

155. Order #527 requisition of Capt. Martin from Cairo to Paducah by order General Mason Brayman.

156. Mason Brayman, report, April 16, 1864, *OR*, 1, XXXII, (1), 507. Twenty-six horses are also mentioned.

those commanders had artillery, had more warning and accurate information, received some reinforcements, had the support of gunboats on the adjacent rivers, had eye contact with Union-occupied territory across the rivers, and could communicate with headquarters.

Some Reasons for the Success of Forrest's 1864 Raid

Although Forrest's skills as a military commander are well known, there were other factors that made this raid easier for him than it would have been at another time or place.

Some favorable circumstances included:

1. Forrest's ability to accumulate 5,000+ cavalry and enter the area almost at will.

2. The support of most of Western Tennessee and Kentucky for the Confederate cause.

3. The removal of the majority of Union troops to the eastern front, along with the absence of a number of the U.S. occupation troops on furlough.[157]

4. Easy entry by horseback into an area defended primarily by scattered infantry.[158]

5. The U.S. high command's low priority for maintaining control over the inland areas of Western Kentucky and Western Tennessee.

6. The Union's ill-advised use of isolated, poorly manned forts.

After March 9, 1864, Grant took command of all federal armies and General William Tecumseh Sherman inherited the oversight of armies left in the west, including those in western Tennessee and Kentucky. He focused, however, on the eastern states where the major part of his command operated. When advised of Forrest's 1864 raid Sherman replied, "The more men Forrest has, and the longer he stays about Mayfield [Kentucky], the better for us." The next day, he wrote that he hoped Forrest would "prolong his visit in that neighborhood."[159] Sherman evidently preferred that Forrest remain in this less strategic area rather than take his troops east. Forrest also preferred to stay in the west.

157. W.T. Sherman to General Banks, April 3, 1864, *OR*, 1, XXXIV, (3), 24.
158. N.B. Forrest to Thomas M. Jack, April 15, 1864, *OR*, 1, XXXII, (1), 608.
159. Mason Brayman, report, May 2, 1864, *OR*, 1, XXXII, (1), 511.

He wrote President Jefferson Davis that he thought he could control West Tennessee if allowed to remain even a month longer and then, if time permitted, Western Kentucky.[160] General Polk, however, ordered him to return to Mississippi.[161]

After the capture of Union City, the massacre at Fort Pillow, and the narrow escapes at Columbus and Paducah, Kentucky, the Union command questioned the wisdom of isolated forts guarded by small forces.[162] They abandoned many small forts,[163] including Union City. The withdrawal of Federal troops left both Confederate and Unionist civilians at the mercy of guerillas and bushwhackers. Forrest bragged in his report to Jefferson Davis that his recent triumphs over the 6th, 7th, and 13th Tennessee Cavalries stopped "their acts of oppression murder and plunder."[164] General Braxton Bragg remarked that this would be gratifying unless marauding bands pretending to be Confederate filled the vacuum.[165] After this time, neither army made much effort to defend the populace of western Tennessee and Kentucky from lawless gangs.

160. N.B. Forrest to Jefferson Davis, April 15, 1864, *OR*, 1, XXXII, (1), 610.
161. *Ibid*, 612.
162. Mason Brayman, report, May 2, 1864, *OR*, 1, XXXII, (1), 510.
163. James B. McPherson to Henry Prince, April 20, 1864, *OR*, 1, XXXII, (1), 516.
164. N.B. Forrest to Thomas M. Jack, April 15, 1864, *OR*, 1, XXXII, (1), 612.
165. Braxton Bragg to Jefferson Davis, April 29, 1864, *OR*, 1, XXXII, (1), 613.

CHAPTER SIX

——◆——

THE REGIMENT ESCORTED TO PRISONS IN GEORGIA, MARCH 24–APRIL 12, 1864

From Union City to Jackson, Tennessee

Thinking that moving 475 prisoners would be cumbersome for the raiders, Hawkins expected Forrest to parole the men and imprison the officers.[1] After releasing the women and children within the enclosure,[2] however, Duckworth hurriedly left Union City on the afternoon of the surrender headed east toward Dresden, Tennessee with the 7th Tennessee in tow. At least a few of Forrest's troops may still have been in the Dresden area. The enlisted men of the 7th walked four abreast with guards in a single file on each side, at least according to Witherspoon.[3] The officers rode their horses. They camped Thursday night at Gardner's Station, Tennessee about 16 miles from Union City.[4]

1. Exchanges of POWs, however, slowed in 1863 even before stopped by Grant in 1864.

2. Mrs. Sutton letter, September 18, 1864, filed in "George W Sutton," #1715, Compiled Service Records 7th Tennessee M395 RG094 roll 65 #1715.

3. William Witherspoon, *As They Saw Forrest*, 105. This late description may or may not be accurate.

4. John W. Beatty, report, April 12, 1864, *OR*, 1, XXXII, (1), 543.

Witherspoon reported two supposed conversations between Confederate officers and Captain Hays soon after capture. First he represented Captain Hays as having claimed that he alone among the officers opposed surrender.[5] In a second conversation, rebel Field and Staff Quartermaster A. B. Crook of Henderson County bragged to Hays about destroying loyal citizens' property at Henderson Station, Tennessee in November of 1862. If true, Crook may have regretted his indiscretion when, after the war, he faced charges concerning that raid and Hayes testified against him.[6]

Since the prisoners remained close to Union City, an attempt could have been made to rescue them. Brayman's borrowed troops, however, constituted the only large Union forces near enough to make the effort. They turned back north, however, six miles before reaching Union City while within about 22 miles of the captives. Brayman later claimed that he favored continuing on and would have rescued the prisoners if the borrowed troops had been at his disposal. He blamed his failure on General Sherman, who insisted the troops be sent east the next day (on the 25th) as scheduled.[7] As it happened, the troops remained in Cairo until March 26 so there would have been time.[8]

At Gardner's Station lieutenants Robert Helmer and Samuel Hawkins, son of the colonel, made their escape. The next day, all the officers accepted parole. They gave their word not to attempt to escape in return for freedom to move about. Colonel Hawkins threatened dismissal from the service for any officer who broke his promise.[9]

Leaving Gardner's Station at daybreak on Friday, the 25th of March, the captors left the Union City to Dresden road and marched the men across country toward Trenton, Tennessee, the location of their previous capture by Forrest in December of 1862. The men had nothing to eat until eight o'clock on Friday night when they received a little bacon and

5. William Witherspoon, *As They Saw Forrest*, 104. Hays might have said this, but it appears to be untrue.

6. Glover, *Report of Committee on Military Affairs*, March 2, 1877. "Rebel Raid on Henderson, Tennessee in 1862." Affidavit by Asa Hays. Crook lost the court case.

7. Mason Brayman, report, March 24, 1864, *OR*, 1, XXXII, (1), 503.

8. Mason Brayman to S.A. Hurlbut, March 26, 1864, OR, 1, XXXII, (1), 505.

9. John W. Beatty, report, April 12, 1864, *OR*, 1, XXXII, (1), 543.

corn bread.[10] Upon arrival at Trenton about noon on Saturday the 26th, the men purchased food from the rebel population. A dozen biscuits went for five U.S. greenbacks and baked chickens for five dollars each.[11] Confederates gladly accepted U.S. currency because its value remained stable in the South while Confederate money continually declined. Fortunately, the men obtained something for their money before their captors stole the rest of it from them.

Prior to their capture, the Army paid the 7th about a year's back wages.[12] In one of the conditions of the surrender, Duckworth agreed that all private property of the prisoners would be respected. At Trenton, however, the captors took the 7th into the courthouse one at a time and robbed them, netting about $60,000. They also took boots, hats, coats, blankets, watches, and pocketknives.[13] Hawkins said he complained to Duckworth, who in turn blamed it on others in Forrest's command and promised to place his own men as guards. The robbery continued, however. When Hawkins complained a second time, Duckworth said that the money would eventually be returned.[14] Duckworth's word meant little in this situation as the money failed to be returned.

At Trenton, an accounting of the prisoners showed 471 men of the 7th Tennessee plus ten of Major Hardy's recruits. The rebels also netted a few of the 24th Missouri Infantry on provost duty at the fort.[15] Not among the prisoners were two companies of colored troops who guarded a bridge near Union City. They attempted to join Hawkins' troops before the attack, but abandoned the plan when rebel troops occupied the area between their position and the fort.[16] In view of later events, they undoubtedly considered themselves very fortunate.

10. Thomas P. Gray, *Joint Committee of 38th Congress*, May 5, 1864, Representative Committee #63, 70.

11. John W. Beatty, report, April 12, 1864, *OR*, 1, XXXII, (1), 543.

12. Mason Brayman, report, March 24, 1864, *OR*, 1, XXXII, (1), 502. Brayman estimated $60,000 was taken.

13. John W. Beattie, *Joint Committee of 38th Congress*, May 5, 1864, Representative Committee #63, 73. Thomas P. Gray, *Joint Committee of 38th Congress*, May 5, 1864, Representative Committee #63, 69, 70.

14. Hawkins Family Letter, *Tennessee Historical Quarterly* (Spring 1987): 38.

15. Thomas P. Gray, report, April 4, 1864, *OR*, 1, XXXII, (1), 545.

16. J. H. Odlin to Mason Brayman, March 24, 1864, *OR*, 1, XXXII, 1, 541.

At Trenton, Lieutenants Bradford, Neely, and Morgan escaped while under oath. Bradford had escaped only a month and a half earlier from Libby Prison in Richmond, Virginia. The remaining officers, with the exception of the colonel and major, reported the lieutenants to the Confederates but to no avail.[17] The escapees brought down retribution on the remaining officers who lost their mounts and had to walk.[18] These parole violations dismayed Colonel Hawkins.[19] All descriptions indicate him to be very much a southern gentleman who would be much embarrassed that his men broke their word.[20]

On Monday, the 28th of March, the prisoners arrived at Humboldt, Tennessee. Here Captain Gray of Company C, Captain Beatty of Company K, and Captain Parsons of Company E violated their oaths. Gray escaped alone to Fort Pillow, then still in Union hands. From there, he proceeded by boat to Memphis to report to General Hurlbut. No record exists for him after this time. Captains Beatty and Parsons traveled to Waverly Landing on the Tennessee River, where they came into Union lines on Thursday the 7th of April.[21] They continued on to Cairo, Illinois, arriving two weeks after their escape.

From Jackson, Tennessee to Mobile, Alabama

The remaining prisoners arrived in Jackson, Tennessee, General Forrest's temporary headquarters.[22] The captors placed the 7th Tennessee's officers in a filthy guardhouse. Friends in Jackson offered to post a $100,000 bond to take Colonel Hawkins to one of their homes. Forrest refused the offer but did decide to place the officers in a hotel.[23]

Hawkins' experiences in Trenton, Humboldt, and Jackson demonstrate how different it could be when locals knew and respected a prisoner being

17. Hawkins Family Letter, *Tennessee Historical Quarterly* (Spring 1987): 38.

18. William Witherspoon, *As They Saw Forrest*, 107. Confirmed by Hawkins Family Letter, *Tennessee Historical Quarterly* (Spring 1987): 39.

19. Hawkins Family Letter, *Tennessee Historical Quarterly* (Spring 1987): 35.

20. John Milton Hubbard, *As They Saw Forrest*, 154.

21. John W. Beattie, *Joint Committee of 38th Congress*, 5 May 1864, Representative Committee #63, 72–73.

22. Frank C. Whitthorne to T.M. Jack, April 2, 1864, *OR*, 1, XXXII, (3), 736.

23. Hawkins Family Letter, *Tennessee Historical Quarterly* (Spring 1987): 38.

taken through their area. In Trenton someone gave Colonel Hawkins a shirt and blanket, in Humboldt a citizen gave him two pairs of socks and a handkerchief. In Jackson he received a cake from Mrs. McCree, a Unionist lady.[24] She may be connected to James McCree, the man Witherspoon later accused of informing the Union authorities that the prisoners were in Jackson.[25]

In Jackson, Hawkins also met with Franklin Hawkins, his rebel first cousin who gave him about $200 in old issue Confederate money. Shortly thereafter, however, a report about their meeting reached the colonel. He hoped, but doubted, that his cousin had been misquoted.[26]

The 7th prisoners spent several days in Jackson at the end of March 1864. While walking on a bridge Hawkins said he met General Forrest, now returned to his temporary headquarters. When the general discovered that the 7th officers' remained on foot, he provided them with the horses of some of his men. The officers rode when the prisoners left Jackson sometime in late March or early April. They camped the first night about 16 miles from Purdy, McNairy County, Tennessee.[27] Here the captors faced the only attempt by Union forces to intercept their movement and perhaps free the prisoners.

The same rescue troops that Brayman borrowed from General Veatch arrived near Clifton, Tennessee by March 28, 1864. When word reached the Federal command that General Forrest might be intercepted near Purdy, Tennessee, a plan evolved to land Veatch's troops at Savannah, Tennessee. They would move westward while troops from Memphis under General Grierson traveled eastward.[28] Frightening rumors circulated among rebels in north Mississippi that estimated the Federal force as 6,000 men.[29] The Union forces, however, never located the prisoners. Only a small fight took place between Purdy and the Tennessee

24. *Ibid.*

25. William Witherspoon, *As They Saw Forrest*, 108. Witherspoon, of course, has a story about how McCree barely escaped being executed by Forrest and how he stopped being "disloyal" or even thinking about it.

26. Hawkins Family Letter, *Tennessee Historical Quarterly* (Spring 1987): 38–39.

27. Hawkins Family Letter, *Tennessee Historical Quarterly* (Spring 1987): 39.

28. S. A. Hurlbut to B. H. Grierson, March 31, 1864, *OR*, 1, XXXII, (3), 204.

29. Samuel Andrew Agnew, *Diary*, April 4, 1864, 228. Call number 923, Manuscripts Department, Southern Historical Collection, University of North Carolina, Chapel Hill.

River, apparently totally ineffective in its purpose.[30] Veatch returned to his ships and continued on to meet Sherman in the east.[31]

Hawkins says Forrest told him he expected the rescue attempt.[32] General Hurlbut confirmed on the 31st of March that Confederates had succeeded in tapping the wires and knew Veatch's movements.[33] Forrest also told him that if the attack materialized, the prisoners would be shot. Witherspoon also remembered the order to kill the prisoners.[34] Apparently Forrest sanctioned killing the nearly 500 unarmed captives in cold blood, even though they had surrendered peacefully at Union City. The events at Fort Pillow, which took place less than two weeks later, should cause little surprise.

From near Purdy the prisoners traveled to within three miles of Pocahontas, Tennessee, where the officers lost their borrowed horses. Taking all the mounts with them, the escort returned to Jackson to prepare for the attack on Fort Pillow.[35] The prisoners, entrusted to a Colonel White,[36] crossed into north Mississippi on foot by April 2, 1864. At Ripley, Mississippi, the escort provided the first food since Jackson.[37] Rumors making the rounds in northern Mississippi listed the prisoners as two regiments, one of them black, captured at Paducah, Kentucky, plus the regiment from Union City, Tennessee consisting of 500–600 of "Hawkins' Tories."[38] This would have totaled 2,000 to 3,000 men, if it had been true.

About 12 miles south of Ripley at Kelly's Mills on April 3 or 4, General Samuel Gholson, having been instructed by Forrest to meet the

30. B. H. Grierson to S. A. Hurlbut, April 5, 1864, *OR*, 1, XXXII, (1), 582. Hawkins Family Letter, *Tennessee Historical Quarterly* (Spring 1987): 39.

31. James C. Veatch to G. M. Dodge, April 7, 1864, *OR*, 1, XXXII, (1), 575–577.

32. S. A. Hurlbut to B. H. Grierson, March 31, 1864, *OR*, 1, XXXII, (3), 204.

33. *Ibid.*

34. Hawkins Family Letter, *Tennessee Historical Quarterly* (Spring 1987): 39. Witherspoon, *As They Saw Forrest*, 108.

35. N. B. Forrest, report, April 4, 1864, *OR*, 1, XXXII, (1), 608. Forrest went to Fort Pillow from Jackson on April 12, 1864, at the same time the 7th Tennessee entered Mobile.

36. Probably T. W. White of the 9th Mississippi. S. D. Lee to Cooper, May 27, 1864, *OR*, 1, XXXII, (1), 606.

37. Hawkins Family Letter, *Tennessee Historical Quarterly* (Spring 1987): 39.

38. Samuel Andrew Agnew, *Diary*, April 4, 1864, 225, 227. No black regiments were captured at Paducah.

prisoners,[39] placed them under the guard of Mississippi State Troops. Gholson furnished Hawkins with a horse. Here also, some of the new Mississippi guards scuffled over a gun, accidentally killing Private Larkin Qualls and wounding two more men of the 7th Tennessee.[40]

After Kelly's Mills, the prisoners encamped at Ellistown, Mississippi. Here Lieutenants Wallace and Allender escaped but were recaptured the next day. From Tupelo, Mississippi, where they spent one day, the captives continued on to Okolona, Mississippi by April 8 and Aberdeen, Mississippi by the 9th. Gholson expected to continue on to West Point, Mississippi that day, where he would place the prisoners on board the newly repaired Mobile & Ohio Railroad on Monday, the 11th of April.[41]

General Sherman's march from Vicksburg to Meridian, Mississippi in February 1864 had wrecked the Mobile & Ohio track. The Confederacy, however, finished repairing the railroad to Mobile, Alabama only a few days before the prisoners arrived at West Point, much to the consternation of the Union commanders,[42] except perhaps Colonel Hawkins. The prisoners, cavalrymen accustomed to riding, walked some 220 miles from Union City, Tennessee to West Point, Mississippi, over a period of 17 days. Boarding the train for Mobile must have been a welcome relief.

From Mobile, Alabama to Prisons in Georgia
April 17–21, 1864

After reaching Mobile about the 12th of April, the 7th Tennessee prisoners resided in a warehouse for several days. Isaac Davenport later described the place as "a cotton shed where the fleas and body lice sucked some of the very life blood out" and where they "numbered" too many

---

39. N. B. Forrest, report, March 27, 1864, *OR*, 1, XXXII, (1), 607. Samuel Andrew Agnew, *Diary*, April 4, 1864, 227–228. Gholson was mortally wounded at the Battle of Egypt Station in December 1864. Major General Washburn, report, January 5, 1865, *OR*, 1, XXXXI, (1), 1,000.

40. Hawkins Family Letter, *Tennessee Historical Quarterly* (Spring 1987): 39. Private Larkin Qualls was killed April 1864. Compiled Service Records 7th Tennessee M395 RG094 roll 68 #1422. Pension application George W. Morgan #107, 788.

41. Samuel Gholson to Leonidas Polk, April 9, 1864, *OR*, 1, XXXII, (3), 762–763.

42. S. A. Hurlbut to W. T. Sherman, April 17, 1864, *OR*, 1, XXXII, (3), 393–394.

for the space.[43] Four men died between the 12th and 17th while the unit remained in Mobile and five died after their removal, undoubtedly too ill to transport. These soldiers have military markers in the Mobile National Cemetery.

While in Mobile, Lieutenant Samuel Hawkins, 21-year-old son of the colonel who had escaped near Union City, Tennessee on his first night as a prisoner, was returned to his comrades after being recaptured.[44] He barely made it in time to join the regiment before it left for the east.

On April 17 the prisoners left Mobile aboard the privately owned *Southern Republic*,[45] a steamship operating in Mobile Bay. In 1862 an English visitor described the boat as a "castle-like hulk," having three stories and "floating on a pontoon." The first floor contained the engine, the second floor a combination dining hall-saloon plus sleeping berths, and the third several small rooms. The metal roof sported a calliope which, according to the visitor, incessantly played "Dixie." Captain Maher, an Irishman, owned the craft and staffed it with slaves.[46] The steamship remained in private hands until late in the war when the Confederacy pressed it into military service.[47]

The *Southern Republic* crossed the bay and continued up the Tensaw River to the town of Tensaw, Alabama. The 7th left there on the 18th of April on the Great Northern Railroad and arrived at Pollard, Alabama, where they spent the night. They needed to change trains at Pollard for the ride to Montgomery, Alabama, which they reached on April 19.[48]

Colonel Hawkins thought the citizens of this "First Capital of the Confederacy" presented a "funeral like appearance." The aforementioned English visitor agreed, describing them as "not very attractive" and the

43. Isaac Noah Davenport, "Andersonville Prison and the Steamboat Sultana's Explosion," in Gordon Turner, *History of Scotts Hill Tennessee* (Southhaven, Mississippi: Carter Printing Co., 1977), 195.

44. Hawkins Family Letter, *Tennessee Historical Quarterly* (Spring 1987): 39.

45. *Ibid.*

46. William Howard Russell, *My Diary North and South* (New York: S. Felt, 1863), 183–189.

47. John Thomas Scharf, *A History of the Confederate States Navy*, 2nd Edition (Albany, NY: Joseph McDonough, 1894), 596. The "Southern Republic" was pressed into Confederate service on April 11 and surrendered on May 10, 1865. George S. Waterman, *Confederate Veteran*, January 1910, 26.

48. Hawkins Family Letter, *Tennessee Historical Quarterly* (Spring 1987): 39.

town as little better.[49] The Montgomery morning newspaper, which was undoubtedly unaccustomed to southern Union colonels, branded Hawkins a "renegade." Given the two parties' mutual disapproval, the departure of the regiment the next morning for Columbus, Georgia must have caused little regret on either side. Changing trains at Columbus, the regiment traveled all night on the South Western Railroad, arriving at Andersonville Prison at 8 A.M. on the 21st of April, 1864.[50] The trip of nearly 750 miles from Union City to Andersonville took three days less than one month.

The Confederate authorities separated Colonel Hawkins, the nine commissioned officers,[51] the provost of the 24th Missouri, and the telegrapher[52] from the enlisted men and non-commissioned officers and sent them by train to an officers' prison at Macon, Georgia. Upon arrival, the men occupied a small city jail.[53] Unpleasant as it seemed, the officers' situation at Macon paled in comparison to the misery the non-commissioned officers and enlisted men encountered upon entering Andersonville Prison.

The 7th Tennessee in Georgia Prisons, April–July 1864

Andersonville Prison (Camp Sumter)

Camp Sumter, the official name for the prison in the little town of Andersonville, Georgia, opened about two months before the arrival of the 7th Tennessee. By May 8, the stockade held 12,213 men, 5,787 of whom (including over 450 from the 7th) entered within the last month. Over 700 deaths had already occurred.[54] Private Isaac Davenport

49. Russell, *My Diary North and South*, 183.

50. Hawkins Family Letter, *Tennessee Historical Quarterly* (Spring 1987): 39–40.

51. Major Smith, Captains Hayes and Moore, Lieutenants Allender, Hawkins, Wallace, Murray, John and Jeptha Robeson.

52. "Capture and Escape of a United States Telegrapher," *New York Times*, July 26, 1864, reprinted from the *Missouri Democrat*. Letter from Edgar B. McNarim to Colonel T. C. Moore, at Columbus, Kentucky, July 18, 1864. Telegrapher was Edgar B. McNarim, a 21 year old Canadian by birth.

53. Hawkins Family Letter, *Tennessee Historical Quarterly* (Spring 1987): 40.

54. H. Wirz to Thomas P. Turner, May 8, 1864, *OR*, 2, VII, 169.

remembered it a "despert [*sic*] looking place" and "very gloomy."[55] Sergeant Henry M. Davidson of the 1st Ohio Light Artillery, an inmate of the prison, noted the arrival of Hawkins' regiment:

> Some five hundred Tennesseans, who had been captured by Forrest…arrived among us; the most of whom were hatless, bootless, and shoeless, without coats, pants and blankets… They were wholly destitute of cups, plates, spoons, and dishes of every kind as well as of all means of purchasing them; they having been stripped of these things by their captors. In their destitute condition they were turned into the stockade and left to shift for themselves in the best manner they could. To borrow cups of their fellow-prisoners was an impossibility, for no one could be expected to lend what, if it were not returned, would insure his own destruction, particularly when the borrower was an utter stranger; there was nothing left for them but to bake their raw meal and bacon upon stones and chips, eat it without moisture, and afterward to go to the brook like beasts to quench their thirst.[56]

The newcomers lived with little protection from the elements. The authorities issued no tents upon entry to the camp. It rained hard most every night during the first month and the sun "blistered" by day.[57] Sergeant Davidson remembered that the men of the 7th "scooped out shallow places in the earth with their hands, and lying down side by side in these, with their bare heads and naked feet resting upon the surface of the ground, their unprotected bodies wet with dews and storms, the wretched men trembled and shivered till morning."[58] Answers on Civil War questionnaires confirm this. Private William Douglas wrote

55. Davenport, *History of Scotts Hill*, 195.

56. Henry M. Davidson, "Experience in Rebel Prisons for United States Soldiers," in *Prisoners of War and Military Prisons* (Cincinnati: Lyman and Cushing, 1890), 234.

57. Melvin Grigsby, *The Smoked Yank* (Sioux Falls: Dakota Bell Publishing Co., 1888), 99.

58. Davidson, *Prisoners of War and Military Prisons*, 234–235.

Photograph of Andersonville Prison marker at
Andersonville National Historic Site

that the men "slept on the ground, nothing under us or over."[59] Private William T. Woods said, "We suffered greatly from exposure."[60]

Much of the misery could have been avoided if the men of the 7th had arrived with the back pay they received preceding capture. It could have been used to buy blankets and equipment from the prison sutler or from hucksters who hawked their wares from every corner of the camp. Some Confederates, unlike the men of Forrest's command, respected the private property of their captives. The nearly 3,000 Union troops captured at Plymouth, North Carolina by the 35th North Carolina came into camp about 12 days after the 7th, bringing all their belongings except arms and military equipment. One captive praised the 35th as a "gentlemanly set of guards."[61] Sergeant Davidson remarked on the contrast in appearance between the Plymouth prisoners with private resources and the 7th Tennessee without.[62] The photograph above shows the tents of those men fortunate enough to have some covering. A prison survivor

59. "William A. Douglas," *The Tennessee Civil War Veterans Questionnaires* 1: 48.

60. "William T. Woods," *The Tennessee Civil War Veterans Questionnaires* 1: 155–156.

61. Davidson, *Prisoners of War and Military Prisons*, 234–235.

62. *Ibid.*

later estimated that about half the prisoners in Andersonville had some resources other than those provided by the prison.[63]

Money to buy food would have been especially helpful since the provisions supplied by the camp proved inadequate and of inferior quality. James Taylor of Buena Vista in Carroll County, Tennessee recalled in later years that the food supply for twenty-four hours represented about half of what a man ordinarily ate for one meal or about one-sixth of the daily requirement.[64] The vegetable allowance, badly needed to ward off scurvy, consisted of "1 spoonful Bow peas a day" according to William Douglas of Henderson County, Tennessee.[65] Joseph McCracken, son of the mayor of Huntingdon, Tennessee, weighed 150 pounds when he arrived at Andersonville and only 75 pounds at release.[66] Isaac Davenport of Henderson County wrote of "our flesh bein reducd we were nothing but skelingtons."[67] Southern apologists make much of the fact that rations supplied to the prisoners compare favorably to those of the guards at the prison. They overlook, however, the opportunities that free men, or prisoners with money, had to supplement their rations.

Inadequate food, overcrowded conditions, and exposure both on the trip south and at camp took their first toll on the West Tennesseans eight days after arrival. The first deaths occurred on April 29 when twenty-eight year old Private Jackson J. Hays of Henderson County, Tennessee died of chronic diarrhea and twenty year old Sergeant George Pickens of McNairy County, Tennessee died of dysentery.[68] The regiment's first full month in prison resulted in six more deaths, half from pneumonia. Sixteen more died in the second full month, fourteen of these from diarrhea. Both northern inmates and rebel administrators thought that corn meal caused diarrhea in the northern digestive system.[69] Diarrhea served

63. Melvin Grigsby, *The Smoked Yank*, 104–105.

64. James Taylor, *The Tennessee Civil War Veterans Questionnaires* 1: 125–126.

65. William Douglas, *The Tennessee Civil War Veterans Questionnaires* 1: 48.

66. *The Goodspeed Histories of Carroll, Henry and Benton Counties* (McMinnville, TN: Ben Loman Press, reprint of 1887), 872.

67. Davenport, *History of Scotts Hill Tennessee*, 195.

68. *Compiled Service Records 7th Tennessee*, M395 RG094 rolls 63-69.

69. James Madison Page, *The True Story of Andersonville Prison* (New York: The Neale Publishing Co., 1908), 154. Ovid L. Futch, *History of Andersonville Prison* (Gainsville: University of Florida Press, 1968), 19.

as the number one cause of death for the West Tennesseans, however, whose diet normally contained large amounts of corn meal. Ninety men succumbed to diarrhea during their captivity.[70]

An increase in the prison population and problems with the "Raiders," a group of lawless inmates who preyed on other prisoners, made even the first two months extremely difficult. In June, over 9,000 new prisoners arrived; by the end of the month, a total of 27,641 men inhabited a prison compound designed to accommodate less than half that number.[71]

July began on a more hopeful note. Union troops stood on Georgia soil and General Sherman threatened Atlanta. Inside the prison, an addition to the stockade helped alleviate overcrowded conditions while a combined force of prison authorities and inmates captured the "Raiders," hanging six of them. The prisoners then formed an internal police force to keep order.[72]

Rumors circulated of an exchange of prisoners to take place on July 7. Reality, however, soon set in when exchanges failed to materialize. By the end of July, the stockade contained 33,443 men.[73] The temperature and the death rate soared. The dead included twenty-six men of the 7th Tennessee among the 1,742 who succumbed within the month of July. This brought the total number of deaths since their capture at Union City to sixty-three or approximately one out of every seven men.

Near the end of July 1864 as hope faded, a petition circulated through the prison begging President Lincoln to take action to effect parole or exchange for the men at Andersonville. One hundred sergeants signed, including Sergeants John M. Rhodes of Company A and Rufus G. Barker of Company H.[74] The Confederate authorities allowed a delegation of prisoners to take the petition to Washington, D.C., but the government never acted on it.

70. *Compiled Service Records 7th Tennessee*, M395 RG094 rolls 63-69.

71. Henry Wirz, report, end of June 1864, *OR*, 2, VII, 438.

72. Grigsby, *Smoked Yank*, 116.

73. Henry Wirz, report, end of July 1864, *OR*, 2, VII, 517.

74. Minutes of sergeants commanding detachments of prisoners at Andersonville, Georgia, *OR*, 2, VII, 618–621. Sergeant Barker later joined the Confederate Army in order to leave prison.

Captured Officers of the 7th Tennessee at Macon, Georgia
from Late April to July 1864

The officers of the 7th Tennessee[75] found very crowded conditions at the city jail, their first place of incarceration in Macon. The pro-Union jailor's wife, however, treated them very kindly, providing food, clothes, and other items. On the 28th of April the authorities moved the men to the county jail where a jailer, without a sympathetic wife, treated them more like enemy prisoners.[76]

About the 10th of May at the county jail, the officers sawed through the floor with knives smuggled in by local Unionists, then dug a tunnel under the wall.[77] Lieutenant William W. Murray, telegrapher Edgar B. McNarim, and a northern officer went out through the tunnel on Saturday, May 14th at 2 A.M. Lieutenant Allender, who had escaped once before being recaptured, also went out, but lost courage and crawled back to the cell. The men evaded being tracked by the bloodhounds by rubbing wild onions on their boots and clothes. They posed as furloughed Confederates and carried forged papers to prove it. Murray, at least, had a southern accent. The three escapees traveled mostly by night. In a month, they covered the 300 plus miles from Macon, Georgia across southeastern Alabama to Choctawhatchee Bay in Florida. There they found and boarded a Union ship on blockade duty. The *New York Times* published a letter about their experiences which was written in Florida by McNarim.[78] Murray and McNarim joined the detachment of the 7th at Columbus, Kentucky in July 1864. An Ohio magazine published a much later and longer account of the escape written by Dr. Murray after the war.[79]

75. Colonel Hawkins, Major Smith, Captains Hays and Moore, Lieutenants Allender, Hawkins, Murray, Robeson, and Wallace, plus telegrapher McNarim and Captain Wyatt Harris of 24th Missouri.

76. Hawkins Family Letter, *Tennessee Historical Quarterly* (Spring 1987): 40.

77. *Ibid.*

78. Letter from Edgar B. McNarim to Colonel Timothy C. Moore, Columbus, Kentucky, July 18, 1864. "Capture and Escape of a United States Telegrapher," *New York Times*, July 26, 1864, reprinted from the *Missouri Democrat*.

79. William W. Murray, "From Macon, Georgia to the Gulf, an Escaping Prisoner's Experience," in *Military Order of the Loyal Legion of the United States, Ohio* 5 (Cincinnati: Commandery, 1902), 88–117.

Moved again on the 18th of May, the remaining officers of the 7th found themselves confined with over 1,000 other officers at Camp Oglethorpe, another prison facility in Macon. Lack of shelter and food made these quarters a little more like those of the enlisted men at Andersonville. Hawkins' son and the other 7th Tennessee officers remained in Macon until August 1864. Colonel Hawkins' residence at this camp, however, lasted less than a month.

On June 10th, the Confederate authorities transferred Hawkins and forty-nine other high-ranking officers to Charleston, South Carolina.[80] They were placed in the O'Connor House,[81] a large mansion inside the city, in hopes of discouraging shelling of the town from Union-occupied Morris Island off the Charleston coast. Asa Isham, one of the officers, remembered, at least in hindsight, that the officers rather enjoyed being under fire. The Union gunners had the range of every part of the city from long practice. Knowing where the Confederates domiciled the officers, the gunners aimed to miss the house and succeeded admirably,[82] as shown in a surviving photograph.

The O'Connor House, 1865 Broad Street, Charleston, South Carolina (Library of Congress Prints and Photographs)

80. Hawkins Family Letter, *Tennessee Historical Quarterly* (Spring 1987): 40. J. G. Foster to Halleck, June 22, 1864, *OR*, 1, XXXV, 144–145.

81. The house, which is privately owned, survives in 2009.

82. *Ibid.* Asa B. Isham, *Prisoners of War and Military Prisons with General Account of Prison Life and Prisons in the South during the War of the Rebellion, including statistical information pertaining to Prisoners of War* (Cincinnati: Lyman and Cushing, 1890), 69.

CHAPTER SEVEN

————•————

REASSIGNMENTS FOR THE DETACHMENT
AND THE PRISONERS

The Detachment at Columbus, Kentucky, May–July 1864

Reorganization and Court-martials at Columbus

Eventually most of the men of the 7th who remained free after the surrender at Union City gathered at Columbus, Kentucky.[1] Nicknamed the "Gibraltar of the West," this heavily fortified post overlooked the Mississippi River 180 feet below. Originally a Confederate installation called Fort DeRussy, it came into Union possession in March 1862 and was renamed Fort Halleck. The town of Columbus, which remained largely Confederate in sympathy, served as the terminus for the Mobile & Ohio Railroad. The Civilian Conservation Corps built the Columbus-Belmont Kentucky State Park on the site of the fort in the 1930s. Attractions include cannon, earthworks, and a large anchor and chain from the Civil War era as well as a small, informative museum.

---

1. Troop Organization, May 31, 1864, *OR*, 1, XXXIX, (2), 67. Some men were still in Paducah, Kentucky, however, on May 31 under the command of Captain Martin.

"Big Bertha" Cannon (left) and Anchor and Chain (right) at the Columbus–Belmont State Park near Columbus, Kentucky

Fort Halleck post returns for June 1864 indicate the presence of 13 officers and 168 enlisted men of the 7th Tennessee detachment, an aggregate of 181. With too few men left to fill six companies, the detachment reorganized on June 18, 1864, into three companies: A, B, and C.[2] Captain James M. Martin led Company A with Lieutenants Elbert N. Royall, James M. Neely, and Marcus Renfro. Pleasant K. Parsons commanded Company B, with lieutenants Robert W. Helmer and James W. Morgan. John W. Beatty led Company C along with lieutenants Robert Y. Bradford, William Cleary, and Francis A. Smith. Frank Travis served as Regimental Quarter Master and Edward Arbuckle as Assistant Surgeon.

Lieutenants Cleary and Smith, plus 27 of the 168 enlisted men at Columbus, belonged previously to Bradford's 13th/14th Tennessee Cavalry. They attached temporarily to the 7th sometime after the defeat at Fort Pillow.[3] Cleary and Smith, the only commissioned officers of the 13th/14th to survive Fort Pillow, wrote extremely accusatory accounts of the actions of Forrest's men during the flag of truce negotiations and after the battle when blacks and southern loyalists attempted to surrender.[4] General Brayman forwarded their reports to the congressional committee investigating the Fort Pillow battle.[5]

2. *Compiled Service Records 7th Tennessee*, M395 RG094 rolls 63–69.

3. Cleary commanded Company A of the 13th/14th Tennessee Cavalry that later merged with Company E, 6th Tennessee Cavalry.

4. Francis A. Smith and William Cleary, report, April 18, 1864, *OR*, 1, XXXII, (1), 563–565.

5. Francis A. Smith and William Cleary, *Joint Committee of 38th Congress*, May 5, 1864, Representative Committee #63, 9.104–105.

By July, the men of the 13th/14th Cavalry no longer remained at Columbus. Eventually they became part of Company E, 6th Tennessee Cavalry, with Smith as captain and Cleary as lieutenant. This reduced the number of 7th enlisted men at Columbus to 141.[6] When Lieutenant William W. Murray rejoined the regiment after his escape from the Macon officer's prison, he became its twelfth officer. Two of those officers soon found themselves in grave difficulty. Captain Pleasant K. Parsons of West Tennessee and Captain John Beatty of Michigan, who escaped together from Humboldt, Tennessee, both faced court-martials.

Parsons' troubles began on July 5, 1864. Fellow officer Captain James Martin, who commanded the attachment at the time, placed Parsons under arrest on charges of misconduct during the time he commanded a scout in McCracken County, Kentucky in May 1864. Martin charged Parsons with keeping money taken from a prisoner and stealing a doormat and a hearthrug, which he used as a saddle blanket. Another complaint said Parsons threatened fellow officer Lieutenant James Wyly Morgan with pistols while intoxicated. Although the testimony appears contradictory, the court declared Parsons guilty on all counts and sentenced him to be dishonorably dismissed from service with loss of all pay and allowance. Something changed, however, since Parsons remained with the regiment until it dissolved and received an honorable discharge.[7]

On July 10, 1864, Assistant Surgeon Dr. Edward Arbuckle brought charges against Captain John W. Beatty, formerly captain of Company K and now captain of the reorganized Company C, for "conduct unbecoming an officer and a gentleman." Arbuckle asserted that Beatty "did bring into camp of the 7th Cavalry a woman and introduce her as his wife, keeping her as such this while he was the lawful husband of another woman." The court found Beatty guilty and he deserted soon after the court-martial.[8]

During the court-martials, Parsons claimed that Captain Martin and two other officers brought the charges against the two captains in order

6. July Monthly Report, Columbus, Kentucky.

7. Witnesses in Parsons' trial: Pvt. John Hale, Pvt. Ulysses Kirk, Lt. James Neely, Lt. James Morgan, Sgt. James Spellings, Lt. Robert Y. Bradford, Capt. James Martin, Lt. Travis, Col. Isaac Hawkins, and Lt. Robert Helmer.

8. Witnesses in Beatty's trial: Lt. James Neely, Capt. James M. Martin, Lt. W.W. Murray, Lt. R.Y. Bradford, Lt. James W. Morgan, Lt. Robert W. Helmer, and Dr. Arbuckle.

that other men could be promoted to their ranks. Beatty claimed Dr. Arbuckle resented an order he gave him.[9] The juries apparently disagreed.

While their fellow soldiers wasted away in Andersonville Prison, the detachment at Columbus continued to perform the usual cavalry assignments. On July 17–18, 1864, Lieutenant Robert Y. Bradford led a scout from Columbus to Hickman, Kentucky in search of the rebel Captain Campbell, who sought recruits, deserters, and conscripts in the area. They captured two of his men but missed Campbell by "some ten minutes, getting his uniform jacket, hat and feathers" plus $50 Confederate money in his jacket pocket. The scout returned to Columbus, with Campbell's wardrobe, by way of Moscow, Illinois.[10] On September 2, 1864, Lieutenant Murray and seventy men engaged rebel forces at Union City, site of the surrender of the regiment five months earlier. This time the detachment of the 7th won, killing six and taking eleven prisoners while losing only one horse.[11]

Colonel Hawkins Released and Returned to the Regiment

On August 3, 1864, the Confederacy exchanged five generals plus Colonel Hawkins and 44 other field officers imprisoned under fire of the Union guns in Charleston, South Carolina for 50 Confederate officers taken from Fort Delaware Prison and placed under Confederate bombardment on Morris Island off Charleston.[12] Federal forces ceased firing while a rebel vessel carrying the officers sailed past Fort Sumter to meet the Union ship *Cosmopolitan*. Shelling commenced again after the return of the rebel ship to port.[13] The released officers spent one day at Hilton Head, South Carolina before sailing to New York on the *Fulton*,[14] reaching there on August 9. Colonel Hawkins thus became the first of the 7th Tennessee Union City captives to be released from prison. Three months elapsed before any more exchanges took place.

9. Proceedings of a General Court Martial convened at Columbus, Kentucky, August 26, 1864.

10. Robert Y. Bradford, report, July 17–18, 1864, *OR*, 1, XXXIX, (1), 360–361.

11. James N. McArthur, report, September 3, 1864, *OR*, 1, XXXIX, (1), 493.

12. R. S. Ripley to A. Schimmelfenning, June 13, 1864, *OR*, 1, XXXV, (2), 132.

13. A. Schimmelfennig, report, August 3, 1864, *OR*, 1, XXXV, (1), 69.

14. J. G. Foster to H. W. Halleck, August 4, 1864, *OR*, 1, XXXV, (2), 212.

Sometime in late August or early September 1864, Hawkins traveled to Columbus where the detachment of the 7th had been stationed since June of 1864. While there on September 2, he vouched for the trustworthiness of a Unionist spy who brought news of a rebel buildup at Trenton, Tennessee.[15] He also heard for the first time the comments made by General Hurlbut about the capitulation at Union City and his accusation of "cowardice" on Hawkins' part.[16]

Asking and receiving permission to "not be immediately placed on duty," Hawkins left to visit his family in Greencastle, Indiana. They had fled Huntingdon, Tennessee when Mrs. Hawkins and her family received threats against their lives. The colonel expressed disappointment that only one neighbor came to his wife's defense.[17] Given the large number of Unionists in Huntingdon, this does seem unchivalrous.

The 7th Tennessee Prisoners August–Fall 1864

The Officers of the 7th Tennessee Relocated

The remaining eight captured officers,[18] plus the provost officer of the 24th Missouri,[19] continued for a time in prison in Macon, Georgia. By August 6, 1864, however, 650 officers already had been moved from Macon to Charleston, South Carolina. Another 1,000 started for Charleston but were diverted elsewhere.[20] This removal resulted from the fear that Sherman's continuing penetration into Georgia might result in release of the prisoners. The officers of the 7th left Macon, spending time in Charleston[21] and/or Savannah.[22] A yellow fever epidemic in Charleston

15. James N. McArthur to P. Paine, September 2, 1864. *OR*, 1, XXXIX, (2), 339.

16. Hawkins Family Letter, *Tennessee Historical Quarterly* (Spring 1987): 41.

17. *Ibid*, 36.

18. John and Jeptha Robeson, Smith, Hays, Hawkins, Allender, Moore, and Wallace. Murray had escaped at Macon.

19. Captain Wyatt Harris of the 24th Missouri wrote an article in 1884 about his unsuccessful attempt to escape from officer's prison in Columbia, South Carolina. Goodspeed, *History of Lawrence Co., Missouri*.

20. Thomas J. Robinson to E. E. Potter, August 6, 1864, *OR*, 1, XXXV, (2), 223.

21. Major Smith's muster roll records mention Charleston.

22. G. W. Moore's pension papers mention his being in prison in Savannah along with J. J. Wallace.

caused the removal of the officers inland to Columbia, South Carolina in October 1864.[23]

The prison at Columbia consisted of a five-acre tract of cleared land outside the city with no fences and no shelters. Guards patrolled a "dead line" and dogs tracked officers attempting to escape. The prison received its nickname, Camp Sorghum, from the sorghum molasses and corn meal issued as rations. The commissary-general supposedly forbade the issuance of meat.[24] Here the remaining officers of the 7th spent the fall of 1864.[25]

The Andersonville Prisoners
from August 1864 until Their Removal to Other Prisons

August began at Andersonville with terrible rainstorms that drenched the unprotected prisoners. The downpours, however, washed some of the filth from the camp and one especially hard rain revealed a spring of fresh water covered during the building of the stockade.[26] The men welcomed a substitute for the polluted stream flowing through the camp and named the new source of fresh water "Providence Spring." Almost every memoir written about the camp mentions this incident.[27] In 1901, the women's auxiliary of the Grand Army of the Republic built a pavilion over the site.

By the end of August 1864, the camp held about 32,900 men.[28] New prisoners arrived almost continuously after Sherman's army entered Georgia. By mid-July recent captives brought the good news that Union troops were encamped as near as Atlanta, only about 110 miles to the north.[29] The camp, however, experienced one of its most disastrous months as nearly 3,000 men died,[30] an average of almost 100 per day. By the end of August, the 7th Tennessee had lost forty-four more men.

---

23. The muster rolls of Jeptha Robeson, Smith, and Wallace all mention imprisonment at Columbia.

24. David Urquhart to S. Cooper, October 26, 1864, *OR*, 2, VII, 1046.

25. Hawkins, Moore, Allender, Hays, Smith, Robeson, and Wallace.

26. Peggy Sheppard, *Andersonville Georgia USA* (Leslie, GA: privately published, 1973), 12.

27. The date of wonder was reportedly March 13, 1864.

28. Dr. Joseph Jones, report, *OR*, 2, VIII, 596.

29. Robert H. Kellogg, *Life and Death in Rebel Prisons* (Hartford: L. Stebbins, 1865), 100, 136.

30. Dr. Joseph Jones, report, *OR*, 2, VIII, 610.

Pavilion built over "Providence Spring" by the women's auxiliary of the Grand Army of the Republic

This brought the death rate since capture to nearly 24 percent, or almost one out of every four.

Gray Rogers of Carroll County accounted for one of the August deaths. George Huffman, a member of the 14th Illinois Cavalry and a friend of Rogers, arrived at Andersonville about four days before Roger's death and left an account of the encounter in a memoir. Rogers, who "had flies all over" and vermin "at work on him," failed to recognize his friend and died of gangrene on August 25. Huffman thought the prison smelled like a dead person and he wondered how anyone would be able to live in such a place.[31]

Private Isaac Davenport remembered the months of seeing so many of his regiment sick and dying. He and a group of his Henderson County neighbors banded together to support each other as much as they could with what little they had. To aid those most afflicted they brought water from the brook or spring, attempted to keep flies away, and offered

31. George Huffman, "My Experience of the Civil War and My Prison Escape," *The Guilford Genealogist* 25, no 2 (Guilford County: North Carolina Genealogical Society, Spring 1998). A very late memoir.

encouragement. To raise their own spirits they talked about home, sang songs, told jokes, and walked about for exercise and diversion.[32]

Removal of Some Andersonville Inmates to Other Prisons
September 1864

In early September, the prison authorities ordered several groups including the 7th Tennessee to be ready for departure for the purpose of exchange. Their actual destinations proved to be other southern prisons rather than freedom. After the Union captured Atlanta, Andersonville became extremely vulnerable. This precipitated the removal of its ambulatory inmates to prisons in Charleston, Florence, and Columbia in South Carolina, plus Savannah, Blackshear, Millen, and Thomasville in Georgia.[33] Conditions in these prisons varied with the location.

The stockade at Florence contained about 32 acres and some 16,000 prisoners by November 1864. Here Jesse Lowry, David Cox, and Thomas Pastures teamed up with West Tennessee neighbor George Hoffman of the 14th Illinois. They dug a hole in the ground about "two feet deep, six feet wide and six feet long" which became their "bedroom, parlor and kitchen." Huffman thought Florence even worse than Andersonville, especially in terms of rations.[34] Mortality rates there reportedly ranged from 30 to 50 per day.[35] Seven members of the 7th died during their incarceration.

More soldiers also died at Millen (16), Charleston (4), and Savannah (16), indicating a presence in those three prisons as well. The men in Savannah most likely moved to Camp Lawton at Millen, Georgia when a yellow fever epidemic hit Savannah.[36] Other records mention men at Blackshear, Thomasville, and Columbia.

---

32. Davenport, "*History of Scotts Hill Tennessee*, 195.

33. George Huffman went from Andersonville to Charlestown, South Carolina to Florence, South Carolina to Goldsboro, North Carolina.

34. George Huffman, *The Guilford Genealogist*.

35. "Where Our Prisoners Are," *New York Times*, November 27, 1864.

36. "Our Prisoners: Their Release from Captivity," *New York Times*, November 26, 1864.

Those Who Never Left Andersonville and Those Who Returned

The removal of the healthiest to smaller prisons reduced the number of inmates at Andersonville from about 33,000 in August to around 2,000 in November. Fifty-two died in September and seven more succumbed at the smaller prisons. This made September the most disastrous month of imprisonment. October saw thirty-six deaths at Andersonville and eight in the smaller prisons. By the end of October, seven months after capture, the death rate reached 48 percent, or nearly one out of every two men (total 210). During the period from October through December 1864, however, the mortality rate dropped sharply. Reasons probably included milder weather, the resumption of prisoner exchanges and less crowded conditions at the smaller prisons.

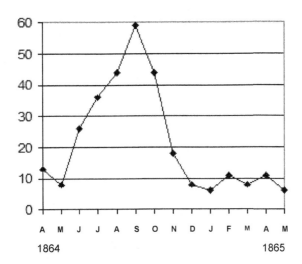

Monthly Prison Deaths of the 7th Tennessee Cavalry

The beginning of 1865 brought a slight increase in the number of prisoners at Andersonville. When federal cavalry raids into southern Georgia threatened to free the Union prisoners at Thomasville,[37] Confederate authorities relocated the approximately 3,500 inmates. After being promised their release, the men—including Private Isaac N. Davenport—marched happily on foot about forty miles from Thomasville to

37. "The War in Florida," *New York Times*, March 23, 1865.

Albany, Georgia, where they boarded a train. To their horror, they found themselves back once again at Andersonville.[38]

Perhaps mounting desperation among the returnees caused seventeen members of the 7th Tennessee to switch sides and take the oath of allegiance to the Confederacy. They left the prison with recruiter Colonel John G. O'Neil on the 28th of February 1865, along with 121 men from other regiments who joined at the same time. As new members of the 10th Infantry CSA, they joined rebel troops defending southwest Georgia from Union troops in Florida and Alabama.[39]Although the South recruited regularly in the stockade, only three men from the 7th had gone over to the enemy in the previous ten months.

Rebel recruiters targeted southern prisoners since a change in allegiance to the South might prove easier for them than for northerners. Southerners comprised around 10 percent of the inmates at Andersonville and a large proportion of those hailed from East and West Tennessee.[40] None of the "Galvanized Yanks"[41] merited full confidence. The probability always existed that they joined only for a chance to leave prison and escape. At least three of the seventeen February recruits reached Union lines within two months of pretending to change allegiances. They promptly gained forgiveness for their indiscretion.[42]

The strategy above, however, involved considerable risk. One might be captured by the Union while still in the southern military. This happened to Privates Nelson Moore and Isaac Smothers,[43] who joined the Confederacy in exchange for release from Andersonville then deserted at the battle of Egypt Station in Mississippi on December 28, 1864. Federal records indicate about 250 former Andersonville prisoners threw down their weapons and deserted at the approach of the Union Army.[44]

---

38. Davenport, *History of Scotts Hill Tennessee*, 195.

39. Ovid L. Futch, *History of Andersonville Prison* (Gainsville: University of Florida Press, 1968), 115.

40. The two largest groups were the 2nd (East) Tennessee Cavalry and the 7th (West) Tennessee Cavalry. Ten percent calculated by number of deaths from southern Union regiments.

41. Warren Lee Goss, *The Soldiers Story* (Boston: Lee and Shepard, 1869), 225.

42. Theophilus Webb, Walter E. Pucket, and Robert C. Hill.

43. Moore and Smothers left in 1864 and were not a part of the 17 who left in February 1865.

44. *Tennesseans in the Civil War, Part 1* (Nashville: Civil War Centennial Commission, 1964), 195. No southern records confirm this information on the battle of Egypt Station.

The Federals took the deserters, including Smothers and Moore, to prison at Alton, Illinois where many volunteered again, this time in the 5th U.S. Volunteers, a regiment of rebel deserters being raised to serve on the plains against the Indians. Both Smothers and Moore then deserted the 5th U.S. Volunteers.[45]

Confederates resented southerners who fought on the Union side even more than they resented northerners. Warren Goss, a Massachusetts soldier in prison at Florence, mentioned in his memoir that Colonel Iverson treated southern men very harshly. Iverson called them "d—d traitors" and asked why they fought against "their country." The northern white prisoners, however, considered Iverson one of the kindest of the prison commanders.[46]

Exchanges of Prisoners, November and December 1864

After seven months without prisoner paroles or exchanges, the warring sides agreed to commence once again. This took place about two months after the removal of the majority of men at Andersonville to the smaller prisons. The first of the men to be exchanged arrived on rebel ships from the prisons at Savannah and Millen, Georgia, the prisons closest to the exchange site at Savannah. Colonel Mulford, who commanded the Union transports, met Captain Hatch, the rebel agent, on the steamer *General Beauregard* at Venus Point on the Savannah River on the 19th of November 1864. They exchanged rolls of the prisoners to be transferred, then the *General Beauregard* went alongside the Union ship and the transfer of men began. These first exchanges purported to be of those prisoners most able to travel. A correspondent from the *New York Times* wondered how men could possibly look worse. Despite their miserable state of health, he reported that the former prisoners cheered and sang as the rebel boat moved away. As soon as possible the ships served hot coffee, ham, and hard bread to the starving men.[47]

45. G. M. Dodge to Major General Pope, February 13, 1865, *OR*, 1, XLVIII, (1), 835. G.M. Dodge to Joseph M. C. Bell, March 5, 1865. *OR*, 2, VIII, 358-359. Records of the 5th U.S. Volunteers.

46. Goss, *The Soldiers Story*, 226, 258.

47. Special Correspondent, "Our Prisoners, Their First Release from Captivity," *New York Times*, November 21, 1864, Port Royal, South Carolina.

The *Savannah News* had similar things to say about the southern soldiers brought by the Union for exchange. Many could not walk, all "were sick or wounded." The citizens of Savannah lit bonfires by the river, a band played, and the ladies served refreshments[48] to welcome the men back south. The celebration[49] may have been less joyous with General Sherman two-thirds of his way from Atlanta to Savannah, his next target.[50]

The first Union transport steamers, the *Atlantic* and the *Blackstone*, filled with paroled prisoners, left Savannah on November 22 and arrived at Baltimore, Maryland three days later. The *Atlantic*, which carried the more critical passengers, docked with 649 men, all in need of hospitalization. Seventeen men died during the passage north.[51] Records exist for 26 men of the 7th Tennessee released through Savannah from November 22 to December 6, 1864.[52]

The *New York Times* came into possession of the official death register for the prison hospital at Savannah (September 12–November 14, 1864) and published it on December 17. It listed fourteen members of the 7th Tennessee as dying in the period immediately preceding the resumption of the exchanges. The military muster rolls fail to list four of these men as having died in prison. The dates of death on the hospital record generally predate those given on the military records.[53]

About three weeks into the prisoner exchange at Savannah, the Confederates announced they could no longer keep up the swap. General Sherman's troops threatened the city and the military needed all transport for defense. On the 5th of December, only 5,500 men had been freed. Colonel Mulford, who headed the Union operation, suggested the exchanges be moved to Charleston, South Carolina and the Confederate authorities agreed. Within a few days, a truce settled over Charleston Harbor and

48. "The Exchange of Prisoners at Savannah," *New York Times*, November 25, 1864, reprinted from *Richmond Examiner*, November 21, 1864, reprinted from *Savannah News*, November 16 (19th), 1864. "Sherman's March," *New York Times*, November 26, 1864.

49. "Release of Prisoners: Their Horrible Condition," *New York Times*, November 27, 1864, reprinted from *The Baltimore American*, November 26, 1864.

50. "Exchange of Prisoners," *New York Times*, November 28, 1864.

51. "Release of Prisoners: Their Horrible Condition," *New York Times*, November 27, 1864, reprinted from *The Baltimore American*, November 26, 1864.

52. About 30 survivors of Andersonville have no place of exchange listed on their muster rolls.

53. "Deaths in the Savannah Prison Hospitals," *New York Times*, December 17, 1864. The four were William Bynum, E. W. Workman, W. Albert, and J. D. Rowe.

Union transports pulled in past the ruins of Fort Sumter, where the first shots of the war had been fired. About 5,000 more men gained release at Charleston, at least 39 of them from the 7th Tennessee. The total release of Union prisoners at Savannah and Charleston from mid-November to late December 1864 totaled 10,500.[54] The muster rolls show around 65 of these to be members of Colonel Hawkins' regiment.[55]

When the exchanges moved to Charleston Harbor, the released men came from South Carolina rather than Georgia prisons. The enlisted men left primarily from the prison camp at Florence and the officers from "Camp Sorghum" at Columbia, South Carolina. Among the officers paroled from Columbia[56] were Major Thomas Atlas Smith of Henderson County (December 14) and Lieutenant John Terrell C. Robeson (December 13). They seem to have been the only two officers of the 7th to gain release in the Savannah-Charleston exchanges.

The prisoners freed on the east coast generally went north by specially fitted hospital ships to Baltimore, then on to hospitals in Annapolis, Maryland. Nineteen-year-old Isaac Reed of Henderson County left through Charleston and died December 9, 1864, aboard the transport *Northern Lights* en route to Baltimore. Reed received burial at sea.[57] Seven men of the 7th Tennessee died in the hospitals soon after arrival. Burial of these men took place in Ash Grove Cemetery in Annapolis.

The Detachment Moves Around in Kentucky

The 7th Tennessee Detachment Assigned to Mayfield, Kentucky, October 1864

In the late summer and early fall 1864, the Union command reassigned a number of the troops at Columbus, Kentucky—the 134th

---

54. "The Union Martyrs: Their Delivery in Charleston Harbor," *New York Times*, December 16, 1864.

55. Some muster roll entries say only that release was at Savannah/Charleston and give no dates.

56. "The Union Martyrs: Their Delivery in Charleston Harbor," *New York Times*, December 16, 1864.

57. Gordon Turner, "Isaac Davenport," in *History of Scotts Hill Tennessee*, 196, and muster roll. Reed's effects were 1 cap, 1 blouse, 1 trousers, and 1 shoes, worth $2.00. Presumably these had been issued on the boat.

Illinois, 34th New Jersey, and a detachment of the 3rd Illinois Cavalry—
to Mayfield, Kentucky, a town about 20 miles to the east. In September
1864, the 156 men of the 7th Tennessee at Columbus left for Paducah,
Kentucky[58] where Colonel Hawkins caught up with them after visiting
his family in Indiana. On October 1, 1864, Hawkins requested to "be
returned to duty"[59] and resumed command on October 5.[60] The regiment
then moved from Paducah to Mayfield, Kentucky. Hawkins remarked
in a letter to his cousin that "quite a force" had been placed at his disposal, which indicates an addition of other troops to his command, most
likely the troops mentioned above as assigned to Mayfield.[61] This larger
command may indicate that his superiors now considered Hawkins jus-
tified in his surrender at Union City, or at least forgiven. Things were
beginning to look better for the colonel.

Only two days after Hawkins resumed command, an intelligence
report placed 1,000 troops within 40 miles of Mayfield awaiting the arrival of Forrest's main troops to join them for an attack on both Mayfield and Paducah.[62] This turn of events was most unfortunate for Colonel
Hawkins. His position was threatened once again by his old nemesis,
General Forrest. Hawkins immediately began preparation for an attack.
He tightened discipline, requiring both officers and enlisted men to mess
and sleep within the camp.[63]

Intelligence reports assumed that Forrest's raiders possessed artillery.
General Buford, said to be occupying Shady Grove in Carroll County,
Tennessee, reportedly had a battery of Dahlgren guns[64] and Forrest "ten
rifled Parrotts." Once again, Hawkins lacked artillery and occupied a post
that would be unable to withstand an artillery attack.[65] The evacuation of

58. Columbus Kentucky Post Return, September 1864.

59. Isaac R. Hawkins to L. Thomas, letter, Oct 1, 1864, *Compiled Service Records 7th Tennessee*, M395 RG094 rolls 63–69.

60. *Day Book*, Special Orders II from Hawkins, October 7, 1864. He replaced Captain Beatty,
who deserted on September 26, 1864, before Hawkins retook command.

61. Hawkins Family Letter, *Tennessee Historical Quarterly* (Spring 1987): 37. In that case, he
would have had at least 652 men, even without the 134th Illinois.

62. S. Meredith to J. B. Dickson, October 7, 1864, *OR*, 1, XXXIX, (3), 144.

63. *Day Book*, Special Orders #3 from Hawkins, October 11, 1864.

64. "The War in Kentucky," *New York Times*, October 30, 1864.

65. James Graham to S. Meredith, October 13, 1864, *OR*, 1, XXXIX, (3), 264.

government property from Mayfield began on October 13[66] and reached completion by October 17.[67] The 7th returned to Paducah, except for 25 men under Lieutenant James Neely who remained at Columbus.[68] The "quite a force" that Hawkins commanded for 12 days evaporated, leaving him with the approximately 160 men of the 7th Tennessee. General Meredith, the commander of the District of Western Kentucky, intended at first to send troops to reoccupy Mayfield when danger seemed to have passed. New information received during the night, however, indicated a possible attack on Paducah, a far more important base. Concern for Mayfield faded.

Rumors persisted that rebels continued to congregate on the Tennessee border[69] and that Forrest and Buford intended to disrupt the upcoming presidential election in November 1864.[70] A major incursion by Forrest into Western Kentucky, however, never materialized. A small rebel force did enter unoccupied Mayfield on October 22, 1864, and burned the courthouse.[71] After attacking Fort Heiman, Kentucky and Johnsonville, Tennessee, Forrest's main force withdrew into Mississippi. Hawkins lost his larger command unnecessarily.

The 7th Tennessee at Paducah, Kentucky
Fall 1864

Paducah in the Declining Days of the War

When the 7th Tennessee moved from Mayfield to Paducah, Kentucky in October 1864, the city contained nearly 6,000 people and had been under Federal occupation since Grant captured it in 1861. The sympathy

66. S. Meredith to James Graham, October 13, 1864, *OR*, 1, XXXIX, (3), 264.

67. S.G. Burbridge to Henry Halleck, October 17, 1864, *OR*, 1, XXXIX, (3), 343.

68. S. Meredith to James Graham, October 13, 1864, *OR*, 1, XXXIX, (3), 264. S. Meredith to J. N. McArthur, October 17, 1864, *OR*, 1, XXXIX, (3), 344. Neely and approximately 25 men remained at Columbus until February 1865 when they joined the regiment at Paducah. *February Post Returns Columbus.*

69. "The War in Kentucky," *New York Times*, October 30, 1864.

70. "From Western Kentucky: Paducah Threatened—Stirring Appeal by General Meredith to the People," *Chicago Evening Journal*, October 18, 1864, copied in *New York Times*, November 23, 1864.

71. "The Rebels Enter Mayfield, Kentucky," *New York Times*, October 23, 1864.

of the natives remained Confederate but with the influx of refugees and war workers, it came to have about the same number of Unionists as Confederates. Paducah prospered from war-related activities[72] including serving as a port for Union gunboats, a staging point for supplies and troop movements, a central site for relaying telegraphs, an oath administering point, and a recruiting station, especially for black troops.[73] When the focus of the war moved east, the threat of attacks on Paducah declined. Even General Forrest forsook raiding in Western Tennessee and Kentucky and joined General Hood's ill-fated forces in Middle Tennessee.

The Command and Men Stationed at Fort Anderson

Colonel Joshua J. Guppey commanded the troops at Paducah[74] and Brigadier General Sol Meredith, who headed the District of Western Kentucky, headquartered there as well. Lieutenant Colonel Hawkins reported to Colonel Guppey, a come down after having been in charge of the installations at Union City and Mayfield. In early December 1864, Guppey's command consisted of:

34th New Jersey Volunteers, 481 men
8th Colored Cavalry (Heavy Artillery), 980 men
7th Tennessee Cavalry and 3rd Illinois combined, 171 men.[75]

By the end of December, the 49th Illinois and the 2nd Illinois Light Artillery replaced the 34th New Jersey and 3rd Illinois. At this time Hawkins' three reorganized companies, A, B, and C,[76] contained about 150 men, the smallest component at the post. The men who had escaped capture at Union City and a few new recruits comprised the majority of the unit. By January 1865 members of the 8th Colored Heavy Artillery, a unit of former slaves raised primarily in Kentucky, outnumbered white

---

72. "Border States after the War," *New York Times*, April 8, 1865.

73. *OR*, 1, XLVII, (2), 229–231, 233–237, 239, 249. *OR*, 1, XLIX, (2), 770.

74. S. Meredith to W. D. Whipple, December 13, 1864, *OR*, 1, XLV, (2), 178. These troops included the 34th New Jersey and the detachment of 3rd Illinois, which also moved to Paducah from Mayfield.

75. S. Meredith to Whipple, December 13, 1864, *OR*, 1, XLV, (2), 178. Meredith was wounded at Gettysburg.

76. Troop Organization December 1864, *OR*, 1, XLV, (2), 464.

Fort Anderson at Paducah, Kentucky
(Library of Congress Prints and Photographs)

soldiers at Paducah almost three to one.[77] After the North accepted blacks into the Union Army, they made up a majority of the garrison forces in Western Tennessee and Kentucky, allowing many white soldiers to remove to the eastern front.[78]

A Description of Fort Anderson

Fort Anderson, built by the Union in 1861 near the junction of the Tennessee and the Ohio Rivers, stood on the banks of the Ohio River in the northwestern corner of Paducah, Kentucky. No part of the fort remains today, but a drawing in *Harper's Weekly* and a photograph in the National Archives show it as a large fortification with very high walls.[79] The enclosure covered about a city block but many buildings, such as the

77. *OR*, 1, XLIX, (1) 802. The 7th Tennessee has added Company I to A, B, and C by February 1865.

78. William W. Freehling, *The South vs. the South* (New York: Oxford University Press, 2001), 131. Freehling estimates about 40 percent of Kentucky's eligible male slaves served in the Union Army.

79. Richard Holland, *Paducah, Portrait of a River Town* (Paducah, KY: Image Graphics, Inc:., n.d.), 19. The large building in the middle of the fort burned in 1863. Library of Congress.

stables, headquarters, and quartermaster buildings, stood outside the walls, as did the regimental camping areas.[80] A Kentucky State Historical Marker on the riverfront marks the site of the fort. A long seawall along the Ohio River to the east of the historical marker has panels depicting Paducah's history. One panel is an artist's rendering of the fort under siege during the battle of Paducah in March 1864, and includes insets of General Forrest, General Grant, and a recruiting station for black soldiers.

The location of the area where the 7th Tennessee encamped outside the fort is somewhat uncertain. All indications, however, point to a region north or northwest of the fort near what is now Shultz Park. The Day Book for the regiment contains orders requiring the digging of trenches from the camp through the stable area to the riverbank. This implies the Ohio River ran close by and the camp stood on low ground. Dr. Edward Arbuckle, the chief medical officer for the 7th, insisted that every man have a bunk at least one foot above the ground. It is known that the tents faced the parade grounds but that site is also unknown.

80. Operator to Lieutenant Mason, March 26, 1864, *OR*, 1, XXXII, (1), 506. Map by Captain John Rziha, 1861.

CHAPTER EIGHT

———◆———

THE REGIMENT IN THE LAST MONTHS OF THE WAR

Prisoner Releases and Exchanges
February–April 1865

Wilmington, North Carolina Exchanges

Sherman's penetration into the Deep South caused disruption in the prisoner exchanges begun in Savannah and then in Charleston in the late fall of 1864. In January 1865, however, the Union Navy took Fort Fisher, and shortly thereafter nearby Wilmington, North Carolina. Exchanges resumed from this port.

Before their release, the six officers still in prison spent their last months at Columbia, South Carolina. At first they had been in "Camp Sorghum," but they later inhabited the yard of the local insane asylum. Lieutenant John J. Wallace escaped from the latter and walked through to federal lines in East Tennessee.[1] The remaining five officers, Captain Hays plus Lieutenants Hawkins, Moore, Allender, and Jeptha Robeson, left Camp Asylum for Wilmington, North Carolina and transportation

1. Wallace's escape gained little. The others were released about the time he made Union lines.

north. They arrived at Annapolis, Maryland on the 8th of March 1865 on the steamer *General Sedgwick*, along with about 500 other officers[2] and 200 enlisted men. About twenty-five enlisted men from the 7th Tennessee also sailed north from Wilmington (Northeast Ferry) from late February through April 1865.

The Fate of the Officers Captured at Union City, Tennessee

By early March 1865, none of the ten commissioned officers taken east after the Union City surrender remained in prison. Lieutenant Murray and the telegrapher escaped from Macon, Georgia in May 1864. Colonel Hawkins gained exchange through Charleston, South Carolina in August 1864.[3] Major Smith and Lieutenant John T. C. Robeson left through Charleston in December 1864 as two of the officers released from the Columbia, South Carolina prison.[4] Lieutenant Wallace escaped at Columbia, South Carolina. Captain Harris of the 24th Missouri tried to escape at Columbia but failed. Harris ended up on the *General Sedgwich* with the five 7th Tennessee officers released through Wilmington, North Carolina. Murray, Hawkins, Moore, Wallace, and Jeptha and John Robeson all returned to duty by mid-March 1865 and remained until the regiment disbanded. Smith, Allender, and Hays took early discharge.

A persistent story in Henderson County families involves an officer of the 7th Tennessee who supposedly posed as an enlisted man in order to enter Andersonville Prison with his men. Most stories identify this officer as Captain Asa Hays of Company C. Records at the officer's prisons, however, clearly indicate that Hays remained with the other officers throughout his imprisonment. If based on fact, the story might be about Wesley Derryberry, who raised Company H but lost his captain's rating long before capture. More likely it refers to Lieutenant James Bar-

---

2. "Arrival of the Steamer General Sedgwick," *New York Times*, April 11, 1865. This ship also had a steam calliope like the "Southern Republic," but it most likely did not play "Dixie." Chapter 3 in David Lear Buckman, *Old Steamboat Days on the Hudson River,* (New York: The Grafton Press, 1907).

3. Bartholomew might have been at Camp Reed, an officer's prison connected to Camp Sumter. He also could have lost his rank when he went AWOL in 1863.

4. "The Union Martyrs," *New York Times*, December 12, 1864. The paper named all 500 officers but no enlisted men.

tholomew, who appears to have been demoted. Both men died in enlisted prisons, Derryberry at Savannah and Bartholomew at Andersonville.

Enlisted Men Released Through Vicksburg, Mississippi
April–May 1865

As late as mid-March 1865, at least 63 enlisted men of the 7th Tennessee remained in prisons in the southeast.[5] Once again the port of exit for exchanges moved. The Confederacy set up Camp Fisk, a parole camp located on the Big Black River four miles east of Vicksburg, Mississippi. It processed prisoners from the Andersonville and Cahaba prisons.[6] The 15 or so members of the 7th Tennessee exchanged at Camp Fisk came from Andersonville, most likely by a combination of walking and rail. At least one, Isaac Davenport, had been returned to Andersonville from Thomasville, Georgia only a short time earlier.[7]

As the men awaited exchange at Vicksburg, two important events took place in the east. On the 9th of April Robert E. Lee surrendered his army in Virginia and on the 14th, John Wilkes Booth assassinated President Lincoln. The news of the assassination reached the parole camp at Vicksburg on April 18. It provoked such a violent reaction among the prisoners that the rebel commissioner of exchange reportedly hid until he could find protection to leave.[8]

Around 5,135 Union soldiers crossed a pontoon bridge over the Black River into Union hands by May 1, 1865. Taken into Vicksburg, they boarded steamers headed up the Mississippi River for Benton Barracks (St. Louis), Missouri and the Ohio River for Camp Chase (Columbus), Ohio. Unfortunately for eight members of the 7th and nearly 2,000 other former prisoners, they boarded the ill-fated steam ship *Sultana* that exploded up river from Memphis on April 27.[9] Over 1,800 men died,

5. John W. Allen, who died February 28, 1865, is the last known member of the 7th Tennessee to die in Andersonville Prison.

6. N. J. T. Dana to Commissary General of Prisoners, May 13, 1865, *OR*, 2, VIII, 554–545.

7. Davenport, *History of Scotts Hill Tennessee*, 195.

8. "The Death of the President," *Chicago Evening Journal*, May 1, 1865 reprinted in *New York Times*, May 8, 1865.

9. Jerry O. Potter, *The Sultana Tragedy* (Gretna, LA: Pelican Publishing Co., 1992), 45.

including six of the men[10] from the 7th Tennessee. The other two spent a terrifying night clinging to debris.[11] A raft picked up Isaac Davenport while John C. Derryberry drifted back to Memphis on a plank.[12] The *Sultana* explosion remains one of the most disastrous events in naval history.

The Enlisted Men Released Through Jacksonville, Florida

The last group of 7th Tennessee prisoners, about 48 in all, made Union lines at Jacksonville, Florida on or about the 28th of April 1865. According to the diary of Jesse Altom, an Illinois soldier, Captain Wirz told the men remaining in Andersonville that the Yankees refused to accept any more prisoners at Vicksburg and that they would be exchanged at Jacksonville, Florida. After a couple more heartbreaking false starts, the remaining men at Andersonville Prison, who were ambulatory, boarded rail cars for Albany, Georgia, walked from there to Thomasville, Georgia, boarded cars again for Live Oak, Florida, and walked to Jacksonville. There the army received them with "open hearts and open arms."[13] Most of this group proceeded eventually to Camp Chase, Ohio.

The End of the Andersonville Experience

The sharp decline in the number of deaths at Andersonville and the smaller prisons in the period from November 1864–April 1865 reflects the reduced number of men still in the prison as the exchanges progressed. The enlisted men who survived the Georgia and South Carolina prisons usually ended up in hospitals rather than returning to the regiment in Kentucky. Occasionally, however, one of them came through Paducah with news about men whose fate had previously been unknown. By the spring of 1865, Stephen Powers wrote home that nearly all the survivors had been released and the others presumed dead.[14] Six members of Pow-

10. Wm. T. Campbell, Meredith L. Davis, Green L Fowler, John Powers, Andrew J. Small, and Isaac M. Smith.

11. Davenport, *History of Scotts Hill Tennessee*, 196.

12. Obituary of Cynthia M. Derryberry, December 19, 1920.

13. James Altom, "Marion County Prisoner of Rebels Kept Diary in Andersonville Prison," *Centralia* (Illinois) *Evening Sentinel*, http://www.goldsbyfamily.into/Diary.htm.

14. Stephen Powers, letter to sisters Emeline, Darkes, and Mary Ann Powers, April 25, 1865.

ers' Henderson County extended family entered Andersonville Prison. Henry M., Joel, Riley, and Willis all died there, and John died in the *Sultana* disaster on the way home. Only Ira and Stephen survived.[15]

About 65 percent of the enlisted men, or nearly two out of three who surrendered at Union City, died from the experience before the end of the war.[16] According to one source, the 7th Tennessee ranked fourth in number of prison deaths for the entire Union Army.[17] Two hundred and seven died at Andersonville, sixteen at Millen, sixteen at Savannah, ten at Mobile, seven at Florence, six on the *Sultana*, four at Charleston, seventeen at northern hospitals, seven en route to and from various prisons or hospitals, two on furlough soon after exchange, and one in unknown circumstances (total 293).[18]

Although monuments to southern Confederate soldiers sprang up immediately after the war and continued to be built for years, very, very few honored the southern Union men. Tennessee soldiers, however, have two monuments in national cemeteries. Solicitation of funds for these monuments fell primarily to the Tennessee Grand Army of the Republic members. Neither the United States nor the State of Tennessee contributed funds for their erection.

The Tennessee Monument at Andersonville remains the only memorial within the confines of the prison to honor southerners who died there. The inscriptions read:

Front: In memory of her Union soldiers and loyal sons who died in Confederate prisons during the war of 1861–65. We who live may for ourselves forget but not for those who died here. 1284 died Tennessee.

Rear: This monument was erected by the voluntary contributions of their surviving comrades and friends.

15. *Compiled Service Records 7th Tennessee*, Rolls 395-68, #1380, #1382, #1383, #1385, #1386, #1387.

16. Calculated by subtracting 17 officers from the 471 men captured leaving 454 enlisted men, 293 of whom died before reaching home.

17. William F. Fox, *Regimental Losses in the American Civil War, 1861–1865* (Albany, NY: Joseph McDonough, 1898), 524. Only two New York regiments and the 2nd Tennessee Infantry had a higher prison mortality rate. Thirteen Richmond deaths are probably also included in the ranking.

18. A surprising number of the Andersonville survivors lived into the 20th century.

The Tennessee Monument at Andersonville Prison

Samuel W. Hawkins, son of the colonel, served on the committee that raised funds for the Tennessee or Wilder Monument in the national cemetery at Knoxville, Tennessee. More imposing than the Andersonville monument, it is in neo-gothic style and reaches 60 feet in height. An inscription on this monument reads "Tennessee furnished for Union Army 31092 men, casualties 6776." Both numbers are too low.

The 7th Tennessee at Paducah, Kentucky 1865

Company I Reorganized

In the early months of 1865 while the last of the prisoners gained release, entered hospitals, or received disability discharges, the active part of the regiment remained at Paducah, Kentucky. As the war wound down and the outcome became increasingly obvious, seventy-five men, most of whom came from eastern West Tennessee, enlisted in the unit from January through April, 1865. This brought the number of active soldiers to about 250 men. Eighteen to twenty-two year old men with no previous service made up half of the new recruits. The majority were placed in the recently reorganized Company I, giving the regiment four companies: A, B, C, and I. Like the original, the reorganized Company I never raised enough men to receive a full complement of officers. Samuel W. Hawkins eventually became its captain on June 5, 1865, only two months before the regiment disbanded. It received some new sergeants from among the recent recruits. Most of the original sergeants died in prison.

The Regimental Daybook, October 1864 to Discharge

Regimental Daybooks document the day to day orders being issued for the running of a regiment. Unfortunately, the earlier Daybooks of the 7th Tennessee must have burned at Union City or been lost along the way. When Colonel Hawkins returned from prison, however, he began a new set at Mayfield, Kentucky and continued them at Fort Anderson in Paducah, Kentucky. This book survives on microfilm at the National Archives and gives insights into the daily life of the regiment that are unavailable for the earlier years, except occasionally in private letters. Mostly the entries deal with attempted solutions to various problems.

1. *The Problem of Camp Sanitation*
Unsanitary conditions resulting from crowded living quarters caused concern to Dr. Arbuckle, the regimental physician. He insisted that the riverbank near the camp needed to be kept clean of human refuse. The men previously relieved themselves anywhere along the bank. On Arbuckle's suggestion, Hawkins ordered each company to dig a hole and construct a screen to "hide them from the public view" along with "a pole placed for a rest."[19] The camp must have been an unhealthy place even with these precautions. Fourteen men died in Paducah of diseases such as typhoid, pneumonia and smallpox between January and July 1865.[20]

2. *Problems with Discipline*
On his return to command after his release from prison, Colonel Hawkins considered discipline a major problem. Perhaps the men grew

19. *Daybook, General Order No. 4*, February 27, 1865.

20. *Compiled Service Records 7th Tennessee*, M395 RG094 rolls 63–69. No one died in action although one died of exposure. Some men were buried first in Paducah then re-interred in the Mound City, Illinois National Cemetery. According to a caretaker at the Mound City cemetery, flooding of the Ohio River has rendered the exact location of many of the graves problematical.

lax during his six months absence or obeying orders may never have been one of their strong points. Both seem likely.

On the 2nd of December 1864, with a view to cutting down on numerous unauthorized absences, Hawkins issued General Orders Number II mandating morning (reveille), afternoon (retreat), and evening (tattoo) roll calls. These included the presentation of weapons. He assigned a commissioned officer to preside and to report all absentees' names immediately to the new adjutant, Lieutenant William W. Murray. Furthermore, the order required a one-hour drill each morning at 8 A.M. for the men and 10 A.M. thirty-minute drill for the non-commissioned officers, after which the officers would receive the duties of the day. As evidence of the difficulty in maintaining compliance with these orders, Hawkins reissued the command for roll calls on June 28th, 1865.

General Orders Number II also complained about the laxity in the watering and grooming of horses. It established regulation hours at which this should be done. On May 22, however, Captain Moore, in charge when Hawkins became ill, again bemoaned the "great irregularity in the watering of horses." Moore even insisted further that all watering be done at the same time, in a line, and in good order.[21] Later entries fail to mention if the men ever complied. It would seem that cavalrymen, who had to depend on their horses, should have been more concerned about the comfort and condition of their mounts.

3. *Dealing with Horse Theft*

The shortage of horses in the last years of the war drove prices to extremes. Hard riding often broke down mounts past usage and horses died in battle along with their riders. Horse thieves scoured the country for any horses still in private hands and sold them to civilians or the military. Soldiers on both sides also confiscated horses from individuals without permission from their commanders. Some members of the 7th may have engaged in this side "business" while on scouting expeditions.[22]

On the 22nd of February 1865, General Orders No. 2 from Colonel Hawkins required a commissioned officer go along with each company on all scouts and marches plus a "sufficient rear guard" to arrest and dismount all stragglers. Under no circumstances would non-commissioned officers impress horses or mules or property of any kind without an

21. *Daybook*, December 2, May 22, June 28, 1865.
22. *Daybook*, February 25, 1865.

attendant commissioned officer. Even those officers who impressed animals in cases of necessity received instructions to obtain the name and address of the owner of the animal and leave a receipt. Hawkins expected this to be done in an "orderly and quiet manner." Upon arrival at camp, the commissioned officer should turn the animal and all information over to the Quarter Master. Any commissioned officer who knew about a proscribed transaction and failed to report it would be court-martialed.[23] The situation, however, remained a serious concern.

When the state of Kentucky passed a law that made mule and horse thievery "punishable by death," Colonel Hawkins sent out General Orders No 3. All soldiers must divest themselves of any horses or mules other than the one issued to them by the government, proof of ownership for any other animal being nearly impossible and therefore unsafe. The order threatened dismissals and court-martials for any soldier who continued to trade in horses or mules and to anyone who knew of the trade without reporting it.[24] As far as known, no member of the 7th received punishment under the new Kentucky law.

4. *Dealing with Frightened Citizens*

Another complaint, this time against all the soldiers at Fort Anderson, came from private citizens across the Ohio River in Illinois. Soldiers from the fort crossed the river "prowling around all night to the terror of the inhabitants." Since soldiers in the colored regiments made up such a high percentage of the soldiers at Paducah, the complaints may also have involved racial fears. The post commander responded by issuing orders for all regiments to see that men answered roll call at tattoo and remained in camp at night. Less demanding than Hawkins, the commander limited his restrictions to night activities and pillaging. Soldiers could continue "going around" and enjoying themselves in daytime.[25] Both the complaint and the lack of daytime restrictions indicate a lack of discipline and decorum at the fort as the war drew to a close. Captain Moore, when he commanded in Hawkins' absence, even found it necessary to order the men of the 7th Tennessee to wear their "prescribed uniforms."[26]

23. *Ibid.*

24. *Ibid.*

25. *Daybook*, June 28, 1865.

26. *Ibid.*

5. Dealing with a Recruitment Problem

The Day Book mentions a volunteer who wanted to wear a uniform but failed to convince the authorities to allow it. The record fails to give the name of this female who attempted to join the 7th Tennessee. It also provides no details of her discovery. Perhaps Dr. Arbuckle gave more thorough entrance physicals than many Civil War physicians. The notation includes only that she tried to enlist but failed in the attempt.[27]

The War Winds Down April–August 1865

During the months of March, April, May, and most of June, Colonel Hawkins' muster rolls list him as "sick and confined to quarters" but give no hint of his malady other than it may have been contagious. Captain George W. Moore, recently released from prison in Columbia, South Carolina, became the acting commander during Hawkins' absence.[28]

The Last Known Military Actions
Which Involved the 7th Tennessee

At least twice during the last months of the war, detachments of the 7th Tennessee left Paducah on cavalry assignments. On April 27, Lieutenants James Matt Neely and John Terrell Robeson received orders to embark on the first boat passing up the Ohio River and take along thirty mounted and armed soldiers equipped with sixty rounds of ammunition per man. Fort Smith, their destination at Smithland, Kentucky, about 15 miles up the Ohio River, guarded the confluence of the Cumberland and Ohio Rivers. They reported to Lieutenant Colonel J. T. Foster, commander of the 13th Colored Artillery,[29] for some unknown purpose and remained only a few days before being re-assigned.

On May 2, scouts reported a rebel force of 120 men operating along the Tennessee and Cumberland Rivers. This took place even after Lee surrendered and the Confederate government fell. Lieutenant Colonel William P. Moore of the 49th Illinois Infantry received orders to command an expedition to intercept the rebels. He took some of his own

27. *Daybook*, no date.

28. "Isaac R. Hawkins," #790, Muster rolls 7th Tennessee, Roll 395-65. *Daybook*.

29. *Daybook*, April 27, 1865. *Special Orders # 20.*

regiment plus men from the 7th Tennessee, including, apparently, Colonel Hawkins,[30] who was no longer ill and confined to quarters.[31]

General Meredith, the commander of the district, told the expedition to board the steamer *Tacony* and proceed to Smithland where they should pick up more cavalry, presumably the thirty men with Neely and Robeson that were sent out at the end of April. They should then continue up the Cumberland River to Eddyville, Kentucky where the 7th should pursue the rebels while the infantry prevented an escape across the river.[32] The effectiveness of this maneuver failed to be recorded.

Release from the Jeffersonville, Indiana Hospital

During the month of May, twenty-five men of the 7th hospitalized at the large Jeffersonville military hospital received medical disability discharges. Ten of them had been in Andersonville Prison; some had transferred to Jeffersonville from Paducah and other hospitals. They left for home through Louisville, Kentucky, across the Ohio River from Jeffersonville. Two men died in the process of discharge: Caleb Blankenship of inflammation of the brain and William B. Wilson of dysentery. Both are buried in the New Albany National Cemetery in Floyd County, Indiana after being re-interred from Jeffersonville Hospital plots.

Discharge of the Entire Regiment
August 1865

Colonel Hawkins resumed command at Paducah on June 25, 1865, relieving acting commander Captain George W. Moore. Immediately upon his return, Hawkins began preparations for the discharge of the three-year men who enlisted in the summer and fall of 1862 and the removal of the remainder of his command to Rockport in Benton County, Tennessee.[33] This community, located where the Rockport-McIllwain Road meets Birdsong Road, barely remains. During the Civil War, it

30. S. Meredith to William P. Moore, May 2, 1865, *OR*, 1, XLIX, (2), 572.

31. "Isaac R. Hawkins," #790, Muster rolls 7th Tennessee, Roll 395-65.

32. S. Meredith to William P. Moore, May 2, 1865, *OR*, 1, XLIX, (2), 572.

33. General Thomas *Special Orders No. 4,* June 27, 1865, *OR*, 1, XLIX, (2), 1041. The order says Rockville, on the Tennessee River, but the *Daybook* says Rockport in Benton County.

served as a steamboat landing and crossing point for troops. No military installation seems to have existed there. Current USGS topographical maps show Rockport Landing on an inlet of Kentucky Lake at about mile 106.3.[34]

The staff at Paducah gathered surplus supplies, made out descriptive lists, and called in all public horses for inspection.[35] The lieutenants of the companies took charge of escorting the first of the three-year men to be mustered out.[36] Instructions for departure included being ready at daybreak on the 9th of July, mounted, carrying three days rations, and several rounds of ammunition. Upon completion of their charge, the lieutenants should return with all papers to the regiment at Rockport, Tennessee or wherever it might be at that time.[37] It seems unlikely that any members of the 7th Tennessee ever arrived at Rockport. The order for deactivation came earlier than anticipated and the place of discharge changed to Nashville, Tennessee.

The entire regiment, consisting of about 265 men, arrived in Nashville, Tennessee on July 27, 1865. The *Nashville Daily Union* newspaper reported that the regiment "had led a most eventful career, and won more than the usual share of honors," flattering words for a regiment that spent much of its career in parole camp or prison. The paper lauded Colonel Hawkins as "not only one of Tennessee's best officers, but one of her ablest civilians." The men mustered out officially during the week of August 7–14, 1865. Only a few of the men who survived Andersonville rejoined the regiment in time to receive discharge with their comrades.[38]

The soldiers who mustered out at Nashville still needed a way home. At least three West Tennesseans mentioned taking a freight train to Johnsonville, Tennessee, the site of the Union depot on the Tennessee River. From there, Sergeant Richard Pinckley rode his horse, Private William Robinson a mule, and Private William King walked to their homes in Carroll County. Private William Woods took a boat from Johnsonville to Perryville, Tennessee, then walked 20 miles to his home in Henderson County. Most members of the 7th Tennessee discharged at Nashville

34. Local confirmation from Jerry Cary to the author, June 9, 2005.

35. *Daybook, Special Orders No. 30*, June 23, 1865. *Special Orders No. 135*, June 28, 1865.

36. *Daybook*, July 8, 1865.

37. *Ibid.*

38. Most were discharged at Camp Chase, Ohio or Jeffersonville, Indiana.

probably took the train to Johnsonville and found other means for the remainder of the distance home. Private William Douglas later declared his hundred miles home as "a right nice trip."[39]

West Tennessee Confederates Feared Assignment of the 7th Tennessee as an Occupying Force

The early deactivation of the regiment meant that members of the 7th Tennessee returned home as civilians rather than as occupation forces. Colonel John F. Newsom of Jackson, Tennessee worried as early as May 10, 1865, that the 6th and 7th Tennessee Cavalries might be assigned to military occupation in West Tennessee. He petitioned General Sol Meredith at Paducah "[i]n behalf of the citizens" of West Tennessee that "none of the men belonging to the command of Colonels Hawkins and Hurst" be assigned near their homes because of the "feeling that exists between soldiers of these commands and the citizens is such that private malice and private revenge might be more the result of such a policy than the restoration of order."[40]

Newsom commanded the 19th/20th Tennessee Infantry, a Confederate regiment raised primarily in Madison, Hardeman, Henry, McNairy, and Lake counties but with members in the Unionist counties as well. The 19th began as an irregular organization but became a part of Forrest's command. It frequently came in conflict with the 6th and 7th Tennessee, USA. Understandably, Newsom's men preferred occupation forces with which they had little or no previous personal contact.

Newsom neglected to mention those citizens in West Tennessee who supported the Union and would have been happy to have the local men as occupiers and might even enjoy their presence. Private Dugal Ross of the 7th, contemplating what his behavior would be toward the "sesesh" population when he returned home, wrote a Union neighbor in Henderson County that his own actions would depend on "how they [the Confederates] conduct themselves."[41]

39. The *Tennessee Civil War Veterans Questionnaires* 1: 48, 78, 104, 126, 156.

40. J. F. Newsom to S. Meredith, May 10, 1865, *OR*, 1, XLIX, (2), 712.

41. Dugal Ross letter to Edmond Gawf, June 1, 1865, published in the Waldron, Arkansas Newspaper, February 11, 1926.

Colonel Hawkins, serving after the war as a representative to Congress, exerted considerable influence on the government to exempt Tennessee from occupation by the federal army. He helped convince President Andrew Johnson that troops from the adjoining states would be sufficient to quell any insurrection or enforce any laws within Tennessee and the Secretary of War agreed.[42] The colonel of the 7th Tennessee Cavalry, at least, turned out to be much kinder to the West Tennessee Confederates than Colonel Newsom anticipated. Not only would there be no 6th and 7th occupiers, there would be no federal occupation forces at all.

Reestablishment of peaceful intercourse proved difficult for both sides regardless of the presence or absence of troops. The former Confederates formed the Ku Klux Klan, an organization that targeted Loyalists as well as former slaves. Unionists organized Loyal Leagues to deal with the defeated majority. Tensions remained high for many years after the war officially ended. In 1921, Irvin Hampton of Company G said he had lived long enough to see his descendants married to those of "the boys who wore the Gray."[43] Fifty years after the war, he seemed surprised.

42. "National Troops in Tennessee," *New York Times*, August 17, 1868.

43. *The Tennessee Civil War Veterans Questionnaires* 1: 63.

---•---

CHAPTER NINE

LIFE AFTER THE WAR AND
CONTRIBUTIONS TO THE CAUSE

The Men of the 7th Tennessee After the War

Politics in Eastern West Tennessee

For a short time, the Unionists had the advantage politically until the federal government restored the rights of the Confederate Tennesseans. Since the vast majority of former rebels voted for the Democrats and the Unionists generally supported the Republicans, the Unionists soon lost out in state elections. The concentration of the 6th and 7th Tennessee Cavalries and their families in the counties in eastern West Tennessee, however, meant that in local politics, the Republicans remained influential for many years. Alvin Hawkins, a Unionist cousin of Colonel Hawkins, even managed to be elected as a Republican governor of Tennessee in 1880 when the Greenback Party and a splinter Democratic group divided the Democratic vote.[1]

Like-minded people within their immediate vicinity may be the reason most members of the 7th remained in West Tennessee even after

1. "A Close Vote in Tennessee," *New York Times*, November 1, 1880.

the takeover of state politics by the old guard. Of the 600 survivors of the 7th whose whereabouts after the war has been determined, 415 continued to live in West Tennessee and many returned to the county from which they enlisted.

Some former members of the 7th and their families, however, moved on. Of the survivors who can be traced, about 44 men moved to Arkansas, 33 to Illinois, 30 to Texas, 26 to Missouri, 28 to Kentucky, 13 to Indian Territory, and six to Kansas. Colorado, Utah, Nebraska, Mississippi, California, Louisiana, Washington, and Indiana received one or more families.[2] Those who immigrated to Illinois, Kentucky and Missouri may have liked what they saw while serving in or near those areas or could have joined West Tennessee refugee families who remained in the north after the fighting ended.

Union Pensions Applications

Invalids (500), widows (543), children (108 sets), mothers (41), and fathers (10) connected to the 7th Tennessee received over 1,200 pensions and probably many, many more. Widows, especially of the men who died at Andersonville, began applying as early as 1865. Unionists fared much better after the war than Confederates in the same situation. For example, in Carroll County, Henry Marion Roark received a Union invalid pension. His Confederate brother Ansel Roark, who lost his eyesight in combat, went on the county rolls as a pauper.[3] The Union could afford to issue pensions, an option unavailable to the former Confederate states for many years. Since 388 men of the 7th Tennessee died during the war or shortly thereafter, and the Andersonville experience disabled many of the survivors, former soldiers and family members filled the pension rolls.

By 1883 the pension rolls for Henderson and Carroll Counties, the two counties with the most soldiers in the 7th, list 57 widows, nine dependent mothers, three sets of minors, and 21 disabled men. Widows of privates received $8 per month, while the wives of officers fared according to the husband's former rank. If no widow survived or if she

2. Numbers determined from pension applications, burials, and census records.

3. Ansel Roark lived with his brother, however, receiving some benefit from the Union pension. Both men are buried in Sellers Cemetery in Carroll County. Henry has a military marker; Ansel does not.

remarried, the pension went to the soldier's children under 16, then to the soldier's mother, then to his father, then to his surviving sister under 16. The amount of a soldier's disability pension depended upon the degree to which the injury or disease incapacitated the veteran.

Given the lack of federal money in the South after the war, eastern West Tennesseans undoubtedly welcomed the infusion of dollars from Union pensions. Widows and disabled veterans who bought provisions at local markets, owned perhaps by former Confederates, would aid the economic recovery of all.

Isaac R. Hawkins' Status after the War

Colonel Hawkins and his family returned to Huntingdon, Tennessee at the end of the war. Given that Captain Beatty reported after the Union City surrender that the men "cursed Col. Hawkins, said he was a traitor and that they would never serve under him again,"[4] the question arises as to his popularity with his former troops and their families after the war.

If winning elections proves good feelings from the populace toward the candidate, then the answer would seem that the surviving men of the 7th Tennessee and the Unionist population either never felt as negative as the Michigan native suggested earlier or forgave very quickly. In August 1865, as the 7th mustered out, Colonel Hawkins won the race for representative from the 7th Congressional District to the U.S. House of Representatives without having placed his name in nomination or making a speech. The military vote of the 6th and 7th Cavalries and their families went to Hawkins. He served from July 24, 1866, to March 3, 1871, having been re-elected in 1867.[5]

In addition, two newspaper comments reveal public favor. *The West Tennessean* in 1868 listed Hawkins as an endorser of an insurance company, an indication that the company considered him to be a man with

4. John W. Beatty, report, *OR*, 1, XXXII, (1), 542–544.

5. U.S. Congress, "Hawkins, Isaac Roberts, 1818–1880," *Biographical Directory of the United States Congress, 1774–1989. The Nashville Daily Union*, August 16, 1865. The vote was 2,643 Hawkins, 904 for Etheridge. The members of the 6th Tennessee voted 72 to 0, and the 7th Tennessee voted 206 to 0.

positive influence in the area.[6] In 1869, the *Carroll County Democrat* mentioned that the Honorable I. R. Hawkins and his cousin, the Honorable Alvin Hawkins, would give speeches at the Saturday temperance picnic in Huntingdon,[7] a definite honor in a small town.

Four years away in the army did little permanent harm to Hawkins' economic well-being. In addition to his salary as a representative, he had income from the law partnership he formed with his son, Samuel W. Hawkins. They even represented some 7th Tennessee men and their families applying for pensions. By 1870 the value of his Hawkins' real estate ($12,000) and personal property ($15,500) had increased over prewar levels, even during hard economic times in West Tennessee.

Isaac R. Hawkins GAR Post #56

Union veterans in Carroll County founded the Grand Army of the Republic (GAR) Isaac R. Hawkins Post #56 at Huntingdon, Tennessee. This post, though primarily made up of men from the 7th, also contained men from several other Union regiments.[8] The new group chose to name the post for Colonel Hawkins, indicating continuing respect for the commander of the 7th by his men and other soldiers some twenty years after the war. Since GAR rules forbade naming posts for living persons, the organization began sometime after Hawkins' death in 1880. The first known membership list begins in the first quarter of 1887. By September of 1889, the *Carroll County Democrat* reported that a number of the members of the Huntingdon GAR post left "in buggies, wagons, and on horseback" to attend an area reunion at Sardis in Henderson County, Tennessee. The GAR Posts at Lexington and Sardis also contained 7th Tennessee veterans. The youngest members would have been about 45 years old at the time.

---

6. *West Tennessean*, Thursday, August 27, 1868. At least seven others from the 7th Tennessee also lent their names to the enterprise.

7. *Carroll County Democrat*, Thursday, July 22, 1869, vol. 2, no. 13.

8. Other regiments represented in Post #56: 10th Illinois Cavalry, 48th Illinois, 52nd Indiana Infantry, 9th Ohio, 6th Tennessee Cavalry, 12th Tennessee Cavalry, 49th Illinois Infantry, 2nd Tennessee Mounted Infantry, 15th Missouri Cavalry, 2nd Kansas Cavalry, 1st Alabama Cavalry, 6th Kentucky Infantry, 27th Wisconsin, 4th Tennessee Infantry, and 10th Tennessee Cavalry. The men from northern units were mostly West Tennesseans, not northerners.

On December 18, 1896, the *Carroll County Democrat* listed the recently elected officers of the Huntingdon Post of the GAR as S.A. Brown, J. M. Tate, John R. Porter, E. G. Ridgley, E. D Bostick, J. D. Thompson, W. S. Worsham, G. W. Vickers, and J. F. Rogers. Tate, Porter, Bostick, Worsham, and Rogers served in the 7th. Brown, Ridgley, Thompson, and Vickers fought in other federal units. In his answers to the Tennessee Civil War Veterans Questionnaire, Samuel Arthur Brown said he served as Commander of the Huntingdon GAR for twenty-five years.[9]

In the early 1920s, the Hawkins' Post held a Memorial Day affair at the Liberty All Methodist Church in Carroll County, in whose cemetery many Union soldiers lie buried. Bob Bennett remembered that in either 1922 or 1923, the Huntingdon High School Brass Band, for which Bennett played drums, entertained the old soldiers with the "Battle Hymn of the Republic" and "The Union Forever" during breaks in the ceremonies. The band received "transportation and a sumptious barbecue dinner" for their efforts. Samuel Brown remained commander and Joe McCrackin served as adjunct of the post at the time. Bennett estimated 40 to 50 Union veterans in attendance.[10] The youngest volunteers in the war would have been nearly 80 years old. This must have been a function for more than one post.

Other GAR posts that existed in nearby areas of West Tennessee included the George W. Moore Post #81 in Lexington, the Nicholas Pitts Post #65 in Sardis, Hugh Neely Post #89 in Austen Springs, Albert Cook Post #76 in Dresden, D. G. Farragut Post #7 in Savannah, Fielding Hurst Post #7 in Adamsville, Jim Grissom Post #72 in Selmer, and William P. Kendrick Post #6 in Waynesboro.

---

9. *The Tennessee Civil War Veterans Questionnaires* 1: 25.

10. Bob Bennett of Jacksonville, Florida, letter to author, March 24, 1986. The author's father remembered his grandfather, Henry Clay Scott, riding horseback around the Carroll County courthouse with other Union and Confederate veterans at Memorial Day celebrations in the early 1900s.

Summary of the Contributions of the West Tennessee Unionist Regiments to the Union Cause

Evaluation by Contemporaries

Given that the Confederates hated the loyal regiments as traitors to the South and the northern army often looked down on them as backward southerners, finding many favorable contemporary evaluations of their contributions seems unlikely. The 5th Iowa records do mention that Colonel Hawkins' 2nd West Tennessee Cavalry "rendered valuable service in the Union Army."[11] Colonel Fry praised their bravery at the battle of Trenton. Among the northern Union officers, Generals Grenville M. Dodge and William Sooy Smith seemed best to understand the eccentricities of the West Tennessee loyalists[12] and to depend on and appreciate the services they rendered. Southerners with rebel sympathies and General Forrest complained the loudest about the Unionist regiments which would indicate, at least to some degree, their effectiveness.

Service as Skirmishers, Scouts and Spies

Even though the West Tennessee Union regiments fought in few large battles, they participated in a tremendous number of small battles and in skirmishes with southern recruiters, guerillas, and small detachments of rebels. Most of these confrontations took place in northern Mississippi, West Tennessee, or Western Kentucky.

The Unionists also served as scouts and spies. Colonel Fry of the 61st Illinois Infantry described the 2nd West Tennessee as "excellent scouts."[13] General Maxey of the Confederate Army complained that Colonel Hurst of the 6th Tennessee knew "every hog-path in the country,"[14] a testimonial from the opposing side. The regiments spent much of their enlistment stationed near home, which provided a tremendous advantage

11. *Iowa Adjutant General's Office: Together with Historical Sketches of Volunteer Organizations, 1861-66* 4 (Des Moines, Iowa: E. H. English Publisher, 1908–1911).

12. Jacob R. Perkins, *Trails, Rails and War: The Life of General G. M. Dodge* (Indianapolis: Bobbs-Merrill Co., 1929), 110.

13. Jacob Fry to J. C. Sullivan, December 15, 1862, *OR*, 1, XVII, (2), 414.

14. S. B. Maxey to G. T. Beauregard, April 30, 1862, *OR*, 1, X, (2), 467.

in an era of poor maps. Genuine southern accents must have helped in spying as well.

Guarding Contrabands and Serving with
Colored Regiments on Garrison Duty

The West Tennessee Unionists regiments also helped protect flee-ing slaves while guarding garrisons to which the "contrabands" fled, as was the case with the 7th Tennessee at La Grange. The loss of the labor force adversely affected the southern economy and added to the Union work force. When the ex-slaves later joined the Union Army, they often served on garrison duty with the Tennessee Unionists as they did with the 13th/14th at Fort Pillow and the 7th at Union City, Columbus, and Paducah. This combination helped the war effort by freeing northern troops to advance to the east. With the bulk of the western army else-where, these Unionists and colored regiments worked to stop Western Tennessee and Kentucky from returning to complete Confederate or guerilla control. Although only minimally successful in maintaining or-der in the final years of the war, they did contribute a great deal to keep-ing the Tennessee, Ohio, Cumberland, and Mississippi Rivers open to Union gunboat and transport traffic.[15]

Serving as a Constant Reminder of Division

The very existence of southerners fighting in Union regiments served as a reminder of division within the Confederacy. This would be especial-ly true where friends, family, and neighbors joined the Tennessee Union regiments and remained stationed in the area, as happened in West Ten-nessee. These regiments contained familiar people rather than faceless foreigners, making the war far more personal. It also encouraged violence among the civilian population, bringing war to the neighborhoods and promoting "war weariness" on the home front.

Even if they often proved no match for Forrest's much larger forc-es, the West Tennessee Unionist regiments seem to have annoyed the

15. The 2nd Mounted Infantry on the Tennessee in Hardin County, the 7th at Columbus and Paducah, and the 13th/14th at Fort Pillow.

general way out of proportion to their size.[16] He frequently called them insulting names, branding Hawkins and Hurst as "renegades" even though both colonels had been duly commissioned.[17] The 6th Tennessee he declared to be "outlaws" not subject to treatment as prisoners of war if caught. He took the time to write letters to the U.S. government demanding that Colonel Hurst of the 6th be turned over to Confederate authorities.[18] His troops even killed Major Bradford of the 13th/14th Cavalry after Bradford had been captured at Fort Pillow.[19] Forrest wrote President Jefferson Davis that he was "gratified" to say that he had broken up the Tennessee units on the 1864 raid.[20] He mentioned specifically that large numbers of "Tories" had been killed or captured[21] and the country nearly freed of them. All of this self-congratulation in spite of the fact that all the loyal regiments in the area never totaled one of Forrest's commands.

The Unionists came back to haunt Forrest. The treatment of the 13th/14th Cavalry, as well as the black troops at Fort Pillow, has remained—rightly or wrongly—the major blot on Forrest's record. The "massacre" and Forrest's part in the founding of the KKK, an organization to control the victorious Unionists as well as the freed blacks, constitute the only information many remember about the otherwise successful military leader.

Depriving the Confederacy of Needed Manpower

Although the southern Unionist regiments obviously made a difference in many needed areas, historian Richard Current maintains that all loyal southern men substantially aided the Union cause even if they did nothing more than enlist in a federal regiment or refuse to serve in

16. At their height the 6th Tennessee averaged about 1,000, the 7th Tennessee about 600, and the 13th/14th Tennessee even less.

17. N. B. Forrest, report, March 27, 1864, *OR*, 1, XXXII, (1), 607.

18. N. B. Forrest to Whom It May Concern, March 22, 1864, *OR*, 1, XXXII, (3), 119.

19. C. C. Washburn to N. B. Forrest, June 19, 1864, *OR*, 1, XXXII, (1), 589.

20. N. B. Forrest to Jefferson Davis, April 15, 1864, *OR*, 1, XXXII, (1), 612.

21. Approximately 174 killed and 668 captured from three regiments.

a Confederate unit.[22] They deprived the Confederacy of manpower, its greatest need. About 100,000 southern white men and 100,000 former slaves enlisted in the Union Army. Given that only about 900,000 men fought for the Confederacy,[23] 100,000 more in the army would have been a substantial addition and the retention of 100,000 farm workers a great help to the southern economy. The 7th Tennessee Cavalry alone took 1,300 eligible men out of the grasp of the Confederate draft and added 1,300 to an army that already greatly outnumbered the rebels. Current sums it up very well: "Surely that loss in manpower is an important, though overlooked, reason for the defeat of the Confederacy and the preservation of the Union."

---

22. The same would be true for men who went north, or hid out in the South, to escape conscription.

23. Current, *Lincoln's Loyalists*, 195–198.

APPENDIX A

———•———

BIOGRAPHIES OF THE OFFICERS
OF THE 7TH TENNESSEE CAVALRY

Lieutenant Colonel

Isaac Roberts Hawkins was born in Columbia, Tennessee on May 16, 1818, and moved to Carroll County, Tennessee at age 10.[1] His parents, Samuel and Nancy Roberts Hawkins, migrated along with Samuel's brother John Milton Hawkins. The numerous sons of these two brothers dominated Carroll County professional life, especially in law, medicine, and journalism well into the 1900s.

Hawkins began practicing law in 1843.[2] He and some of his cousins took time off to volunteer in Company B of the 2nd Regiment Tennessee Infantry during the Mexican War, 1846–47. He attained the rank of lieutenant at age 26. In 1861, when war seemed likely, Hawkins gained national attention by serving as a delegate to a peace conference in Washington, D.C. He became a circuit judge in 1862 at age 44 but entered the federal army shortly thereafter as a colonel.

1. "Isaac R. Hawkins," *Biographical Directory of the United States Congress 1774–Present: Bicentennial Edition.*

2. *Ibid.*

Issac R. Hawkins

The Hawkins cousins held opposing opinions about secession. Samuel Hawkins' sons Isaac and Lucian supported the Union. John Milton Hawkins favored the Confederacy but his eleven sons divided, brother against brother. William H., Albert G., Elvis B., and Franklin fought with the Confederacy.[3] Ashton W. became a captain in Isaac's federal regiment. Alvin, who later became governor of Tennessee, remained a civilian but supported the Union as well. The majority of noncommissioned men of the area who fought alongside the Hawkins men in both armies had little in common with these well-educated, town-connected, doctors, lawyers, judges, and journalists.[4]

Issac R. Hawkins commanded the 2nd West Tennessee Cavalry (later the 7th Tennessee Cavalry) from the 1st of September 1862 through July 1865. He participated in the battles at Lexington and Trenton, Tennessee in December 1862. Captured at Trenton, he spent time in parole camp at Camp Chase, Ohio January–June, 1863. Captured again at Union City, Tennessee in March 1864, he spent four months in prisons in Georgia and South Carolina. He was stationed at Trenton, Grand Junction, Saulsbury, La Grange, and Memphis, Tennessee, plus Paducah, Kentucky, each time under higher ranking officers. Hawkins commanded the posts at Union City, Tennessee and Mayfield, Kentucky. Upon his discharge, he became a brevet colonel and brevet brigadier general.[5]

---

3. William H. in Carroll Guards, Elvis B., in 19th/20th, and Albert G. in 55th.

4. William H. Hawkins edited the *Carroll Patriot* and *People's Paper*, Camilus edited the *McKenzie Banner*, and Ashton W. *The West Tennessean*. Isaac, Alvin, John C., Milton and Lucian L. were lawyers. Albert G. was Chancellor of Southern Normal University. Elvis B. and Ashton W. were doctors.

5. He received both brevets on March 13, 1865, when the War Department gave one or more brevets to many, if not most, officers then on duty, weakening the honors considerably.

After the war, he returned to his law practice in Huntingdon, Tennessee. He also served as representative of the 7th Congressional District in the 39th, 40th, and 41st sessions of the U.S. Congress from July 24, 1866, through March 3, 1871, running first as a Unionist and twice as a Conservative Republican.[6] He died in Huntingdon on August 12, 1880, at age 62. He lies buried in the small Hawkins family cemetery near Highway 22 south of Huntingdon. The Tennessee Historical Commission placed Marker 4A 27 near the entrance to the cemetery. It mentions his service as an officer in the Federal Army, but fails to give his rank or the name of the regiment he commanded.

Major

Thomas Atlas Smith was born in Randolph County, North Carolina on the 6th of July 1817, but resided in the 11th District of Henderson County, Tennessee at enlistment. At age 33, he already owned property worth $1,000. Before the war, he served as constable, justice of the peace, colonel commandant of the militia, steward of the poor house, and county magistrate.[7] Smith recruited many of the men of Company A and mustered as their captain on August 18, 1862, at age 45. Three months later, he received a promotion to major. Captured at both Trenton and Union City, Tennessee, Smith spent time at parole camp in Columbus, Ohio, and in Confederate prisons at Macon, Georgia and Columbia, South Carolina. He mustered out early in 1865 due to disability.

Active in public life and Republican politics, Smith also served as census taker and county registrar after the war. He owned about 500 acres of land. Smith died in October 1891 and is buried in Lexington Cemetery without a military marker.

Assistant Surgeons

Joseph Williams McCall, a native of Henderson County, Tennessee, began studying medicine under his brother, Dr. Henry McCall, in Clarksburg, Tennessee in 1853. He graduated from the University of

6. "Isaac R. Hawkins," *Biographical Directory of the United States Congress.*

7. *The Goodspeed Histories of Henderson, Chester, McNairy, Decatur and Hardin Counties* (McMinnville, TN: Ben Loman Press, reprint of 1887), 841–862.

Nashville in 1857, which gave him better credentials than many Civil War era doctors. At age 30, McCall received an appointment on October 15, 1862 as an assistant surgeon for the 7th Tennessee. He enlisted for only one year and left the military on Sept 1, 1863. After discharge he continued to serve the unit by contract, as did his brother Henry McCall. In 1869, Joseph McCall graduated from the College of Physicians and Surgeons in New York, New York. He continued his education at Vanderbilt and Tulane Universities and received an honorary degree from the University of Tennessee. He became an examining surgeon for pensions and gained national attention for the successful treatment of a family of seven with trichinosis. In the 1890 veteran's census, he gave his connection with the 7th Tennessee as 1862–1866. McCall died of a stroke on August 10, 1923, at age 91 and was buried with Masonic ceremony in Clark Cemetery, Huntington, Tennessee. His military marker lists him as a surgeon.[8]

Edward Arbuckle, born in Kentucky in 1821, resided near Como, Tennessee when he joined the 7th Tennessee in December 1863 at age 42. He was assisted by Emily Dark, a "servant." Captured at Union City, Tennessee in March of 1864 and taken to Mobile, Alabama with the regiment, Arbuckle gained release on the 6th of May 1864, slightly over a month after his capture. He may have been paroled or exchanged for a Confederate doctor. Shortly thereafter, he joined the detachment of men at Columbus, Kentucky who had escaped capture. While there, he brought charges of immoral behavior against Captain John Beatty which resulted in Beatty's court-martial conviction. At Paducah, Kentucky, Arbuckle issued several health directives that undoubtedly benefited the men. He served as the regimental doctor until the unit disbanded in August 1865. Dying on September 16, 1883, he is buried in Phelps Cemetery in Henry County, Tennessee.

Edmond D. Bostic volunteered in Company D in August of 1862. Appointed Hospital Steward by Colonel Hawkins, he served out his one-year enlistment and seems to have become a contract physician for the regiment. A pension dispute lists him as having been Acting Assistant Surgeon in 1863. Bostick continued to practice medicine after the war and served as an officer of the Grand Army of the Republic (GAR) in

8. *The Goodspeed Histories of Carroll, Henry and Benton Counties* (McMinnville, TN: Ben Loman Press, reprint of 1887). Obituary in *The Nashville Banner*, August 3, 1923.

1896. He is buried in Parsons Cemetery in Decatur County, Tennessee and has a military marker.

Regimental Quartermaster

Franklin Travis was a well-to-do merchant in Huntingdon, Tennessee before the war. He joined the 7th Tennessee in Company F as an orderly sergeant but re-enlisted at the end of his one year and became a regimental quartermaster in June 1864. Travis received assistance from Emmons Douglas, a "servant."

A military record exists for Emmons Travis in the 4th U.S. Colored Heavy Artillery. He gave his birthplace as Carroll County, Tennessee, where Franklin Travis resided. He may have been a slave or servant of Travis and went along with him into the war. Emmons joined the military on September 20, 1864, at Columbus, Kentucky where Travis was stationed and could have taken the Travis surname after emancipation. Thirty years old and six foot tall, Emmons rose in the ranks to sergeant by December 1864. His rank was reduced, however, on January 25, 1865. After the war, he went to Pine Bluff, Arkansas.

Franklin Travis returned to Huntingdon, Tennessee and became a partner in McCracken and Company. Appointed Collector of Internal Revenue for the Seventh Collection District of Tennessee in 1867, he absconded with $27,038.69 collected as taxes on distilled spirits and tobacco. He and his family fled Huntingdon sometime after 1870 and before 1876. The men who signed sureties for him lost personal assets due to his dishonesty.[9]

Lieutenants Who Served as Adjutants

Milton W. Hardy was adjutant for one year, 1863–64, before leaving for another regiment.

Robert Y. Bradford became acting adjutant at Columbus, Kentucky in 1864.

9. John S. Blair, ed., *The Washington Law Reporter* (Washington, D.C.), March 2, 1887, volume XV, 132–133. The men were Young W. Allen, Wilburn H. Graves, Eli T. McGill, Priestley E. Parker, Henry McCall, and Jasper Ballew. J.W. McCall, J.N. Belew and G.T. McCall acted as administrators for Henry McCall.

William W. Murray served as adjutant at Paducah, Kentucky in 1864 until May 13, 1865.

John J. Wallace became adjutant at Paducah, Kentucky on May 13, 1865.

The Commissioned Officers

Captains of the Companies

Thomas Atlas Smith (see Major Smith) served as captain of the original Company A for only three months before promotion to major. 1st Lieutenant Alexander Hart seems to have commanded the company until reorganization in 1864, when James M. Martin became captain.

George W. Moore replaced Captain Martin by appointment from the governor of Tennessee on the 20th of January 1864 at age 47. Born in Iredell County, North Carolina, Moore resided in Henderson County, Tennessee. He enlisted first in Company F then re-enlisted in Company A. Captured at Union City, Tennessee after being a captain only two months, Moore survived officer's prison in Macon and Savannah, Georgia. Exchanged through Wilmington, North Carolina on March 1, 1865, he returned to command Company A. He served as the acting commander of the regiment in Paducah, Kentucky when Colonel Hawkins became ill in 1865 and mustered out with the regiment at Nashville, Tennessee in August 1865. Moving to Hardin County, Tennessee by 1876, he died in 1889. Moore is reportedly buried in Shady Grove Cemetery, but he has no marker.

James M. Martin received his commission as captain of Company B on August 25, 1862, at age 36. He escaped capture at Lexington and Trenton, Tennessee in December 1862 and frequently commanded the detachment in the spring and fall of 1863 while stationed at La Grange and Grand Junction, Tennessee. Martin also escaped capture at Union City, Tennessee. He became the captain of the reorganized Company A in 1864 at the reorganization at Columbus, Kentucky in June 1863. He brought charges of drunken gunplay and theft against Captain Parsons of the reorganized Company B while stationed at Columbus. Martin resigned in October 1864 due to chronic dysentery and scorbutic affection of the general system. He returned to Carroll County, Tennessee after the war and represented the county in the House of Representatives of the Tennessee 35th General Assembly. He served only one session due to his death on April 21, 1868, of chronic hepatitis and malaria at age 33. Buried in Martin's Cemetery in Carroll County, he has a Masonic emblem on his tombstone but no military marker. Lieutenant William W. Murray of the 7th Tennessee replaced him in the legislature.

Asa Nelson Hays was born in Roane County, Tennessee on the 4th of August 1818. He reportedly served as a youth in the Indian wars and obtained his nickname "Black Hawk Hays."[10] At age 46, he recruited Company C from among his family and neighbors in the Bear Creek area of Henderson and Decatur Counties in Tennessee. He escaped capture at Lexington, Tennessee in December of 1862 but faced court martial in January of 1863, presumably in connection with the battle. Apparently acquitted, he sometimes commanded the detachment in the spring and summer of 1863 at La Grange and Grand Junction, Tennessee. In 1864, Hays surrendered with the regiment at Union City, Tennessee and spent time in officers' prisons in the southeast along with the other 7th Tennessee officers. The often repeat-

Asa Nelson Hays

ed story that he chose to enter Andersonville Prison with his men can be easily debunked. After release from prison, he received an early discharge on March 12, 1865. Hays, an unquestionably colorful character, returned to Decatur County after the war and inspired many stories of doubtful veracity. One story suggests he had 60 children, most of them illegitimate. He died in 1887 and is buried in Bear Creek Cemetery near Parsons, Tennessee. He does not have a military marker.

Thomas P. Gray has no muster rolls. He surrendered, however, with the regiment at Union City, Tennessee. Breaking his parole oath by escaping at Trenton, Tennessee, he traveled to Cairo, Illinois where he

10. If Hays served in the Black Hawk War, he would have been only about 14 years old. Most participants came from Illinois, not West Tennessee. He is not listed on the Black Hawk War database, but does have later documentation in the Indian wars in Florida.

wrote a critical report about the surrender at Union City, Tennessee in which he calls himself the captain of Company C. In April he testified before a joint committee of Congress, once again speaking very critically about Colonel Hawkins. At that time, he said he had been "holding the place of captain in Company C" of the 7th Tennessee for four months but had "not been mustered in yet."[11] Gray's previous service had been in Company G, 12th Illinois Infantry. The records of the 12th Illinois list him as mustered out on August 13, 1864, so he apparently went back to his old regiment.

John A. Miller was born in 1834 and taught school before the war. Captured at the battle of Trenton, Tennessee in December 1862, he spent time in parole camp at Camp Chase, Ohio. He was part of a prisoner exchange in June of 1863 and returned to duty at Saulsbury, Tennessee, where he was mustered out with his company in October 1863 at the end of his one-year enlistment. Rather than re-enlist in the 7th Tennessee, Miller became the captain of Company M, 12th Tennessee Cavalry, in August 1864. Several members of his former company enlisted with him. This new command saw action in the battles of Franklin and Nashville, Tennessee. After the war, Miller returned to Henderson County, Tennessee. His daughter's boyfriend shot him through the heart when Miller charged at him with an open knife at Wildersville, Tennessee in 1876.[12] He has a military marker in Mount Pisgah Cemetery within Natchez Trace State Park.

John Terrell Robeson, a 2nd Lieutenant at age 27, acted as captain for Company H from November 1863 to March 1864, but the surrender at Union City, Tennessee took place before he mustered at that rank. Robeson survived officers' prisons in the southeast and was an active detachment commander at Paducah, Kentucky. He became captain of the reorganized Company C on August 3, 1865, just six days before the regiment disbanded. At discharge he received a brevet to colonel, a title he occasionally used rather than captain after the war, especially when attending veterans' activities.[13] Robeson became colonel of the State Guards,

11. Thomas P. Gray, Joint Committee of 38th Congress, May 5, 1864, Representative Committee #63, 68–71.

12. *Whig and Tribune*, Jackson, Tennessee, February 5, 1876.

13. "Grant Among Comrades: Dining with Companions of the Loyal League," *New York Times*, November 4, 1880.

1866–1868, during the reorganization of Tennessee government. He
received an appointment as the U.S.
Consul to Tangiers, Morocco by 1869
and continued in the consular service
for twenty years, serving as consul in
Beirut, Syria, Tripoli, Scotland, and
Turkey. He considered New York City
home base during that period.[14] The
New York Sun listed his residence as
523 Manhattan Avenue, New York,
when his wife, Lizzie D. Robeson,
died in March 1897. Robeson died in
1906 and is buried in Oak Hill Cemetery in Huntingdon, Tennessee. His
tombstone says he was a captain in the
7th Tennessee, but it makes no mention of his stellar diplomatic career.

John Terrell Robeson
(Tennessee State Library & Archives)

Pleasant K. Parsons, born in South Carolina on the 14th of August 1826, served first as a lieutenant in the Mexican War, 1846–47.
A resident of Carroll County, Tennessee, he raised Company E at age
40. Escaping capture at Lexington and Trenton, Tennessee in 1862, he
spent much of 1863 at the forts along the Tennessee-Mississippi line.
Captured at Union City, Tennessee in 1864, Parsons and Captain Beatty broke their parole oath—to the dismay of Colonel Hawkins—and
left the other prisoners to face the consequences. Parsons testified before a joint committee of Congress and criticized Hawkins' decision to
surrender the fort, calling it "cowardly." He became captain of Reorganized Company B at Columbus, Kentucky in June 1864. Captain Martin brought charges of theft and dangerous behavior against him in the
fall of 1864. Parsons was convicted and sentenced to be dishonorably
discharged. Something changed, however, and he remained with the
regiment until he was honorably discharged on August 7, 1862. Parsons moved to Green County, Arkansas and became a merchant and a
physician. He died on March 5, 1894, and is buried in the Providence
Cemetery in Union, Green County, Arkansas.

14. *Register of the Empire State Society of the Sons of the American Revolution.* Personal Data #8733.

Ashton W. Hawkins was born in Bath County, Kentucky. He served as a corporal in Company B, 2nd Regiment Tennessee Infantry during the Mexican War 1846–47 alongside his cousin Lieutenant Isaac R. Hawkins. Returning to Carroll County, Tennessee, he became a physician. When Isaac Hawkins raised the 7th Tennessee Cavalry, Ashton Hawkins became captain of Company F at age 37. He was captured at the battle of Trenton, Tennessee and spent time at the Camp Chase, Ohio parole camp. While in Ohio, he obtained permission to visit his family in Alton, Illinois. He mustered out on the 9th of September 1863 when the one-year enlistment of his company ended. Hawkins published a newspaper in 1868, and a year later President Grant appointed him United States Assessor of Internal Revenue for the Seventh District of Tennessee.[15] He died in 1888 and is buried in Clark Cemetery in Huntingdon, Tennessee without a military marker.

Captain Thomas Belew was born in Giles County, Alabama and

moved to Clarksburg, Tennessee with his family as a child. At age 39, he raised Company G mainly from among his neighbors in the area around Clarksburg. Captured at Trenton, Tennessee with the regiment in December 1862, he spent time at parole camp at Camp Chase, Ohio. He resigned his commission there and received an honorable discharge on April 10, 1863, after only nine months service. After the war, he returned to farming and may have owned a saloon for a time in the Clarksburg area. He applied for and received restitution from the Southern Claims Commission for losses during the war. Belew has a military marker with no dates in the Bennett-Belew Cemetery near Clarksburg. He died about 1875.

Thomas Belew

15. Senate Executive Journal, Tuesday, April 13, 1869.

Michael Wesley Derryberry began life in Warren County, Tennessee. When the war began, he preached at the Union Baptist Church in Henderson County, Tennessee. He raised a portion of a company from among his neighbors around Chesterfield, Tennessee and for a time was considered its captain. Unfortunately, Company H never became a full company and Derryberry was demoted, becoming a private at age 41. Lieutenant John T. C. Robeson commanded Company H unofficially for a time, but was captured and never became its captain. Derryberry spent time in Andersonville Prison and died in prison in Savannah, Georgia on November 1, 1864, of scurvy and chronic diarrhea.

Samuel W. Hawkins was the oldest son of Colonel Isaac R. Hawkins. Born in Carroll County, Tennessee in 1844, he was only 18 when he accepted the appointment to 2nd Lieutenant in Company F, a one-year company. Hawkins re-enlisted and raised Company I, but it had low enlistment and failed to merit a captain. Hawkins led the company as its 1st Lieutenant until he was captured at Union City, Tennessee in 1864. He was able to escape his captors, but was recaptured and spent time in officers' prisons in the southeast. While the majority of the regiment remained in prison, only the reorganized companies A, B, and C existed. Colonel Hawkins reinstated Company I by adding new enlistments at Paducah, Kentucky, where the regiment encamped from late 1864 to July 1865. After release from prison, Samuel Hawkins became captain of Company I about a month before the regiment disbanded. After the war he practiced law with his father, becoming a prominent citizen in the state. From 1889 to 1894, he served as U.S. District Attorney for West Tennessee. Hawkins died of heart trouble at his residence on East Paris Street in Huntingdon, Tennessee on Saturday, the 29th of December, 1906, at age 62.[16] Buried in Oak Hill Cemetery in Huntingdon, Tennessee, his only tombstone is his military marker.

John K. Beatty, a native of Ireland and a sailor by profession, enlisted in the 3rd Michigan Cavalry in Detroit, Michigan as a sergeant on Sept 8, 1861. Transferring to the 7th Tennessee, he recruited Company K and became its captain on July 6, 1863.[17] Captured with the regiment at Union City, Tennessee on March 24, 1864, he escaped near

---

16. *Dresden Enterprise*, obituary of Captain Samuel W. Hawkins, January 4, 1907.

17. Record of Service of Michigan Volunteers in the Civil War 1861–1865. Kalamazoo, MI: Ihling Brothers and Everard H.

TOOK HIS OWN LIFE

Veteran of the Old Third Michigan Infantry.

James Beatty Takes a Fatal Dose of Morphine.

James Beatty, an inmate of the Soldiers' Home, hired a room at the Hotel Grand on Canal street Thursday night. He was called in the morning but told the porter that he wished to stay in his room. He was not again disturbed until 10 o'clock Friday night. At that time Proprietor McLeod went to Beatty's room. He found his guest asleep and a paper of morphine upon a center table aroused his suspicions. He attempted to awaken the sleeper but failed and summoned Drs. Best and Dillon.

The physicians managed to partially arouse the unfortunate man and took him to the Soldiers' Home in the ambulance. There he was given all possible aid but died in a few hours.

John Beatty was admitted to the Soldiers' Home two years ago last June. He was a member of Company B, Third Michigan infantry, and was 67 years of age.

Tombstone and obituary of John W. Beatty

Humboldt, Tennessee, violating his parole oath.[18] On April 12, 1864, he wrote a damaging report and gave testimony before a joint committee of Congress about the surrender at Union City. Beatty became captain of the reorganized Company C for a short time. While at Columbus, Kentucky, he was declared guilty of a morals offence[19] and deserted on September 1, 1864. Beatty managed by some means to gain admission to the Old Soldier's Home in Grand Rapids, Michigan in June 1896. In January 1898, he overdosed on morphine at a local hotel and died a few hours later.[20] Buried in the Old Soldier's Home Cemetery, his military marker and his obituary fails to mention anything about his service in the 7th Tennessee, his court-martial, or desertion. It only gives his service in the 3rd Michigan and lists no rank.

18. Hawkins letter, 38.

19. He married Mary W. Wilcox in Obion Co, Tennessee on December 10, 1863. She had "inflammatory action of female organs" (Dr. Arbuckle testimony) which caused Beatty to believe her "no proper wife."

20. *Grand Rapids Democrat*, January 23, 1898, 5.

The Lieutenants of the 7th Tennessee

William Francis Allender was a native of Daviess County, Indiana and a blacksmith before the war. He transferred to the 7th Tennessee from an Illinois regiment. After the war, he lived in several states and died in the Soldiers Home at Los Angeles, California on March 4, 1910. He has a military marker.

James Oliver Bartholomew, a native of Henderson County, Tennessee, died of scrobutus at Andersonville Prison in Georgia on October 12, 1864. His presence in an enlisted man's prison is puzzling unless he had been demoted.

Robert Young Bradford, a Benton County, Tennessee resident, escaped from the enemy twice but died of either delirium tremors or pneumonia at the Paducah, Kentucky Post Hospital on the 2nd of February 1865. He is buried in the National Cemetery at Mound City, Illinois.

Henry Clayborn Butler, 2nd lieutenant and a native of Carroll County, Tennessee, resigned from the military on May 5, 1863, and died of unknown cause on September 14, 1865, near Ramsey, Layette County, Illinois. His widow returned to Carroll County after the war.

Joel W. Chambers spent one year in the 7th Tennessee before joining Major Milton Hardy's Battalion (15th Cavalry). When the 15th became part of the 2nd Mounted Infantry after Hardy's death, Chambers served as Captain of Company G, which contained a number of men from the 7th. He is buried in Hampton Cemetery, Carroll County, Tennessee with a military marker but no dates. He died sometime before 1871.

William Cleary, a native of Illinois only temporarily attached to the 7th Tennessee at Columbus, Kentucky after most of his unit died at Fort Pillow, was reassigned to Company E, 6th Tennessee Cavalry, on February 14, 1865. Afterward Cleary became a cadet in the United States Military Academy at West Point, but died before the completion of his course.[21]

Newton Cox, a native of Carroll County, Tennessee, deserted his command in September 1863 and was dismissed from the military on July 14, 1864. He lived in southern Illinois after the war.

Milton W. Hardy, a native of Carroll County, Tennessee, left the 7th Tennessee in 1863, formed a unit called Hardy's Battalion, a part of

---

21. "Wm C. Cleary," *Historical Encyclopedia of Illinois and History of Morgan County* (Munsell Publishing Company, 1906).

Milton Hardy Monument

the 15th Cavalry, and became its major. He was killed attempting to kidnap or assassinate former Tennessee Governor Isham Harris in Henry County, Tennessee on March 21, 1864. Hardy is buried in Wilson Cemetery in Henderson County, Tennessee. His grave has an impressive monument donated by his comrades in arms.

Alexander T. Hart, a resident of Henderson County, Tennessee, commanded Company A after Captain Thomas Smith became a major. Hart resigned on the 1st of March 1864 after being diagnosed with tuberculosis and chronic hepatitis. He became a doctor by 1870 and graduated from the Louisville Medical School in 1889, but died on February 1, 1890. Hart is buried in the Olive Branch Cemetery in Henderson County, Tennessee.

Robert W. Helmer enlisted as sergeant in Company A of the 3rd Michigan Cavalry in 1861 at Saugatuck, Michigan, but accepted promotion to 2nd lieutenant of the 7th Tennessee on June 27, 1863. He commanded the reorganized Company B after October 31, 1864, when Beatty deserted. Resigning his commission on the 12th of June 1865, he returned to Michigan and became a sawyer and a highway commissioner. He died May 12, 1885, and is buried in the Richter-Tanner Cemetery, Dorr, Michigan. His monument is a York Rite, Royal Arch Masonry stone.

Joseph Crawford Miller, a native of Henderson County, Tennessee, commanded Company D, June 20, 1863–September 20, 1863. He left the military after one year and became a resident of Millbrook, Illinois until his reenlistment in 1865. Sometime after 1873, he moved to Indian Territory and died in Blair, Jackson County, Oklahoma, on January 28, 1916.

James Wyley Morgan was the acting lieutenant of the commissary beginning December 9, 1863, and supervised refugees at Paducah, Kentucky, 1864–65. After the war, he became a deputy marshal and farmed near the Decaturville Post Office in Decatur County, Tennessee. He was disabled from having his leg and foot smashed during the war. Morgan died on March 17, 1891, and is buried in the Campground Cemetery in Decatur County. He has a military marker.

William W. Murray, born in Georgia but a resident of Carroll County, Tennessee, served as a physician before the war. He commanded Company I from February 1864 until captured at Union City, Tennessee. After the war he served in Tennessee House of Representatives, became a lawyer, served as U.S. District Attorney for West Tennessee (1877–1882), and a U.S. judge, holding court as far away as Santa Fe, New Mexico. He owned a gold mine in Dahlonega, Georgia,[22] edited the *Tennessee Republican* (1871), and even found time to write a memoir of his escape from officer's prison in Macon, Georgia. He died on the 28th of November 1907, and is buried Oak Hill Cemetery in Huntingdon, Tennessee. His house still stands in Huntingdon.[23]

James Matt Neely, a member of the 5th Iowa before transferring into the 7th Tennessee, led Company M, which had no captain in 1864. After the war, he returned to Carroll County, Tennessee where he had been a school teacher. Although he had spinal paralysis from being thrown from his horse, he served as sheriff 1866–1870. Neely died October 16, 1905, and is buried in Antioch Cemetery #2 without a military marker.[24]

John Newton Park, a resident of Carroll County, Tennessee, was born in North Carolina. He returned to Hollow Rock, Tennessee after the war and farmed. He died August 24, 1904, and is buried in Park Cemetery, Carroll County.[25]

Frank (or Francis) M. Reed deserted while under arrest on February 13, 1864. He returned to Henderson County, Tennessee and farmed. Reportedly dying in a hunting accident in 1874, he is buried in Union Church Cemetery in Henderson County.

Mark M. Renfro, born in Decaturville in Decatur County, Tennessee, was a lieutenant in Company C. He died of dysentary at the Cumberland Hospital in Nashville, Tennessee on the 6th of August

---

22. *Carroll County Democrat*, Huntingdon, Tennessee, December 11, 1896.

23. Carroll County Historical Society, *Carroll County* (McKenzie, TN: McKenzie Banner, 1972), 68.

24. *History of Carroll County, Tennessee* 1 (Paducah, KY: Turner Publishing Company, 1987), 275.

25. *Ibid*, 285. There is a picture of John Newton Park in later years in this book.

1864. Renfro is buried in Derryberry Cemetery in Henderson County, Tennessee and has a military marker.

Jeptha Lafayette Robeson, a steamboat pilot before the war, was captured at Union City, Tennessee and spent time in southeastern officer prisons. He became a farmer in Carroll County, Tennessee after the war. Dying in 1888, he was buried in Oak Hill Cemetery in Carroll County near his brother Captain John Terrell Colfax Robeson.

John Terrell Colfax Robeson was commissioned a lieutenant by the Tennessee Military Governor Andrew Johnson on November 15, 1863. He spent most of his military career as a lieutenant but became a captain on August 3, 1865, a short time before his discharge.

Elbert N. Royall was promoted from sergeant to lieutenant by the governor of Tennessee to fill a vacancy. After the war, he left Carroll County, Tennessee for Arkansas. By 1871, he lived in Greene County, Arkansas and may have been in Clay County, Arkansas at some point.

John J. Wallace

Applying for an invalid pension in 1904, he died in 1905.

Francis A. Smith originally enlisted in the 13th Cavalry and was temporarily attached to the 7th Tennessee after the battle at Fort Pillow, Tennessee. He became captain of Company E, 6th Tennessee Cavalry, on July 1, 1865.

John J. Wallace, a resident of Michigan, enlisted originally in 3rd Michigan Cavalry. He resigned to become a 2nd Lieutenant in Company K, 7th Tennessee. His later whereabouts are unknown, but a child received a minor's pension in Kansas.

Deaths among the Officers

No member of the Field and Staff of the 7th Tennessee, including the lieutenants who served as adjutants, died during the war. All the captains survived except for former Captain Derryberry, who died in prison at Savannah, Georgia. Two lieutenants, Bradford and Renfro, died of disease, and former Lieutenant Bartholomew died in Andersonville Prison. Lieutenant Milton Hardy died in battle after he had joined another regiment. One sergeant died in battle from "friendly fire" and nine died of disease at various camps. Eighteen sergeants died in southeastern prisons, fifteen of those at Andersonville, Georgia.

APPENDIX B

———•———

STATISTICS OF THE
7TH TENNESSEE CAVALRY

Statistics[1]

I. Number of Men in the Regiment with Records: 1,362
II. Number of Known Deaths during Service: 399 or almost one-third
    A. Causes of Known Deaths
        Gunshot and wound deaths: (15)
            Inside Andersonville Prison (2)
            Union City, Paducah, Parker's Crossroads battles (1 each)
            Accidents (2)
            At home by guerillas or citizens (5)
            Skirmishes or unknown (3)
        Prison related deaths during the war: (303)
            (Starvation and exposure were the underlying causes.)
        Deaths from illnesses other than those while in prison (75)
            Pneumonia (24), Typhoid (6), Diarrhea (5),
            Smallpox (6), Erysipelas (5), Dysentery (4),

---

1. Statistics obtained from the muster rolls. Since some records are incomplete and some numbers are unreadable, actual numbers may be higher but will not be lower.

Measles (3), Brainfever (2), Consumption (2),
Chills (1), Congestive Fever (1), Frostbite (1),
Spinal Meningitis (1), Remittent Fever (1),
Dibilitus (1). Deaths listed only as caused
by disease (12)

Deaths from the *Sultana* steamship explosion (6)

B. Known Places of Deaths during the War: (disease, starvation, and gunfire)

Andersonville Prison, GA (207)	La Grange, Saulsbury, Grand Junction, TN (14)
Annapolis, Baltimore, MD (10)	Memphis, TN (4)
Benton, Jefferson Barracks, MO (5)	Millen, GA Prison (10)
Benton, Carroll, Madison counties, TN (5)	Mobile, AL Prison (11)
Cairo, Metropolis, IL (4)	Okolona, MS (1)
Camp Chase, OH (16)	Paducah, KY (22)
Charleston, Florence, SC Prisons (11)	Richmond, Danville, VA (13)
Columbus, KY (2)	Savannah, GA (12)
Decatur, Hardin counties, TN (3)	Sultana Explosion (6)
En Route (6)	Trenton, TN (5)
Henderson County, TN (13)	Union City, TN (11)
Jeffersonville, IN (2)	

III. Information Gleamed from the Descriptive Lists (685 recorded)

A. The Descriptive Lists

About one half of the men in the 7th have descriptions with their muster rolls. For some unknown reason about one-half of the men, in all but one of the companies, lack this information. Some have suggested that Duckworth destroyed all the records at Union City, Tennessee, but 82 of the men at Andersonville have descriptions though 144 lack them.

B. The Six Categories of the Descriptive Lists

1. *Height*: The median height of the men was 5' 9," while the average height was 5' 8." No one was below 5,' the largest group was 5' 6" to 5' 11," and 99 men stood 6' or more.

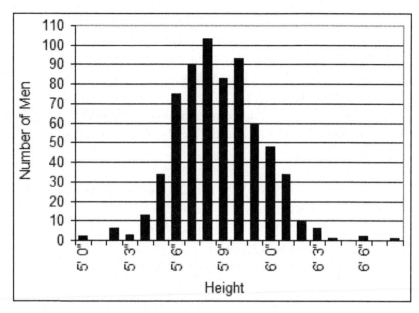

Distribution of Heights at Enlistment

2. *Complexion Color*: Assuming the clerks to be at least somewhat observant, four-fifths of those described had light complexions. The clerks used "fair" for two-thirds of these, "light" for nearly one-third, with five men described as "sallow." All but three of those with darker complexions had the label "dark." Two of the other three had "brown" and one "black." One would have expected a group of farmers to have dark complexions.

3. *Eye Color*: About two-thirds of the men had light colored eyes. Of these, three-fourths had blue eyes, about one-fourth grey, and seven termed "light." Dark eyes were "black" (65), "dark" (60), or "brown" (5). Eighty-six men had eyes of a yellow/greenish color. Most (83) of these were "hazel," but two were described as "yellow" and one "green."

4. *Hair Color*: Although more complexions and eyes tended to be light, hair color proved to be dark. About 58% of the men had dark hair and 42% light. Darker included "dark" (274), "auburn" (25), "black" (76), and "brown" (24). Light hair listed as "grey" (9), "light" (269), "red" (2), and "sandy" (5).

5. *Place of Birth*: Tennessee had the highest number of recorded births (556); North Carolina second highest (60), and Kentucky third (30). Other states included Virginia (12), Alabama (12), Illinois (8), Ohio (2), South Carolina (2), Georgia (2), Arkansas (2), Maine (1), and Indiana (1). Four men were foreign born: Switzerland, Ireland, Canada, and Germany.

Nearly half of the recorded births took place in Carroll (179) or Henderson Counties (147). Benton (31), Decatur (21), Weakley (19), Gibson (17), Henry (17), McNairy (12), Obion (7), Hardeman (4), Dyer (3), Madison (2), and Haywood (1) brought the West Tennessee total to 460 or about two-thirds of the men with recorded birth places. Middle Tennessee births added 61 more. Adding the East Tennessee counties and those that list only Tennessee as the place of birth (64) gave Tennessee a total of 585 out of 685.

The men born in North Carolina usually came from the Piedmont counties and resided in West Tennessee when they enlisted. Those born in Kentucky and Illinois usually enlisted when the regiment occupied Columbus or Paducah, Kentucky. The men born in Alabama and Mississippi came from counties near the Tennessee line.

6. *Occupation at the Time of Enlistment*: The clerks failed to fill in many of the occupation blanks, presumably because many young men had no occupation as yet. The most frequent answer was "farmer" (623 out of 660). The other 37 men said mechanic (6), blacksmith (5), carpenter (3), clerk (3), grocer (2), physician (2), saddler (2), steamboat worker (2), plus one plasterer, artist, sailor, brick mason, miller, musician, laborer, renegade, boot maker, shoemaker, engineer, and dentist.

IV. Enlistment Information

A. Date of Enlistment

Only about 60 men out of the 1,312 with muster rolls failed to have a date of enlistment on their records. Therefore, the data should be very close to the actual numbers of men who enlisted in any given month.

August 1862 saw by far the highest number of enlistments (441) with September 1862 the second highest (154). The first four months account for over half (671) of the total enlistments for the regiment. The early enthusiasm waned by October 1862. This proved true even before the regiment lost at Lexington and Trenton, Tennessee in December 1863. Only 34 men volunteered October through December 1862.

Recruitment continued to be low while most of the regiment spent time in parole camp in Ohio. January through April 1863 saw only 29 new recruits added to the men who remained free. In May 1863, when the new officers transferred in from the 3rd Michigan to lead the new Company K, a recruitment drive added 77 more men.

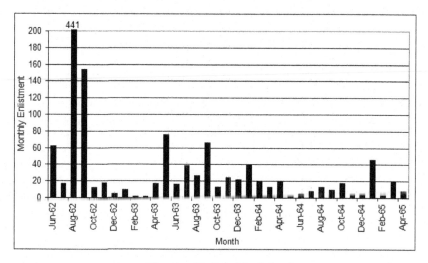

Number Enlisted by Month

Colonel Hawkins returned from parole camp in June 1863. General Hurlbut sent him to Union City, Tennessee in late fall specifically to recruit more men. From that time until the regiment surrendered at Union City on the 24th of March 1864, another 268 men volunteered.[2] In the months after the surrender, however, new additions fell off significantly during the time the majority of the unit starved in the prisons of the southeast.

2. Hurlbut to Sherman, October 24, 1863. *OR*, 1, XXXII, (1), 720.

B. Age of Enlistment by Month

The graph below gives the distributions of the median and average enlistment ages in the 7th Tennessee by month. The ages never dipped below 20 except in months with fewer than 10 recruits. This regiment consisted largely of men in their mid 20s rather than 18 and 19 year olds. The Union Army, having a large pool from which to draw, could afford

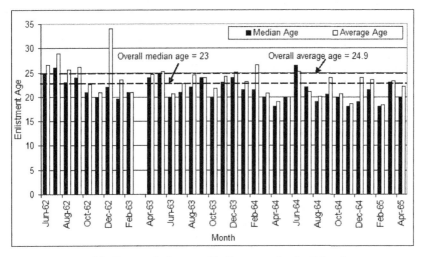

Median and Average Enlistment Age by Month

to reject those volunteers below 18. To be under 18 in the 7th Tennessee meant the recruit lied or brought written parental consent. Few seem to have done so. Since almost half of the regiment enlisted in August and September of 1862, the median and average ages shown in the graph are strongly influenced by the enlistment ages in those two months.

C. Places of Enlistments in Tennessee

Information about the places of enlistment has survived for 1,224 men. Over half of the men in the 7th enlisted in Carroll and Henderson Counties. In addition, most of the men who enlisted in Madison County lived in Henderson County, Tennessee. The known information about the places of enlistment is given in the table below. Tennessee had the most enlistments with 1,024 out of 1,224.

Carroll County (total 466)
 Buena Vista (17)
 Clarksburg (13)
 Huntingdon (122)
 Oak Grove (1)
 Shiloh (2)
 Town not given (311)

Henderson County (total 216)
 Friendship (2)
 Lexington (149)
 Scotts Hill (5)
 Town not given (60)

Madison County (total 113)
 Jackson (111)
 Town not given (2)

Gibson County (total 83)
 Milan (1)
 Trenton (74)
 Town not given (8)

Obion County (total 49)
 Union City (46)
 Town not given (3)

McNairy County (total 38)
 Adamsville (30)
 Bethel Station (1)
 Montezuma (3)
 Town not given (4)

Hardeman County (total 22)
 Grand Junction (1)
 Saulsbury (21)

Decatur County (total 10)
 Town not given (10)

Fayette County (total 7)
 La Grange (7)

Benton County (total 6)
 Town not given (6)

Shelby County (6)
 Memphis (6)

Weakley County (total 5)
 Boydsville (4)
 Dresden (1)

Henry County (total 4)
 Paris (4)

Lauderdale County (total 1)
 Fort Pillow (1)

Humphreys County (total 1)
 Johnsonville (1)

Hardin County (total 1)
 Savannah (1)

D. Places of Enlistments in Other States (total 200 out of 1,224)

Camp Chase, Ohio (1)
Corinth, Mississippi (6)
Metropolis, Illinois (1)
Kentucky (total 192)
    Fort Heiman (6)
    Fort Columbus (26)
    Paducah (160)

V. Economic Statistics of Soldiers in Carroll County, 1860

The author studied the economic status of the families of 398 Union and 390 Confederate soldiers resident in Carroll County, Tennessee in the 1860 census. Given the high percentage of men in the 7th Tennessee from this county, the results for the Union men are most likely representative of the regiment. (Refer to Tables 1 and 2.)

Carroll County contributed about the same number of landless men to each side (125 USA, 110 CSA). About three-fourths of the Union families owned no property or had property valued at $1,000 or less. On the other hand, nearly half of Confederate families owned real estate of $1,001 or more. The average value of all Unionist property was a mere $812, while that of Confederate families averaged $2,427. In Carroll County, it can be said that generally small farm owners or their sons fought for the Union while medium and large landowners and their sons joined the Confederacy.[3]

Confederate families in the county also far outstripped Unionists in personal property. Since slaves were considered property, their value accounted for much of the difference. About 25% of the families of Confederate soldiers owned slaves in contrast to only 5% of Union families. The average personal property evaluation of $4,609 for rebels, as compared to $857 for loyalists, reflects those percentages.

3. Comparison of the families of Confederate and Union soldiers in Carroll County, Tennessee by the author using the real estate, personal property figures and Slave Schedules in the 1860 census.

Table 1: Value of Real Estate (Carroll County 1860 Census)

| Value | Numbers of Soldiers' Families | | | |
| | CSA | | Union | |
	Number	%	Number	%
Landless	106	34.8	125	37.2
$0–$500	14	4.4	67	19.9
$501–$1,000	37	11.7	66	19.6
$1,001–$2,000	45	14.2	41	12.2
$2,001–$3,000	32	10.8	25	7.4
$3,001–$4,000	15	4.7	6	1.8
$4,001–$5,000	23	7.3	1	0.3
$5,001–$10,000	23	7.9	4	1.2
$10,001–$25,000	12	4.1	1	0.3

Table 2: Value of Personal Property (Carroll County 1860 Census)

| Value | Numbers of Soldiers' Families | | | |
| | CSA | | Union | |
	Number	%	Number	%
$0–$1,000	163	51.6	283	84.2
$1,001–$5,000	68	21.5	45	13.4
$5,001–$10,000	38	12.0	4	1.2
$10,001–$15,000	19	6.0	3	0.9
$15,001–$20,000	12	3.8	1	0.3
$20,001–$25,000	10	3.2	0	0.0
$25,001–$30,000	0	0.0	0	0.0
$30,001–$50,000	6	1.9	0	0.0

A Composite Soldier of the 7th Tennessee

Given the information in the descriptive lists, a typical member of the 7th Tennessee would be 24.9 years of age and born in either Carroll or Henderson Counties in Tennessee. He would stand 5' 8 ½" tall, have a light complexion, blue eyes, and dark hair. He would make his living as a farmer or live with parents who farmed.

A composite economic description from the 1860 census of a Union soldier, at least in Carroll County, would include the following. He would be either landless, own a small farm, or be from the family of a small farmer or landless person. The value of his or his family's personal property would be less than that of his typical neighbor fighting for the Confederacy, and neither he nor his family would own slaves. After the war the vast majority of the enlisted men who survived returned to farming.

——— ◆ ———

PLACES CONNECTED TO THE
7TH TENNESSEE CAVALRY

1. **Trenton, Tennessee** has a self-guided driving tour on the site of the Battle of Trenton. This battle took place on December 20, 1862, and resulted in the capture of a little over half of the 7th Tennessee by Forrest's troops. City Hall provides copies of the tour route to visitors.

2. **Jackson, Tennessee** has a small display situated at the site of the battle of Salem Cemetery located on Cotton Grove Road that includes a map of the ambush of Forrest's raiders by Union troops, which included members of the 2nd West Tennessee. The Tennessee Room at the Jackson-Madison County Library, located at 433 East Lafayette Street, has good information and directions to the cemetery.

3. **La Grange, Tennessee** has several Civil War houses that date to the time a detachment of the 7th was stationed there. One mansion served as General Sherman's headquarters and received an unwelcome visit from General Grant and his wife. A historical marker about Grierson's raid stands beside an interesting local restaurant,

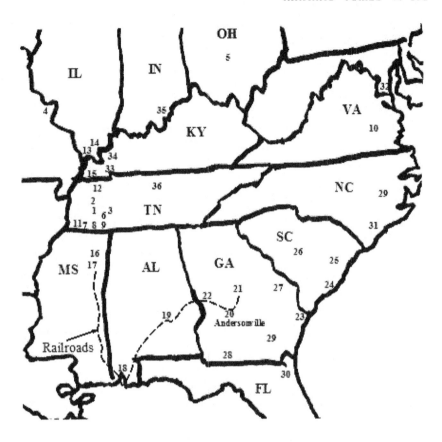

1. Humboldt, TN	13. Cairo, IL	25. Florence, SC
2. Trenton, TN	14. Mound City, IL	26. Columbia, SC
3. Lexington, TN	15. Columbus, KY	27. Millen, GA
4. St. Louis, MO	16. Tupelo, MS	28. Thomasville, GA
5. Columbus, OH	17. West Point, MS	29. Goldsboro, NC
6. Jackson, TN	18. Mobile, AL	30. Jacksonville, FL
7. La Grange, TN	19. Montgomery, AL	31. Wilmington, NC
8. Grand Junction, TN	20. Andersonville, GA	32. Annapolis, MD
9. Saulsbury, TN	21. Macon, GA	33. Mayfield, KY
10. Richmond, VA	22. Columbus, GA	34. Paducah, KY
11. Memphis, TN	23. Savannah, GA	35. Jeffersonville, IN
12. Union City, TN	24. Charleston, SC	36. Nashville, TN

but little effort has been made to attract tourism to this charming small town. Plan to find a motel elsewhere.

4. **Richmond, Virginia** has lots of Civil War sites, but most commemorate the "Lost Cause." Men of the 7th spent time there in Libby Prison and on Belle Island. Both sites are marked. Thirteen men died and are in cemeteries in the area. The Chimborazo Medical Museum, housed in an old Confederate hospital, has Civil War medicine exhibits.

5. **Union City, Tennessee** has a small Civil War museum with a model of the Union City fort that Hawkins surrendered to Duckworth. If the museum is closed, as it usually is, ask at the library about the person to contact to open it. A monument to the unknown Confederate dead buried nearby reportedly was the first such monument to be erected.[1] The old M & O Railroad track still runs through town.

6. **Mound City, Illinois** has a national cemetery where several men of the 7th who died in the Kentucky and Illinois area are buried.

Mound City National Cemetery

The graves had to be moved from an earlier site due to flooding.

7. **Columbus, Kentucky** has the Columbus-Belmont State Park on the site of the fort where a detachment of the 7th was stationed in the spring and summer of 1864. The site overlooks the Mississippi and has picnic facilities. A farmhouse has been made into a small museum that is worth visiting.

8. **Mobile, Alabama** National Cemetery has military markers for the nine men of the 7th buried there after they died in a cotton warehouse while prisoners on the way to Andersonville.

1. R.C. Forrester and Bill Threlkeld, *Roads Less Traveled: Self-Guided Tours to Historic Sites and Scenic Areas in Obion County, Tennessee* (Union City, TN: Lanzer Printing and Office Supply Company, Inc., 1996), 62.

9. **Andersonville, Georgia** is the primary site for those interested in the 7th Tennessee since 207 men died there and lie buried in the national cemetery. The stone on the left honors Corporal Hardy H. Worrell, a Carroll County native.

Military marker at
Andersonville Prison

10. **Florence, South Carolina** has a National Cemetery. Land has been purchased on the actual site of the prison and is being developed for tourism.

11. **Paducah, Kentucky** has a historical marker where Fort Anderson was situated. It also contains a long flood wall mural which includes an artist's interpretation of the fort and the battle of Paducah in 1864. Civil War interest runs high, but the sympathy of the current residents is definitely Confederate. The Lloyd Tillghman House and Museum contains Civil War memorabilia.

12. **Parker's Cross Roads**, just north of where Tennessee State Highway 22 crosses Interstate 40, has a well-developed site, including a self-guided tour with explanation. Marker number one is north of the crossroads on Highway 22. Members of the 7th who escaped capture at Lexington and Trenton fought alongside other Union forces against Forrest's command during this battle.

Company C, 7th Tennessee Cavalry Reenactors

An active company of Civil War reenactors has been in existence for several years. They portray either the 7th Tennessee Cavalry USA or CSA as the situation demands. For more information about this group and their schedule of events, see their website at www.c7tenncav.com.

Reenactors at Collierville,
Tennessee encampment

APPENDIX D

———◆———

SOME MEMBERS OF THE
7TH TENNESSEE CAVALRY

Photographs in this section are courtesy of family members.

Thomas J. Broddie
(Died exposure, Paducah)

John Washington Christopher
(Survived the war)

Henry Martin Douglas
(Survived the war)

George Newton Frizzell
(Survived the war)

Granville H. Grogan
(Killed by bushwhackers)

John H. Grogan
(Killed by bushwhackers)

Hezekiah Bradbury Harris
(Survived the war)

Thomas Herndon
(Survived the war)

Henry Parker Ingram
(Survived the war)

Thomas Edward Jones
(Survived the war)

Alexander Heutine Manual
(Survived the war)

Eli Martin Morris
(Died typhoid, Paducah)

William T. Melton
(Survived the war)

James C. Riles
(Died smallpox, POW,
Richmond, VA)

Joseph Riley Ward
(Survived the war)

Henry Clay Scott
(Survived the war)

APPENDIX E

———•———

THE MEN LISTED ON
THE MUSTER ROLL OF THE
7TH TENNESSEE CAVALRY

Aaron, John P

Aaron, Wiley J

Aber, Aaron

Able, John T

Ables, John T

Acox, Francis M

Adams, Archibald

Adams, Green

Adams, Harmon

Adams, William Henry

Adkinson, James

Akens, George W

Aldridge, G W

Aldridge, Thomas

Allen, G W

Allen, John F

Allen, John W

Allen, Lewis A

Allen, S R

Allender, William F

Altom, David Crockett

Altom, John

Altom, William

Andrews, James H

Andrews, Sertain B

Andrews, William F

Anglin, William

Arbuckle, Edward

Arbuckle, Samuel T

Archer, James Thomas

Arnn, John Madison

Arnold, Ezekiel

Asbel, John

Ashby, Charles L

Ashby, Joshua F

Atkins, Thomas J

Atkinson, Richard A

Atkinson, William

Autery, Durgan T

Autery, Jacob

Autery, John P

Autry, James P

Autry, Samuel Walter

Autry, William

Aybill, John

Bailey, James F

Bailey, William

Baker, James W

Baker, William

Baley, Elisha

Baley, John T

Balinger, John

Ball, David J

Bane, Henry

Bane, Robert

Barker, Rufus G

Barker, Samuel A

Barnes, Frederick B

Barnes, James H

Barnes, James T

Barnes, William B

Barnes, William Carroll

Barnhart, Doctor F

Barnhart, George W

Barnhart, Jacob

Barrow, John Jackson

Bartholomew, Edward A

Bartholomew, James O

Bartholomew, Milton B

Bartholomew, Thomas

Bass, James T

Bateman, Green

Bateman, John J

Batey, John H

Batten, Daniel

Beard, Miles C

Beaten, Christopher C

Beaton, William

Beatty, John W

Belew, Aaron

Belew, John G

Belew, Thomas

Bell, William H

Bennett, Benjamin

Bennett, Samuel

Bennett, Samuel F

Bennett, W R

Bentley, Franklin Evan

Benton, William B

Bevel, David R

Biggs, James T

Binum, William

Birdwell, Albert H

Birkett, William D

Bishop, Wiley

Blakely, Benjamin

Blankenship, Caleb

Blankenship, Martin

Blankenship, Pleasant H

Bledsaw, John

Bloodworth, W Rufus

Bo(w)man, James Wiley

Bo(w)man, Jonathan

Bo(w)man, Simeon

Bo(w)man, William

Boatwright, Annanias

Boatwright, Samuel

Bodkins, Weakley

Bollard/Ballard, David C

Bolton, William P

Bond, Andrew J

Bond, Jacob M

Bond, John

Bond, Robert J

Bonds, James K Polk

Boren, John

Boren, Lawson B

Bostic, Edmond D

Boswell, Jesse T

Boswell, John I/J

Boswell, William M

Bowlin, John W

Box, Edward/Edmund

Box, James A

Box, William B

Boyd, Jabez T

Boyd, Robert T

Boyd, Thomas Butler

Bradfield, Elisha L

Bradford, Hugh Elison

Bradford, Robert N

Bradford, Robert Y

Branch, Joseph J

Branch, Lewis K

Branch, William M

Brandon, Chronicle S

Brandon, Harrison S

Brandon, John D

Bratton, Alex

Brent, John

Brewer, Cornelius C

Brewer, Edmond

Brewer, Henry

Brewer, Isaac Newton

Brewer, John Franklin

Brewer, Joseph C

Brewer, Lucian

Brewer, Patrick

Brewer, Patrick B

Brewer, William T

Brewer, William W

Bridges, William A C

Brinkley, Silas

Britt, Dempsey B

Britt, George W

Britt, Green Lee

Britt, Noah

Britt, Pinckney

Britt, Wiley

Britt, William A

Britton, Charles

Broddie, Thomas J

Brodie, Lud

Brown, James W

Brown, Joseph

Browning, John K
Browning, Robert C
Browning, Robert Lee
Bruff, Greenville M
Bryant, Charles
Bryant, James L
Bryant, Needum J
Buchanan, Daniel A
Bullington, Robert
Bullion, Joseph
Bundrant, John W
Burcham, Christopher C
Burchum, James D
Burchum, John A
Burgess, George
Burkett, Isaac F
Burkett, James Franklin
Burkett, William H
Burnes, James A
Burnes, James H
Burns, Martin V
Burton, George Wade
Burton, James Allen
Bush, E
Bush, Elisha P
Bush, John J
Bush, Richard
Bush, William E
Butler, Alexander T
Butler, Clark S
Butler, Elias Gray
Butler, Franklin J
Butler, Galston Ward
Butler, Henry Clayborn
Butler, Henry H
Butler, John J
Butler, John Riley

Butler, John T
Butler, Wiley W
Butler, William J
Cagle, Benjamin F
Cagle, Henry C
Caldwell, Hugh D
Calhoun, John A
Calhoun, Thomas C
Camp, Benjamin F
Campbell, Arthur W
Campbell, William P
Campbell, William T
Cannon, Joseph Fulton
Cantrel, Andrew J
Cantrel, James K P
Carden, Alexander K
Carden, James E
Carden, Wiley F
Carey, Felix
Carey, Harrison H
Carliles, Franklin
Carllyle, George W
Carpenter, Emanuel
Carter, Graves
Carter, Jesse Madison
Carter, John Wesley
Carter, William H
Carver, James W
Cary, Alexander
Cary, James Monroe
Cary, Thomas
Cary, William Elbert
Cash, John J
Caviness, Mathew C
Caviness, William H
Cazey, Edward
Chambers, Aaron D

Chambers, Benjamin R
Chambers, Joel W
Chase, Alden P
Chasteen, Benjamin
Childers, James
Childers, William E
Childers, Zachariah D
Christopher, John W
Chumney, Beverly R
Chumney, John T
Clark, James
Clark, John
Clark, Nelson C
Clark, Richard
Clark, William H
Cleary, William
Cleaver, Albert E
Clements, Stephen M
Clever, William
Coffman, Samuel M
Coffrey, James
Cole, George
Cole, Jasper Newton
Collins, Frank
Collins, James F
Collins, Richard
Cook, Lycurgus D
Cooley, Joshua
Cooper, Elbert Y
Cooper, George W Jr
Cooper, George W Sr
Copeland, Simpson
Cottrill, George W
Cowell, James F
Cox, John H
Cox, Newton
Cox, Thomas

Cox, William David
Craig, George W
Crane, Linville
Cranford, George W
Cranford, Martin V
Creacy, Stephen P
Crenshaw, William
Crews, William
Criswell, David
Cruise, Elisha
Cunningham, Elijah
Cunningham, Willis H
Curtis, Charles F
Cutmoore, Charles H
Darnell, Nathaniel
Darnell, Thomas H
Davenport, Isaac Noah
Davidson, William
Davis, James
Davis, John D
Davis, Leroy
Davis, Levi
Davis, Meredith L
Davis, Samuel
Davis, William T
Deer, Harvey
Deer, Milton B
Deer, Richard
Delaney, Josephus
Dennison, Levy H
Dennison, William H
Derrossett, William E
Derryberry, Elisha H
Derryberry, John Calvin
Derryberry, M Wesley
Derryberry, William A
Derryberry, William H

Dill, Stephen F
Dodd, Benjamin L
Dodd, Charles
Dodd, Harbert H
Dodd, John C
Dodd, Samuel F
Dodd, Stanley
Dodd, Stanley H
Dodd, Thomas J
Dorety, Asa H
Doss, Charles Wesley
Doss, John C
Doss, William J
Doty, James Samuel
Douglas, Henry M
Douglass, William A
Douglass, William H
Drummonds, Joseph M
Drury, Robert H
Duke, Benjamin
Duke, G B
Duke, J P
Duke, James
Duke, W D
Dunaway, David C
Duncan, Henry
Dunn, Benjamin C
Dunn, George H/B
Dunn, George R
Dunn, James Barney
Dunn, Tillman J
Dunn, William
Dunning, James M
Dunning, William H
Dyer, William
Dyer, Winship
Eastwood, Wiley

Edmondson, James
Edwards, Felix J
Edwards, James N
Edwards, John
Edwards, Lint B
Edwards, Miles B
Edwards, William A
Edwards, William R
Elinor, Benjamin F
Elinor, Robert
Elkins, Aaron E
Ellis, John
Enloe, Thomas E
Esra, Thomas D/N
Essary, John F
Essary, Nathan C
Essery, George W
Eubanks, Edward C
Evans, Drury
Evans, Elias C
Evans, James F
Evans, James M
Evans, Wiley
Everett, James K
Everett, William H
Feland, Lafayette F
Ferguson, James Polk
Finch, Adam
Finch, Hampton
Finch, Isaac B
Fisher, Henry B
Flippin, George
Flowers, Henry
Flowers, James
Forest, James S
Forshee, William R
Fowler, Green L

Francisco, Robert
Frederick, B Frederick
Freeman, Daniel D
Freeman, Elijah C
Freeman, Thomas
Freeman, William
French, Richard E
Frizell, Abraham
Frizell, George N
Frizell, Thomas J
Fry, George W
Gaitley, Isaac
Gaitley, William
Gamble, James
Gamble, Moses
Gamblin, Joshua M
Gardner, Samuel
Gardner, William R
Garison, Elbert W
Garner, Frank
Garner, Franklin A
Garner, Franklin C
Garner, Isaac
Garner, James W
Garner, Thomas W
Garrison, Elbert
Gaskins, Amos L
Gaskins, Thomas J
Gately, William
Gatlin, William
George, Ezekiel
Gibson, Green B
Gilbert, J
Gilbert, Jackson J
Gilbert, Jesse
Gilbert, Michael
Gilbert, Thomas J

Gilbert, William
Giles, Enoch J
Giles, John A
Giles, Marques C
Gill, George W
Ginn, Benjamin F
Glosson, Alexander
Glosson, James
Goff, Edmond
Goff, Elias Perry
Goff, Robert Edmond
Goff, Thomas M
Golden, John H
Gooch, Littleton O
Gooch, Pumphrey W
Gooch, William M
Gooch, Willis C
Goodman, Thomas T
Gordon, Pleasant W
Gowers, George W
Graves, Joseph
Gray, Robert
Green, J D R
Green, James C
Green, James H
Green, John C
Green, Joshua G
Green, Richard F
Green, William Henry
Greenway, James
Greer, Benjamin F
Greer, James
Greer, James O
Greer, Jesse C
Greer, William L
Grice, William Riley
Griffin, Thomas B

Griffin, William A
Grimsley, Meredith M
Griswell, Thomas J
Griswell, William H
Grizzard, John C
Grogan, John H
Groom, Isaac R
Groom, James M
Groom, William H
Gunter, Adolphos W
Gwinn, James E
Hadgins, Asberry N
Haggard, John
Hail, Charles Nathaniel
Hail, Ivy
Hair, John
Halbrooks, Joseph
Hale, John W
Hall, Edward G
Hall, James Newton
Hall, James Riley
Hall, John L
Hall, William Riley
Hallenack, John R
Hallmark, John
Hamilton, Samuel
Hamilton, William J M
Hammett, John Wesley
Hampton, Andrew B
Hampton, Charles B
Hampton, Elvis S
Hampton, Hiram H
Hampton, Irvin R
Hampton, James E
Hampton, Thomas
Hampton, William H
Haney, Absalom C

Hardy, Milton W

Hare, Francis M

Harny, William H

Harris, Alex Coleman

Harris, Hezekiah B

Harris, James

Harris, James W

Harris, W B

Harris, William

Harris, William H

Harris, William R

Hart, Absolom

Hart, Alexander T

Hartley, Hardin

Hatch, George D

Hatch, Sidney I

Haulmark, George W

Haulmark, Phenias

Hawkins, Aston W

Hawkins, Isaac R

Hawkins, Samuel W

Hawks, William H

Hayes, James E

Hays, Asa Nelson

Hays, Isaac M C

Hays, Jackson J

Hays, James M

Hays, James R

Hays, John B

Hays, John Crockett

Hays, Samuel L Jr

Hays, Samuel Leon

Hays, William

Hays, William Henry H

Haywood, Henry H

Haywood, James Riley

Haywood, Jeff Green

Haywood, William T

He(a)rn, James M

Heathcott, William H

Hedges, Benjamin F

Hedges, Henderson C

Hedges, Isaac

Hefley, Samuel M

Heflin, Allen S

Heflin, Thomas H

Helmer, Robert W

Hendricks, William H

Herindon, Thomas D

Herrington, John W

Hester, James A

Hester, James Irving

Hetnimsproger, Fredrick

Hickman, William

Hicks, John P

Hicks, Willis G

Higdon, William T

Higgs, Levi

Hill, Elijah P

Hill, John L

Hill, Robert C

Hilton, Duncan B

Hipkins, James G H

Hodge, James M

Hodgin David M

Holbrook, John H

Holland, Louis

Holliday, William H

Hollowell, Hensley

Hollowell, Stephen

Holmes, A M

Holmes, George P

Holmes, Miles F

Holmes, William E

Holt, Wiley A

Hood, Franklin Robert

Hood, Wiley A

Hooks, John L

Hoosier, Thomas J

Horn, Major B

Hornbeck, Joshua

Horne, James F

House, Tennessee

Houston, George W

Howell, David

Huey, William M

Huffman, Charles D

Huffman, James F

Huistis, Andrew J

Huistis, Stephen W

Hutchins, William C

Hyett, David

Hyett, Leonard

Ingram, David C

Ingram, Dotson

Ingram, Parker

Ivey, Henry

Ivey, Joseph W

James, Hiram

James, William

Jarred, Thomas J

Jenkins, Henry Kelly

Jenkins, James R

Jenkins, William

Johnson, Alexander

Johnson, Andrew

Johnson, Cary

Johnson, Charles J

Johnson, Charles M

Johnson, Charles M

Johnson, Edmond D

Johnson, Edwin W
Johnson, Eli
Johnson, Emanuel
Johnson, Falton
Johnson, Henry K
Johnson, James
Johnson, James K
Johnson, James M
Johnson, Rufus D
Johnson, Samuel
Johnson, Samuel L Jr
Johnson, Sherode
Johnson, Silas
Johnson, William
Johnson, William F
Johnson, William H
Johnson, Willis
Joiner, John A
Jolley, Marion E
Jones, Gaston L
Jones, George B
Jones, Green A
Jones, Henry T
Jones, Randel D
Jones, Thomas E
Jones, William H
Joplin, Lucian F
Jowers, J J
Joyner, James Milton
Joyner, Moses
Joyner, Nathan Green
Kee, John
Kee, John W
Kee, William Riley
Keen, Elisha
Keen, George W
Keen, Isaac

Keen, James Thomas
Keen, Jeptha
Keen, William R
Kelly, N
Kemp, Bazil D
Kenn, James Thomas
Kennard, Thomas
Kilbreath, Moulton A
Killbreath, George W
King, Alfred
King, James A
King, James Thomas
King, Stephen Gray
King, William Pressly
Kinman, Moses
Kirby, Smith C
Kirk, Alvin H
Kirk, Ulyssus
Kyle, Robert Erastus
Lacy, William
Lambert, James
Lambert, Thomas
Lammons, Archibald
Lammons, William C
Lampley, James M
Lane, Nathaniel M
Latham, Carter C
Lawler, James G
Lawler, John A
Lawler, Robert J
Lawrence, Harwood J
Lawton, W H
Laycock, John Sims
Laycook, John C
Leathers, Thomas F
Ledbetter, Isaac J
Lee, Berry D

Leonard, Isaac M
Lester, James L
Letsinger, George Lewis
Lewis, Moses Vandever
Lewis, Zacharias
Lindley, William
Lindsey, Berry G
Lindsey, James
Lindsey, John L
Lindsey, William
Lindsey, William J
Lipe, James D
Listen, William H
Little, Edward D
Little, George M
Little, George W
Livingston, Mark
Loftus, Thomas
Logan, Preston
Lovell, Lindolph
Lowe, James M
Lowery, Jesse H
Lowing, John
Lynn, Nathaniel
Mackey, Henry T
Madaris, Joel B
Madison, John
Mainess, Mark
Malone, Lawrence H
Maness, Richard L
Maness, Stephen W
Manley, Jasper
Manuel, Alexander H
Manus, James W
Marbry, Isaac Francis
Marcum, William C
Martin, Benjamin M

Martin, Henry P
Martin, James Franklin
Martin, James L
Martin, James M
Martin, William H H
Massey, Andrew D
Mathews, Melvin R
Mathias, Hugh H
Mathias, Spencer
Mattox, Napoleon
Maxfield, G W
Maxwell, James H
Maye, Joseph H
McArthur, William Alexander
McCall, Joseph William
McCallister, William Thomas
McCaslin, J Riley
McCaslin, W H
McCauley, James C
McClum, George
McCollam, Samuel
McCord, Jesse
McCracken, Joseph
McCracken, Josephus
McElyea, Robert D
McFarland, John
McFarlin, James
McGee, William
McGill, Jesse
McGinas, Andrew
McGuire, Merriman
McKinney, James H
McKinney, John P
McKinney, Lafayette A
McKinney, Napoleon B

McLeod, John A
McLeod, Norman H
McMackin, Wesley
McMorris, James A
McMullen, Cullen D
McMullen, Dempsey
McMullen, Robert L
McNeely, Thomas W
Meals, Asa Harper
Meals, Daniel J
Meals, Samuel J
Medlin, John A
Medlin, Robert L
Melton, Beverly N
Melton, Merritt
Melton, Reuben R H
Melton, William P
Melton, William Tiley
Middleton, Alfred W
Miller, Alfred H
Miller, Benjamin F
Miller, Finice E
Miller, George W
Miller, George W
Miller, James
Miller, John Alexander
Miller, Joseph C
Mitchell, James L
Mitchell, Willis
Mizzell, Andrew
Mizzell, Robert A
Montgomery, Samuel J
Moore, Alfred N
Moore, Ephraim
Moore, George W
Moore, J W
Moore, James D

Moore, James T
Moore, John
Moore, John H
Moore, John W
Moore, Nelson M
Moore, Robert
Moore, Thomas
Moore, Thomas J
Moore, William C
More, James J
More, John A
Morgan, Benjamin F
Morgan, Edward D
Morgan, Francis Marion
Morgan, George H
Morgan, George W
Morgan, Granville H
Morgan, Hugh Joyner
Morgan, James Wyley
Morgan, John A
Morgan, Jonathan B
Morgan, Pleasant G
Morris, Eli Martin
Morris, Felix W
Morris, Richard Harvey
Morris, William C
Morris, William L
Moss, Thomas A
Mullins, James R
Mullins, Richard
Mullins, William R
Murray, William W
Muse, Calab
Myracle, Chester F
Myracle, J P
Nance, John C
Nealy, James W

Neely, Columbus C
Neely, James Matt
Neighbors, Henry
Neighbors, J F
Neighbors, John Ashley
Nelson, John A
Nelson, Robert W
Newbill, William G
Nicelar, Robinson M
Nichols, William J
Nicler, James H
Nolen, Real D
Noles, James Edmond
Norvell, William R
Norwood, Thomas J
Norwood, William
Orr, John
Osburn, Robert T
Overman, Nathan
Owens, Joseph
Owens, Redding S
Ozier, Levi
Padgitt, Abraham
Page, William C
Palmer, D P
Palmer, Edmund B
Palmer, William G
Paris, Henry S
Parish, Samuel H
Parish, Sion
Park, James
Park, John Newton
Park, Robert Wilson
Park, Ross T
Parke, Luther R
Parker, Henry O
Parker, Robert

Parker, Wesley
Parker, William Green
Parrett, John
Parrett, Reuben L
Parsons, Pleasant K
Pasteur, Thomas E
Pate, Edmund
Pate, Joseph B
Pate, Thomas I
Patterson, Isaiah
Patterson, Isaiah M
Patterson, Robert H
Patterson, Stokely
Peagram, William A
Peak, Francis M
Pearson, James N
Pendergrass, John W
Pendergrass, John W
Pendergrass, William M
Perdew, Irwin T
Perdew, John
Perdu, Elbert T
Perdu, William C
Perry, Allen M
Pettigrew, Alfred
Petty, Wesley
Phelps, George W
Phillips, Abner L
Phillips, Andrew Franklin
Phillips, Benjamin F
Phillips, Columbus P
Phillips, James
Phillips, Neil S Brown
Pickens, George W
Pickens, Richard C
Pickett, Joseph D
Pickler, Jesse

Pierce, Thomas
Pinckley, Allen
Pinckley, Clark
Pinckley, James T
Pinckley, Richard K
Pinckley, Scott
Pinckley, William C
Pinkston, Elijah
Pinkston, Hamilton
Pinkston, Napoleon B
Pomroy, Isaac M
Pomroy, John A
Pond, Darling A
Pope, James E
Port, John
Porter, David Granville
Porter, John Robert
Porter, John Robert
Porterfield, Alfred D
Powell, Aaron
Powell, Benjamin A
Powers, Henry M
Powers, Ira
Powers, Joel
Powers, John
Powers, John
Powers, Riley
Powers, Stephen L
Powers, Willis
Preslar, James
Preslar, Minton T
Preslar, William C
Pressen, Ellis T
Pressen, Richard L
Presson, Henry T
Presson, John W H
Presson, Thomas H H

Prewett, James

Prewett, John E

Prichard, William D

Pritchard, Nathan Clark

Pruett, Robert M

Pruett, Simpson B

Puckett, Walter E

Pugh, John

Pugh, Walter C

Pully, James W

Purdon, Benjamin C

Qualls, Larkin

Quick, Richard L

Quillian, Jesse

Radford, William P

Rafferty, William

Rainey, James H

Ray, William J

Read, Isaac S

Reaves, Jesse

Redding, William A

Reed, Frank M

Reed, John C

Reed, Robert J

Reed, Sirrineus

Reede, George W

Reeves, Richard F

Reives, Elisha G

Renfro, Mark M

Renfro, Thomas J

Renshaw, Henry G

Rhoads, William B

Rhodes, Edward H

Rhodes, James P

Rhodes, John M

Rhodes, William G

Richardson, Jasper

Richardson, William

Ridings, Thomas H

Riggs, James

Riles, Alfred

Riles, James C

Ringold, Warren

Ritter, Henry

Ritter, James

Ritter, John

Roach, John W

Roark, Henry Marion

Robbins, Joseph A

Roberts, Charles

Roberts, Fanteroy R

Roberts, Fayette M

Roberts, J G

Roberts, James

Roberts, James M

Roberts, William

Robertson, Asa R

Robeson, Jeptha L

Robeson, John Terrell

Robinson, Alfred B

Robinson, Andrew J

Robinson, David

Robinson, Henry L

Robinson, James

Robinson, James A

Robinson, Lemeul

Robinson, Wilie D

Robinson, William M

Robinson, William V

Rogers, A Gray

Rogers, Alex A

Rogers, Christian

Rogers, David C

Rogers, Green W

Rogers, James F

Rogers, John H

Rogers, Levey

Rogers, Taverner

Rogers, William F

Rollins, Jesse E

Roney, Thomas J

Rose, William

Ross, Dugal W

Ross, James

Ross, Joseph A

Rowe, John D

Rowe, John M

Rowe, John W

Rowe, William J

Rowland, Amos

Rowland, Ebin

Royall, Elbert N

Rushing, John G

Rushing, William H

Rushing, William R

Russell, Samuel J

Rust, John

Rust, John Y

Sanders, Benjamin A

Sanders, Ferman C

Saudling, J H

Saunders, Thomas

Scarlett, Shadrick M

Scates, Green

Scott, Charles M

Scott, Daniel H

Scott, Gabriel

Scott, Henry Clay

Scott, Henry G

Scott, James J

Scott, Jesse Right

Scott, John
Seavers, Joel B
Seay, Henry L
Sellers, Jesse L
Settemyre, John W
Sharp, John F
Shaw, James
Shaw, John P
Shaw, John P
Shear, James D
Shelton, James B
Shlass, Isaac R
Short, Leonard H
Simmons, Samuel C
Simons, William B
Simpson, Charles B
Singleton, James P
Singleton, John
Singleton, John W
Singleton, Leonard
Singleton, Wyatt R
Sisson, James R
Slater, Andrew J
Small, Andrew J
Smith, Addison R
Smith, Britoen
Smith, Daniel
Smith, Edward H
Smith, Isaac M
Smith, James M
Smith, John
Smith, John W
Smith, Joseph
Smith, Sidney
Smith, Thomas
Smith, Thomas Atlas
Smith, William H

Smith, William M
Smothers, Isaac
Smothers, James F
Smothers, Sebron S
Spain, Abner H
Spain, Hezekiah
Spain, Wilbur
Spane, Samuel
Spears, J W
Spears, William
Spellings, James M
Spellings, John
Spires, John
Spires, Joseph
Spires, Robert
Spoon, Elijah
Springer, Hosea
Springer, Reny B
Steel, James L
Steel, John T
Stephens, John
Stewart, Edward
Stewart, James R
Stewart, John R
Stewart, Levi
Stewart, Thomas J
Stone, Reuben
Stone, William Jr
Stone, William Sr
Stratton, John L
Stratton, John M
Stricklin, Peter
Stublefield, Dallis
Sugg, Joel M
Sutton, George W
Swafford, John
Swafford, John W

Tarpley, Frances P
Tate, Elisha
Tate, Jesse M
Tate, John William
Taylor, Archibald F
Taylor, Green D
Taylor, James Franklin
Taylor, James T
Taylor, Jarrott
Taylor, Lindley M
Teague, James A
Teague, Jasper N
Teague, Leander
Teague, Samuel
Teddlar, James
Tedford, George W
Tedford, William E
Terrell, Alfred T
Thacker, Simon G
Thomas, Andrew
Thomas, Jackson
Thomas, James H
Thomas, John Harrison
Thomas, John R
Thomas, John W
Thomas, William H
Thombrough, William
Thompson, Calvin L
Thompson, George W
Thompson, James S
Thompson, John C C
Thompson, William J
Tice, Stephen J
Tidwell, John F
Tomlin, Albert
Tomlinson, Henry W
Tosh, Lafayette Mancil

Touhey, Stephen

Townsell, George W

Townsend, Joseph H

Townsend, Joseph R

Townsend, Nathaniel

Trauburger, Benjamin F

Travis, Franklin

Trout, Granville

Tubbs, Elijah

Tucker, Erasmus

Tucker, George W

Tucker, George W

Tucker, John Wesley

Tucker, Thomas J

Turner, Jesse Frank

Tyler, John

Umstead, Daniel

Umstead, Squire

Uptigrove, Elijah

Vannoy, Cornelius R

Vaughn, Matthew H

Veteto, Albert J

Via, Simpson Harper

Vickers, Francis M

Vickers, Thomas J

Wadley, J R

Wadley, Thomas M

Waggoner, John W

Waites, Thompson

Walker, James A

Walker, W J

Wall, John W

Wallace, George W

Wallace, John J

Wallace, Robert R

Wallace, William

Waller, William

Walpole, Benjamin F

Ward, John T

Ward, Joseph R

Ward, Thomas Allen

Ward, W Robert

Watson, James A

Watson, John

Watson, Simon P

Watson, William M

Waugh, James Willis

Waugh, Stanfield

Weakly, R L

Weaver, William

Webb, Henry

Webb, John Richard

Webb, Martin L

Webb, Theophilus

Webster, Daniel

Webster, William

Wells, John

Welsh, James H

Welsh, William J

West, Edgar W

Westerman, Richard

Wheatley, George W

Wheeler, John L

Whitaker, James P

White, Fenelroy

White, George W

White, Harmon L

White, Joseph

Whitehurst, William

Whittle, Hartwell

Whittle, John J

Wiley, Addison J

Wilkerson, John

Wilkes, George W

William, George W

Williams, Benjamin F

Williams, Burrell T

Williams, Christopher C

Williams, George N

Williams, John F

Williams, John F

Williams, Robert C

Williams, Samuel

Williams, Sanford N

Williams, Thomas

Williams, William M

Williamson, George W

Williamson, William W

Willy, Thomas W

Wilson, Adonijah A

Wilson, Charles M

Wilson, Erastus E

Wilson, Francis A

Wilson, John

Wilson, Martin V Buren

Wilson, Matthew M

Wilson, Nathan C

Wilson, Thomas C

Wilson, W B

Winberry, James

Winbery, George W

Winn, Alvan E

Winn, Robert Allen

Wise, George W

Wise, James F

Wise, John

Wofford, William F

Wood, Huston George

Wood, Jesse L

Wood, Jessee L

Wood, John

Wood, Thomas H
Wood, William
Wood, William H
Woodard, Peter H
Woods, J Martin
Woods, James F M
Woods, Lasson
Woods, Samuel C
Woods, Thomas
Woods, William T
Woodside, Milus M
Woodson, Thomas
Wooley, Andrew J
Worden, John A
Workman, William
Worrell, Hardy H
Worrell, John
Worsham, William S
Wright William J
Wright, Andrew J
Wyatt, Henry H
Wyatt, John
Wyatt, William B

INDEX

CPSIA information can be obtained
at www.ICGtesting.com
Printed in the USA
BVOW10s0356210717

489702BV00008B/163/P